THE AFRICAN NOVEL C

The African Novel of Ideas

PHILOSOPHY AND INDIVIDUALISM IN THE AGE OF GLOBAL WRITING

Jeanne-Marie Jackson

PRINCETON UNIVERSITY PRESS
PRINCETON & OXFORD

Copyright © 2021 by Princeton University Press

Princeton University Press is committed to the protection of copyright and the intellectual property our authors entrust to us. Copyright promotes the progress and integrity of knowledge. Thank you for supporting free speech and the global exchange of ideas by purchasing an authorized edition of this book. If you wish to reproduce or distribute any part of it in any form, please obtain permission.

Requests for permission to reproduce material from this work should be sent to permissions@press.princeton.edu

Published by Princeton University Press
41 William Street, Princeton, New Jersey 08540
6 Oxford Street, Woodstock, Oxfordshire OX20 1TR

press.princeton.edu

All Rights Reserved

Library of Congress Cataloging-in-Publication Data

Names: Jackson, Jeanne-Marie, author.
Title: The African novel of ideas : philosophy and individualism in the age of global writing / Jeanne-Marie Jackson.
Description: Princeton : Princeton University Press, 2021. | Includes bibliographical references and index.
Identifiers: LCCN 2020032380 (print) | LCCN 2020032381 (ebook) | ISBN 9780691186443 (hardback) | ISBN 9780691186450 (paperback) | ISBN 9780691212401 (ebook)
Subjects: LCSH: African fiction (English)—20th century—History and criticism. | African fiction (English)—21st century—History and criticism. | Philosophy in literature. | Thought and thinking in literature.
Classification: LCC PR9344 .J33 2021 (print) | LCC PR9344 (ebook) | DDC 823.9109—dc23
LC record available at https://lccn.loc.gov/2020032380
LC ebook record available at https://lccn.loc.gov/2020032381

British Library Cataloging-in-Publication Data is available

Editorial: Anne Savarese and Jenny Tan
Production Editorial: Sara Lerner
Cover Design: Pamela L. Schnitter
Production: Danielle Amatucci
Publicity: Alyssa Sanford and Amy Stewart
Copyeditor: Cynthia Buck

Cover Credit: "Head in the clouds." Photo of Smasheriico, by Lidudumalingani

This book has been composed in Miller

Printed on acid-free paper. ∞

Printed in the United States of America

10 9 8 7 6 5 4 3 2 1

For my son, Benjamin Eyiku Andoh Awotwi, and
the ideas to which he may one day lay claim

CONTENTS

Acknowledgments · ix

Introduction: Disaggregating Liberalism	1
Book Structure	19
Chapter Summaries and Conceptual Guide	23

PART I	NATIONAL HORIZONS	29
CHAPTER 1	*Ethiopia Unbound* as Afro-Comparatist Novel: The Case for Liberated Solitude	31
	Comparison between the Global and the Decolonial	33
	J. E. Casely Hayford and Philosophy as Historical Redemption	49
	Flash-Forward: Implications for the Postcolonial Anglo-Fante Novel	60
CHAPTER 2	Between the House of Stone and a Hard Place: Stanlake Samkange's Philosophical Turn	68
	The Public Intellectual in Late Rhodesia	70
	The Mourned One and the Search for Replicable Selfhood	79
	Hunhuism or Ubuntuism: Philosophy as Way of Life	90
	Coda: Samkange's Literary Surrounds	96
PART II	GLOBAL RECESSIONS	105
CHAPTER 3	A Forked Path, Forever: *Kintu* between Reason and Rationality	107

[vii]

"The Great Ugandan Novel" as Periodizing Device   109

Reading Kintu's *Twins: Individuation versus Subjectivization*   123

Curses as History in Recent East African Fiction   137

CHAPTER 4   Bodies Impolitic: African Deaths of Philosophical Suicide   145

Philosophical Suicide as a Conceptual Tool   147

Tendai Huchu's Maestro of Lonely Learning   156

Imraan Coovadia's Measured Thinking   166

Coda: Masande Ntshanga's The Reactive *and the Rewards of Self-Affliction*   175

Conclusion   180

Epilogue: Speculations on the Future of African Literary Studies   181

Notes · 191
Works Cited · 199
Index · 213

ACKNOWLEDGMENTS

AS BEFITS A book about the interplay of intellection, individualism, and common cause, *The African Novel of Ideas* came to fruition alongside many colleagues, friends, and family members. I am lucky to work amid an astonishing array of sharp and humane thinkers, from my grad school cohort to my home institution to the participants in my overlapping fields.

First, I am grateful to my colleagues at Johns Hopkins, in and beyond the Department of English. Though it is not exactly known as a warm and cuddly place, the truth is that I love going to work. Jared Hickman, Drew Daniel, Mary Favret, Andrew Miller, Larry Jackson, Chris Cannon, Jesse Rosenthal, Mark Christian Thompson, Doug Mao, Nadia Nurhussein, Chris Nealon, and Sharon Achinstein make faculty meetings decidedly sufferable. (Thanks for the open-door policy in our hallway, Jesse.) As chair during the eventful year before this book was published, Mark deserves special acknowledgment for his insight, advocacy, and attention. I have also been glad to share the Homewood campus with Yi-Ping Ong, Anne Eakin Moss, Dora Malech, Bécquer Seguín, Lester Spence, Robbie Shilliam, Katrina Bell McDonald, and fellow Africanists Liz Thornberry, Pier Larson, and Mike Degani. It was a delight to host Ankhi Mukherjee at Hopkins for the spring 2019 term; she is now a lifelong academic "big sister." You are the individuals who make the institution worth anything at all.

Elsewhere in academia, I am in frequent conversation—in person and, for better or worse, online—with an extended range of scholars of the novel, novelists, linguists, and philosophers. In no particular order, I would not have written this book, in this way, without Michaela Bronstein, Chris Grobe, Nan Z. Da, Cóilín Parsons, Olufemi O. Taiwo, Barry McCrea, Len Gutkin, Lucas Klein, Jonathan Kramnick, Denis Ferhatović, Omedi Ochieng, Christopher Bush, Lidudumalingani Mqombothi, Peli Grietzer, Tyran Steward, Mark de Silva, Taff Gidi, Hardy Matewa, Fanie Naude, Elnathan John, Henrietta Rose-Innes, Eben Venter, Tendai Huchu, or Imraan Coovadia. Imraan and Tendai, in particular, have been key interlocutors both in print and in person, the definition of "intellectual friendship." Lidudumalingani lent me his vision for the cover photo, and much else. For keeping my faith in African literary studies, especially, as a safe haven for deep engagement without professional ill will, I am indebted to

Cajetan Iheka, Tsitsi Jaji, Nathan Suhr-Sytsma, Magali Armillas-Tiseyra, Madhu Krishnan, Bhakti Shringarpure, Ainehi Edoro, Yogita Goyal, Stephanie Bosch Santana, Monica Popescu, Lily Saint, Kwabena Opoku-Agyemang, Adwoa Opoku-Agyemang, Isabel Hofmeyr, Ashleigh Harris, Stefan Helgesson, Kirk Sides, Lindsey Green-Simms, Wamuwi Mbao, Simon van Schalkwyk, Ebony Coletu, Andrew Van der Vlies, Thando Njovane, Akin Adesokan, J. B. Amissah-Arthur, and Abdul-Karim Mustapha. There is no other way to describe my senior postcolonial colleague Sangeeta Ray than as my disciplinary partner in crime, and I am honored to count Ato Quayson among my most valued mentors and models.

For reading and commenting on pieces of this book and/or related projects at various points along the way, I am grateful to Doug Mao, Lily Saint, Nathan Suhr-Sytsma, Leon de Kock, Olakunle George, David James, and the two thoughtful readers for Princeton University Press. For shepherding it to completion, I thank Princeton's Anne Savarese. Parts of the project were also "auditioned" for myself in the literary magazine *n+1*, for which I wrote regularly during the time it evolved. Nikil Saval, as its editor at the time, has had a more profound effect on my writing than perhaps anyone else. I received voluminous and astute verbal feedback during invited talks on individual chapters at Duke University, Wits University, the University of Cape Town, the University of Houston, Northwestern University, the University of Maryland, New York University, Stanford University, the University of Ghana at Legon, Pennsylvania State University, Oxford University, Queen Mary University of London, and the University of Bristol. For invitations to the above I respectively (and respectfully!) thank Nancy Armstrong, Christopher Thurman, Greg Fried, Sebastian Lecourt, the comparative literature graduate students at Northwestern, Sangeeta Ray, Ato Quayson, Nancy Ruttenberg, Kwabena Opoku-Agyemang, Magali Armillas-Tiseyra and Hoda El Shakry, Ankhi Mukherjee and Elleke Boehmer, Shital Pravinchandra and Andrew Van der Vlies, and Madhu Krishnan and Kirk Sides. I am additionally indebted to Liz Thornberry, Pier Larson, and Michael Degani for their great feedback on the book's introduction at Hopkins's Africa Seminar.

I had a baby while writing this book, and so it is my pleasure to thank the close scholar-friends who have journeyed toward toddlerhood on more or less the same chaotic schedule: Maria Taroutina, Tsitsi Jaji, and Theresa Runstedtler. You have amplified the joys and made the frustrations bearable. Ally Vitale and her staff at the Bar Method Baltimore helped me feel like myself again and contributed to my sense of community in our adopted city. I also owe more than I can say to the loving staff at Kiddie

Academy, aka "baby school"—especially Asia, Najah, Erica, and Shanika—without whose good work it would be impossible to do mine.

Small portions of this project—scattered, reworked sentences, paragraphs, and a few pages here and there—have appeared in essays or chapters published in *Novel*, the *Cambridge Journal of Postcolonial Literary Inquiry*, the *Oxford Research Encyclopedia of Literature*, Wiley-Blackwell's *Companion to African Literature*, *n+1*, and *Public Books*. I thank the editors of each of these venues for their contributions to the final product.

It would be unthinkable not to acknowledge my parents, Ralph and Ellen, as well as my sister and brother-in-law, Erin and Joe. I am profoundly grateful to my mother for her bond with my son, and for her frequent, helpful weekend trips from New Haven to Baltimore over the past two years. My sister came all the way to Ghana for her nephew's naming ceremony despite her demanding work schedule, and the values she's helped me foster permeate this book even where it is far from obvious. During its writing, I also gained new siblings, and so I thank the Awotwi family—Francesca, Effuah, Maame Yahan, Jonathan, and Egyeiku—for sharing so much of their knowledge with me, and in turn, showing such interest in mine. Medaase pii.

Finally, I offer my abiding gratitude to my husband, Kwamina Awotwi, and our son, Benjamin Eyiku Andoh Awotwi, who have taken my life by storm in the most soothing way. If there is a unifying sensibility behind this project, then it is surely Kwamina's as much as mine, whose cosmopolitanism, acumen, and unremitting fair-mindedness are a gift I could never have anticipated. Benji, I hope, may one day read this book and find it a worthy rival to *Good Night, Octopus*. You two are the center that holds.

THE AFRICAN NOVEL OF IDEAS

INTRODUCTION

Disaggregating Liberalism

The irony is that all too often we anti-imperialists, in the name of anti-imperialism, enter into an unwitting complicity with the value separatists and supremacist ideologues of Western exceptionalism. We assent to their claim that a signal value, say, individualism, is a Western thing, a cultural particular, a bad one at that; and that we have or ought to have an aversion to it because it is Western and because it is bad and bad because it is Western.

—ATO SEKYI-OTU, *LEFT UNIVERSALISM,
AFRICACENTRIC ESSAYS* (2019)

IN 2010, a Zimbabwean writer named Tendai Huchu published a debut novel that found ready uptake as an exploration of postcolonial African identity. The story of a young gay man's struggles to navigate the social rigidities of Zimbabwe's capital, *The Hairdresser of Harare* was a book that critics knew how to champion. Among its timely concerns are gender roles, state corruption, and the yawning wealth gap between Zimbabwe's political elite and its poor majority, all to further a main plot of queer self-becoming. With lines like "Could it really be that independence had become a greater burden than the yoke of colonial oppression?" (loc. 1784) and its reams of unemployed youth, Huchu's novel is also a veritable goldmine for anti-neoliberal critique. Neither a reading based in gender and sexuality nor one that foregrounds economic precarity is misguided: *The Hairdresser of Harare* indeed does much to showcase Zimbabwe's richness as a post-settler-colonial, post-democratic social setting. Amid these urgent themes and their appeal for attendant methodologies, however, there is a *weirder* and overlooked strain of inquiry. Stuck between a chapter on ruling party loyalty and one on an anti-gay attack against the main character, Huchu has imagined a non-institutional philosophy club, a circle where young men sit streetside to contemplate Diogenes the Cynic and Plato's *Republic*. Asked for directions to the club by the narrator, one jobless young man volunteers that "everyone knows those lunatics," before instructing her to "head for those rocks over there," where they can be found "talking nonsense" (2530, 2538). This "nonsense," as it happens, also raises a series of questions that anchor *The African Novel of Ideas*.

First, what would emerge from seeing the explicit philosophical interest in Huchu's book not as a side note, but as its interpretive crux? And second, what might the longer tradition of the African novel look like were it reoriented around the philosophy club's concerns, including such matters as a priori truth, the possibility of pure form, and the search for resilient sources of moral authority? A number of other prospects flow from here. What kinds of reading and which writers and texts would be privileged by viewing the African novel as a source of *thinking about thinking*, a site of agile negotiation between private minds and public spaces? *The Hairdresser of Harare*, in this light, is an instructive example of how critical priorities put on political resistance and cultural representation can sometimes serve as blunt instruments, dull blades taken to fresh voices. The novel's philosophy circle promotes a spirit of inquiry whose search for answers extends beyond the fraught conditions of modern Zimbabwe, even as they are the clear basis of its emergence. "We try to discover the truth for ourselves here," its leader Fungai explains. "We do not refer to the Bible as an authoritative text. To us it is just one of many philosophical texts and while we do pay it attention we do not place it on a pedestal" (2554). To recognize the sharpness of Fungai's position demands some knowledge of Zimbabwe's religious landscape, particularly the pervasiveness of charismatic forms of Christianity. But the ambition to give ideas and those who pursue them their own space, adjacent to yet unsprung from Harare's economic woes, is a palpable part of a book whose setting might least seem to support it.

It would be naive, at best, to suggest that a philosophical pursuit of truth can easily "rise above" life-determining social and economic problems. Nonetheless, Huchu asks his reader in this scene to proceed *as if* this were the case. He does so, moreover, in order to foment a more expansive and self-justifying range of social possibilities, in this instance as regards human sexuality. Identities are converted into Manichaean abstractions as circle participants are guided to "assume that there are two types of sexuality since everything is made in pairs, light and dark, good and evil, etcetera. The one we shall call heterosexuality, which is an attraction of opposites, and the other we shall call homosexuality which is an attraction of matching subjects" (2563). After their discussion works deliberately through bisexuality, hermaphroditism, and the distinction between truth and illusion, the group's leader arrives at what is here a socially radical conclusion that "man and woman may not be as distinct as they seem" (2571). Perhaps surprisingly, this outcome's liberatory potential is tethered to clear, systematic explication. As the circle's men depart in anger at Fungai's assertion that homosexuality is not only natural but "necessary," he maintains equanimity through what he views as an objective commitment to intellectual virtue. "In our reasoning we can only turn to Lady Philosophy," he avers. "Those who have preconceived notions of where she will lead us must leave because they are not seekers of truth" (2580). Would-have-been philosophers peel off two by two, leaving Fungai shunned and alone with his insistence on what he inexactly calls "natural" as opposed to "man-made" laws and ultimately leading to the group's dissolution. Huchu's exercise nonetheless serves as a gauntlet thrown down in a critical arena whose bundled suspicions of rationality, universality, and individualism have become reflexive: from the economic ruins of the postcolonial state, he gathers a strong and autonomous truth-seeking self.

The African Novel of Ideas shares this goal of peeling away the sticky associational layers that have accreted to the notion of "individualism" in postcolonial-cum-globalist literary and theoretical debates. If the book has a grand claim, it is that African intellectual traditions are rich in work where a separate space for the thinker corresponds to a separate space for the thought—where ideas, that is, are granted a force and even ontology of their own by a turn to narrative designs that advance individual integrity, as against porosity or dissolution. As Justin E. H. Smith notes in his book *The Philosopher: A History in Six Types*, defining a philosophical practice depends on characterizing those who do it. "Philosophy," he writes, "is often held to be the activity that is concerned with universal truths, to be discovered by a priori reflection, rather than with particular truths, which are to be discovered by empirical means" (4). This is an especially apt summary in the present, fictive frame. To call something a "novel of ideas" is to contemplate the figures in novels who *have* ideas: their structural role and situation; how their thoughts are given narrative shape; and the realms between which they mediate, to use Smith's term—for example, "between the immanent and transcendent," or the material and the ideal (14). Inasmuch as philosophy is performed, however, it is crucially not reducible to its embodiment. Sophie Oluwole goes so far as to declare that it is "about what people say rather than what they do" (Ajeluorou), while Raymond Geuss writes, "Philosophy takes place when someone . . . begins to try to look for a way out which might include transforming the framework of some situation, changing the rules, asking different questions" (5). Though work on the novel, in Africa and elsewhere, has moved away from its once-definitional emphasis on the representative individual in favor of topics like networks, ecology, and the transmission of popular genres, it remains the case that the form is particularly well suited to pivot between the embedded thinker and the abstract thought.[1]

Crucially, the novel can also present philosophical individualism as a *fantasized* space, rather than only a historiographic sticking point. ("Transforming the framework," per Geuss, might be both materially impossible and discursively compelling.) The form no doubt articulates the conditions of capitalist modernity in the sense that it is, well, modern: in this way, it may seem ripe for discussion of "universalism" as invoked by, for example, Vivek Chibber's attempt to reassert a shared sociology of subjective coherence against what he sees as the self-defeating cultural particularism of postcolonial theory. Nonetheless, its scalar versatility means that it is an unreliable social diagnostic tool in an ultimate sense.[2] The novel is a fickle mediation: it can foreground dimensions of thought and experience that offer historical insight in one frame without being attuned to its farthest-reaching historical (or for that matter, cognitive) derivation.[3] I mean fantasized "space" in this formulation quite literally, in that the presentation of both thinkers and ideas must, in a novel, take up more or less actual room on a page, interwoven more or less fluidly with other textual features. It is this space and the fate of its perceived constraints with which I am most concerned. For reasons I discuss at greater length later in this chapter, African philosophy provides an essential though largely untapped resource for thinking about individualism as a tool for demarcating thought. Unlike disciplines more widely identified with Africanist scholarship and its penchant for broad social structures, such as history or anthropology, philosophy is accountable not to empirical standards of evidence so much as it is to the *design* of a conceptual apparatus. A debate like that between the Ghanaian philosophers Kwasi Wiredu and Kwame Gyekye over whether or not personhood is an "achieved" status in their shared Akan ethnic group—is one born a person, or does one earn the label?—is a brief but powerful instance of what I mean.[4] The cultural practices invoked as a point of origin, such as different burial norms for different age groups, are not in question, nor, really, is their cultural implication: Wiredu and Gyekye both have deep knowledge of Akan customs and agree that they esteem elders. Their discord hinges, rather, on whether it is more apt to see personhood *itself* as an incremental construct, or to distinguish among earned statuses within a given category. This question, in turn, reinflects the most fundamental political, narratological, and even cosmological terms of analysis across language traditions, including the notion of individuality itself.

I want to pause briefly now and reflect on a particular philosophical individual who was often in mind as I wrote this book, because I think he is revealing of these stakes and their transformation across the African twentieth century. My late father-in-law, David Eyiku Awotwi, or Nana Ekow Eyiku I, was born in 1922 to a prominent family from the then–Gold Coast town of Elmina. He was a decolonial intellectual very much of his time: after completing a master's degree at the London School of Economics, he served in various government roles under Kwame Nkrumah, Ghana's first prime minister and president, and then in Ghana's Second Republic. Also a Fante chief, revered family elder, and head of the *anona* (parrot) clan, Awotwi's communal bona fides are self-evident. This account is not intended as hagiography; Awotwi was without doubt subject to the blind spots shared by most men of his time and place. I am, however, struck by the difficulty I have faced in finding a critical language to make sense of his life as recounted to me, a life in which self-determination featured equally as richly as affiliation. He spent long hours in his study, reading voluminously from both Western and African traditions, and ultimately wrote a learned history of Elmina that affords it the depth of Fante perspective he thought was lacking from previous efforts. Though Ghana's capital city of Accra is not known for its walkability (nor was it then), Awotwi would rise each morning before dawn to stroll briskly around his busy neighborhood of Osu. Such reflective discipline and self-boundedness, in the tradition of J. E. Casely Hayford's *Ethiopia Unbound* as I foreground it in this book's next chapter, was a key part of his civic leadership model. One might say after Frédéric Gros that walking was, for Awotwi, an act by which "the body's monotonous duty liberates thought. . . . It is then that thoughts can arise, surface or take shape."

These words from Gros's *A Philosophy of Walking*, as it were, describe Immanuel Kant and his iconic daily perambulations around Königsberg. It is an obvious point of comparison with the glimpse of Awotwi's life offered here, revealing in its differences and similarities alike. The cliché of Kant's walks is of almost hermetic containment: neither marrying nor ever leaving the small Prussian city in which he was born, he becomes an emblem either of dogged commitment to the pursuit of a priori truths (the good version) or, more commonly now, of flawed Enlightenment notions of truth's extrication from social meaning and consequence. Awotwi's life, on the other hand, was cosmopolitan in every sense: he saw no contradiction between the knowledge bequeathed by his metropolitan education and his activism on behalf of the Fante language and culture. As a dedicated civil servant, he traveled often between Ghana and London, returning to oversee a household of many children and whatever relations, liberally defined, might be there for an extended stay. If it is easy to see how a life like Kant's would be impoverished by a lack of social accountability, it is harder to remember that a life like Awotwi's, with its seemingly endless list of communal responsibilities, also entailed an abiding commitment to a Kantian ideal. Their walks thus represent two extremes of what intellectual self-sequestration asks of critical thought at our own aspirationally pluralist juncture. The first cries out for the (ongoing) revision of stock Enlightenment norms to accord with social interdependence, while the second calls for recognition of how essential an almost naive-seeming life of the mind might feel to people steeped in unquestioned communal obligation.

At the same time, the restoration I am proposing of the strong individual mind as a tool for charting African novels' stake in ideas, as such, comes with baggage. The fate of the individual in postcolonial studies has long been bound to the field's critique of "the liberal subject," seen broadly as the creation of (or alibi for) a larger liberal-developmentalist agenda that is bound to Western imperialism, neoliberal capitalism, and racial slavery, to list only a sampling of its grisly associations. Variations on this line of argument are ubiquitous enough that it will strike at least some readers as a given. Achille Mbembe offers a neat summary of its logic in *Critique of Black Reason* when he states, "The modern idea of democracy, like liberalism itself, was inseparable from the project of commercial globalization. The plantation and the colony were nodal chains holding the project together" (80). Rather than really reckon with humanity's seeming opaqueness across great cultural divides—its appearance as "indefinable and incomprehensible"—the educational, legal, and commercial institutions by which European powers in the eighteenth and nineteenth centuries sought to realize "an experience of the world common to all human beings" demanded conformity. Only upon satisfying certain ethnocentric conditions of conduct, this assimilationist story goes, would the status of "full individual" be granted (87). And yet, as Mbembe movingly chronicles in that book's search for a form of self-authorship that can somehow persist *even so*, it is easier to do away with individualism as a theoretical proposition than to relinquish its foundational lived power. *The African Novel of Ideas* breaks away from seeing the cohesive, systematically reflecting individual as the fulfillment of civilizational exclusivity. Instead, it suggests the novelized philosopher as the threshold of world-expanding abstraction.

It is worth noting at the outset that this book is nonetheless not a "defense" of liberalism on the order of, for example, Amanda Anderson's *Bleak Liberalism* from 2016, which seeks to restore a fuller systemic capability to the intellectual apparatus supporting the "free-standing and autonomous" subject (4) that is so readily allied with free-market ideology. For better or worse, liberalism's hypocrisies are necessarily more glaring in texts from former British colonies than they are in scholarly work on Dickens, a fact that has often been illustrated with pointed reminders that the Universal Declaration of Human Rights was adopted in 1948 by numerous powerful seats of empire. In his essay collection *Reordering the World*, Duncan Bell makes a powerful case that settler colonies, as contrasted in particular with India, offered an ideal space for the development of liberal British doctrine. The ostensible "blank slate" of these lands, including those of present-day South Africa, "offered liberals a way of celebrating expansion and rule cleansed of traditional anxieties about foreign conquest," he writes. "Instead, they were premised on a comforting fantasy about the occupation of new lands" (48). And as Chris Taylor argues in their book *Empire of Neglect: The West Indies in the Wake of British Liberalism*, liberalism to its imperial subjects had little to do with feelings, intentions, or aesthetics and everything to do with the cold, hard effects of its institutionalization. In Taylor's words, "Approaching metropolitan thought and practice from the colonial world requires a methodological consequentialism" (4).

What the present book *is*, then, is an effort to move beyond liberalism's conception as a prepackaged collusion between the integrous self and the civilizational violence of Western colonial rule, looking instead to the philosophical individual's purposive intellectual formation by African writers whose moral and political terms are largely homegrown. In this I most closely join the Ghanaian philosopher Ato Sekyi-Otu in *Left Universalism, Africacentric Essays*, from which this introduction's epigraph is drawn. "Yet the simple or rather complex truth is that there can be and there are transcultural value commitments not because or only because someone echoes another," he writes, "although that is also true in the nature of human affairs, but because these commitments speak for ill or good to shared human necessities, desires, claims and dreams" (158). Rather than downplay the role of individualism *in* liberalism in order to redeem a worldview that has been sullied by tepid inaction or outright hypocrisy, I look precisely to what appear as narrativized instances of both "reason" and "autonomous selfhood" whose complicity with imperial models is not foreordained. Some of the challenge that *The African Novel of Ideas* takes on is semantic: if someone walks like a liberal, and talks like a liberal, in a context where liberalism is *not* the dominant ideology—or at least, where it is not dominant in the sense of having been painfully and lucratively exported around the world—is "liberalism" the right word to use? I am frankly not sure. Individualism, for this reason, will serve here as a more precise yet pliable home base. As Bell suggests, liberalism has been variously identified as "a squabbling family of philosophical doctrines, a popular creed, a resonant moral ideal, the creature of a party machine, a comprehensive economic system, a form of life," and indeed, it "was all of these and more" (2). Even in Bell's stellar work, however, there is little to assist us in determining what to do with "global liberalisms" whose consequences are not only not the same as, but are often opposed to, their British expressions. There is something deeply presumptuous about assuming that liberal ideals—including the most basic humanistic premise that safeguarding individual integrity of thought is the ultimate justification for whatever social puzzles we undertake to solve—are intrinsically or irredeemably Western.[5]

Caveats aside, I have titled this introduction "Disaggregating Liberalism" in order to signal an interest in patient parts over slippery wholes. Too often, individuality as a narrative tool—not to mention an existential commitment—is a baby thrown out with the bathwater of well-meaning structural critique and collective exposition. African literature has long been an especially ripe setting for oppositions between liberalism and radicalism, and between individualism and collectivity, owing not just to an inordinate focus on independence-era texts but also to its long-standing significance as a "foil" of various sorts to Western norms *within* Western academies. Some of this has been useful, and some of it less so. In the first category, top scholars of the field often built names at British and US institutions, in part through astute, early-career explications of canonical African novelists, for example, Simon Gikandi's *Reading the African Novel* (1987) as well as *Reading Chinua Achebe* (1991); Ato Quayson's *Strategic Transformations in Nigerian Writing* (1997); or Adéléké Adéèkọ́'s *Proverbs, Textuality, and Nativism in African Literature* (1998). For all intents and purposes, such work was obliged to unseat Eurocentric misconceptions about how novels are "supposed" to work via a realism of fine-grained description and psychological depth, as in Gikandi's exposition of how the "literature of praxis is informed by a belief that 'structure' or 'history,' or the 'mechanics of society' provide man with referents which enable him to know himself and the world" (1987, 113). Following Abiola Irele's essay "The African Imagination" in its efforts to shore up the distinctive features of African literature in light of various *other* efforts to do so, it is also a body of texts with a closer proximity than most European ones to orality as what he calls its "basic intertext" (56). African literature, in this way, was influentially institutionalized as something unlike the Western traditions against which it was often condescendingly measured.

At the same time as the field gained this important foothold in Europe and the United States, however, a less geographically anchored kind of postcolonial critique also came into its own, in the process absorbing Africa into a broader currency of "otherness." Building on the poststructuralist imperative to dismantle hegemonic claims to truth, postcolonialism in both its "discursive" and "materialist" strains was mostly a negational enterprise. In some of the more powerful Marxist postcolonial work (Peter Hallward's *Absolutely Postcolonial* from 2001, or Neil Lazarus's *The Postcolonial Unconscious* from 2011, for example), former colonies in Africa and the Caribbean are a means of insistence on "the concrete," standing in valiant opposition to the struggle-obscuring singularities of postcolonial theory. A poststructuralist negation of "the West" as the font of universalism begets a negation of the negation, both of which, in retrospect, have merit but leave little room for taking African quandaries over form and representation on their own terms. Rey Chow's *Ethics after Idealism*, from 1998, diagnosed the tense convergence of what she calls "critical theory" and "cultural studies" in similar terms that remain relevant. Critical theory, she writes, upholds an intellectual culture "in which marks of distinction . . . are achieved, paradoxically, by attempts to be negative and subversive, attempts to blast open the generality of the Western logos with the force of an exotic species/specialization from within" (xvii). At the time, Chow was also right to point out the inadequacies of a culturalist counterweight to this tendency, which too often advanced a neatly packaged brand of locality that did not delve into the full extent of its internal stakes, contradictions, or oddities. In her words, this is because "localization is revered as the basis for a pluralism with all its 'diversities' and ultimately for a stable, respectable liberalism" (xviii).

It remains the case that locality often plays too gestural a role in our critical debates, no longer in juxtaposition to poststructuralist "high theory" but as a strike against a voracious global framework that swallows up the difference it means to distill. Following Chow's work, the present book eschews both the grand scale of "theory" in its newer, global permutation—recent debates about world literature have for me run their course—and the righteous specificities of "culture" as a guiding methodological tool. It opts for philosophy instead, with the aim of being more systematic than theory and less self-reifying than culture. At the same time, I do not in any sense claim that the philosophical investments of the books, writers, and traditions I treat here represent African literature as such any better than some other frames might; thankfully, the field now occupies a prominent enough position in the discipline at large to make this unnecessary. What I do claim is that philosophy—accessed, as I have stated, through its individual novelistic avatars—is *an* important investment for *some* very interesting African novelists that has been obscured by previous debates about African literature's difference from Western models. *The African Novel of Ideas* is not especially concerned with the well-trod terrain of alterity, in other words, but with the sorts of concerns that battles *about* alterity have left on the table. One of these concerns is the narrativized "doing" of philosophy, which bears an intimate relation to the individual philosopher and has thus been prey to postcolonialists' obligation and/or persistent desire to perform a critique of liberalism for mostly Western peers.

At this point, philosophers and historians of liberalism and its afterlives have entered something of a golden age of writing about its complex and often conflicted development across centuries: in addition to Bell's book, notable efforts include Larry Siedentop's *Inventing the Individual: The Origins of Western Liberalism* (2014); Edmund Fawcett's *Liberalism: The Life of an Idea* (2014); Helena Rosenblatt's *The Lost History of Liberalism: From Ancient Rome to the Twenty-First Century* (2018); and Adom Getachew's *Worldmaking after Empire: The Rise and Fall of Self-Determination* (2019). In the meantime, much postcolonial scholarship that approaches liberalism from literary and cultural studies continues to labor under obscure and historically overreaching definitions. Taylor's argument against redeeming liberalism through a hermetic textual exercise is the most trenchant sort of rebuttal: whether or not one agrees, it clearly distinguishes between discursive genealogies and material effects, even as it charts their interrelation through deep engagement with a geographically located archive. Many others, however, make claims of a looser associational sort. Julietta Singh's *Unthinking Mastery: Dehumanism and Decolonial Entanglements* (2018) is an apt case in point. It takes the diffuse notion of "mastery" as key to explaining and then undoing the ways in which "colonization is masterfully coextensive with liberal globalized life today" (176), often invoking the "liberal subject" as if readers anywhere and everywhere know just what emplaced ends it serves. An assertion like "humanitarian fetishism applies not strictly to those who work in explicit spaces of aid but is also a critical compulsion of liberal subjectivity itself" (103) would require more than a motley assemblage of recent novels to be persuasive. There is no analytic apparatus in such work for moving between micro- and macro-, or between normative and descriptive claims.

Mine is less an ideological objection, in other words, than a methodological and dispositional one. For every literary example of individualism's rejection as a symptom of global capitalism, there is a countervailing example of a writer using individualism as a bulwark against precisely its dehumanizing effects. And yet for many postcolonial and anti-imperial critics, it is almost axiomatic that "the liberal individual" we might encounter in a novel, as intrinsically defined by others' exclusion from that category, reflects the logic of unevenly allocated private property, free trade, and citizenship, all of which support the global regimes of inequality on which "freedom" has paradoxically been based. Lisa Lowe's 2015 book *The Intimacies of Four Continents* offers a quintessential version of the sort of argument I refer to here in a description of "the individual person within the liberal private sphere" (21). It thus bears longer quotation:

> This mythic and affective individualism is central to the constitution of domestic household as the property and privileged signifier of the liberal person and articulates the disciplining of gendered subjectivity and desire in relation to family and home. Further, intimacy as interiority is elaborated in the philosophical tradition in which the liberal subject observes, examines, and comes to possess knowledge of self and others. Philosophy elaborates this subject with interiority, who apprehends and judges the field of people, land, and things, as the definition of human being. (21)

The upshot is that "possessive" individuality, defined as a right to foster a paradigm of intimacy through private ownership, has abetted "the racialized distributions of freedom and humanity" (36) characteristic of Western colonialisms. Lowe contends that we can trace the emergence of liberal individualism's dependence on ownership through Locke, Rousseau, Kant, and Hegel, the last of whom sees "the individual's possession of his own person, his own interiority," as "a first sense of property" (28). A deep accounting for the vast and disparate philosophical canon invoked here is beyond the scope of this introduction. But even were this incontrovertibly true, this way of arguing risks falling into the category of closed textual exercise of which Taylor is rightly wary. If individualism is "liberal" not only at points of particular historical emergence but in *essence*, how do we make sense of the many ways in which it is embraced by people who are not to any meaningful degree complicit with Western violence?

Put otherwise, there is at least room to argue that individualism—alongside other norms that may attend it, such as rationality or civility, both of which are addressed in later chapters of this book—works to different effect in different places, at different times. Liberal traits and practices in one frame may not serve pejoratively or even recognizably liberal political ends in another. Grand theoretical generalizations about how the "logic" of the liberal (autonomous) subject enforces cultural and economic hierarchies end up entrenching precisely the Eurocentrism they aim to discredit. The examples Lowe marshals to "prove" the connection between liberal individualism and the material realities of slavery and colonialism are from literary texts such as Thackeray's *Vanity Fair*, in whose domestic spaces colonial commodities like cotton feature heavily. It is a compelling argument, and not at all surprising that a Victorian novel by a white Englishman would seem to naturalize—to literally domesticate—a racist economy. By painting in such broad strokes, however, the harder philosophical problems that should be at the fore of thinking through which moral and political commitments to uphold amid global hyperpluralism recede to the background. The crucial question that this book pursues, and which the writers it features also address, is that of how what we might call liberal notions such as individuality, universality, rationality, sovereignty, civility and even *philosophy itself* are informed by the contexts of their emergence and elaboration *outside* the West. In some ways, globally minded books like *The Intimacies of Four Continents*, or perhaps Debjani Ganguly's *This Thing Called the World* (2016), are sympathetic interlocutors on whose insights I aim to build. For better or worse, however, I am ill at ease with the scale of the claims such work advances. "*Liberalism*, as I use it here," Ganguly writes, "is shorthand for a modern political imaginary that, at least since the French Declaration of the Rights of Man and Citizen, established an international system of sovereign nation-states governed by the principles of individual liberty, private property, and equality before the law" (6). Yes, fair enough. But all of the truly vexed questions of how to balance ideas qua ideas with ideas' implications in their various local historical manifestations go missing in this representative summary.

It is my contention that they can be found in Africa, across various settings in which literary intellectuals seek a deep understanding of the relationship among self-determination, universal moral principles, and a localized imperative to social equality. In an interview spanning such weighty topics as American educational culture, African humanism, and the difference between social concepts and artistic theories, the South African writer Es'kia Mphahlele describes his individuality as "the sense of self, while at the same time not wanting to isolate myself from the context, from the environment. Still living the context but seeking a corner where I can try to understand things" (Samin and Mphahlele, 192). He goes on to differentiate his African individualism from "the European" one (ibid.) and identifies the former with the "contemplative aura" of South African rural life (194). An organic fit between rural settings and intellection is also a hallmark of the career of the South African–Botswanan writer Bessie Head. Defiant of categories of race and sexuality that could not accommodate her mixed origins and bisexuality, as well as admired now for what was once received as a confounding "coolness and detachment" in her style (Nyabola), Head has become a touchstone figure for African literary individualism. As Nanjala Nyabola writes in a poignant 2018 essay for *Popula* on Head's career, she was often "out of step with the dominant themes of her time; eschewing post-colonial moralising to centre on a deeply interior and personal experience." Though it does not feature in this book's coming chapters, Head's 1971 novel *Maru* is a fascinating, if enigmatic novel of ideas in the sense that it is about an attempt to build a person *from* one. Its plot begins with a cerebral white missionary named Margaret adopting a daughter from a "Bushman" (aboriginal) woman who dies giving birth, whom she imagines as "a real, living object for her experiment" (11) of prioritizing environmental over hereditary factors in human development.

Mphahlele's words here, and the imputation of inwardness to Head, are almost but not quite the primary concern of this book. I am less interested in textures of thought, what Mphahlele calls "[feeling himself] think" (199), than I am in how cohesive individuals mark space in the novel for philosophy itself. In this way, "intellection" as conceived by *The African Novel of Ideas* is distinct from, say, the Ghanaian writer Kofi Awoonor's ecstatic description, in an essay called "Tradition and Continuity in African Literature," of the novelist as a "visionary" who represents *processes* such as integration, transformation, fragmentation, and "self-generating ecstasy" (665–66). Similarly, while I find much to admire in Wole Soyinka's elaboration of African cosmological "self-apprehension," developed to rebuff Western-originating "universal-humanoid abstraction" (x), in his classic *Myth, Literature, and the African World*, its emphasis on *consciousness*—expressed via what he calls "psychic emanations"

(2)—as the path to understanding "cosmic totality" (3) is slightly beyond my purview. It would be fair to say that this book is concerned with something a bit more prosaic, which is humanity in its more or less recognizable and earthbound forms. Its working sense of the individual is more narratological and conceptual than psychological, so that interiority is often referenced or "marked" as an attribute without becoming a representational preoccupation. Yuri Corrigan has usefully suggested the promise for narrative forms of "substitutes for indwelling principles of identity" (395), in his case the "external soul" but also in broader reference to outward projections of selfhood rather than their psychic terrain.[6] Likewise, I follow Martin Puchner in an essay on J. M. Coetzee as far as his notion of intellection as "something that allows us to leap outside of ourselves," with the "primary drama" of the novel as "the work of grounding otherwise free-floating ideas" (5).

Whereas our current critical climate has, to some degree, backed away from the notion of intellectual understanding as an end in itself, casting it as elitist, masculinist, or problematically disembodied, Mphahlele suggests the complementarity of ordered thought and collective belonging. If the Zambian writer and American literature scholar Namwali Serpell captures something essential about our moment when she says, on the website Africa in Words, that "to understand is only one of many ways to read and it is not always the most important," then *The African Novel of Ideas* takes the opposite tack. What *of* understanding, it asks—as distinct from feeling, observing, or even agitating—as a mainstay of literary ambition? Another way of asking this might be, what becomes of philosophy amid a culturally restituting turn to lived-out "stories" and away from a meta-analytic and epistemologically evaluative set of investments? In terms of the conjuncture between literary archive and critical method, there are often formal differences between texts that prioritize philosophical understanding and those that may appear to have more democratic commitments, for example, to capturing a social affect or blurring generic lines. The novels included in *The African Novel of Ideas* share a focus on marking off ideas via their thinkers in a quite literal sense, through a range of techniques, including long cerebral reflections, philosophical dialogues, and "bracketing" overtly conceptual passages so that readers but not other characters are privy to them.

These methods can seem disruptive, what the Sri Lankan–American philosopher and novelist Mark de Silva has memorably called "putdownable prose" in *3:AM Magazine*. But they facilitate what is perhaps the one thing that a critical mass of philosophers seem to agree on in terms of what constitutes philosophy's elusive definition: some measure of analytic distance, as expressed by the power to order ideas and then make choices about their relative value. The Ghanaian luminary Kwasi Wiredu, in an interview with Michael Onyebuchi Eze and Thaddeus Metz, refers to African philosophy as "the investigation into various fundamental concepts of human thought," and to philosophy in general as what happens "when you investigate or you try to make a coherent picture from your worldview" (86, 87). Paulin J. Hountondji similarly argues in *African Philosophy: Myth and Reality* that the "mode of existence of philosophy" is "that of a text or set of texts, that of a piece or pieces of explicit discourse" (xii). The word "explicit" packs a polemical punch, especially in the context of African philosophy, which spent much of the 1970s and '80s embroiled in tense debates about the merits of "ethnophilosophy." Ethnophilosophy has typically been defined as the philosophy *of* a people—a conceptual essence as indicated by traditional practices, proverbs, religious beliefs, and the like—rather than the philosophy produced *by* a people and marked as such. It has been criticized for its culturally essentialist qualities on that score (with the seminal text often cited to both points as the Belgian missionary Placide Tempels's *Bantu Philosophy* from 1945).

While Hountondji is committed to the idea of investigating the "worldviews and value systems of traditional African societies," he insists that their status as philosophy requires a minimum threshold of "empirical" documents that express an "intellectual quest" (8). Recording the process of thinking with an eye to *ordering* one's thoughts is essential to meet the philosophical standard of self-reflexivity. Philosophy, in his view, is not merely "wisdom," since it must exceed the transmission of truth to arrive at its structured interrogation (105). Arguably, then, granting thought a philosophical status—even where it is concerned mainly with *collective* conceptual life, or social ideals—entails an intrinsic methodological priority on individuation. Appiah suggests something similar, drawing on work by Hountondji, Wiredu, and others, when he too defends philosophy's preference for a written medium. "Oral traditions have a habit of transmitting only the consensus, the accepted view," he asserts, while "those who are in intellectual rebellion . . . often have to begin in each generation all over again" (1992, 92). This may or may not be true, but it points to a salient norm of ideas' contestation rather than their widespread cultural fulfillment, which, Appiah argues elsewhere with Mudimbe, is at any rate *easier* to identify in a textual tradition (1993, 132). Wiredu advances an inverse claim to the same argumentative end, in "An Oral Philosophy of Personhood: Comments on Philosophy and Orality," by reinstating a textual principle in the Akan tradition of "talking drums," even though writing is not technically present. As drums are beat in patterns to sound like the human voice, conveying "deep reflections about reality and human experience," only those who are privy to "the given drum language" will be able to understand. From this, Wiredu concludes that "something is going on not altogether dissimilar to the reading of writing . . . to the extent that the method of preserving the drum text is almost as formalized as in the case of written text" (11). In foregrounding the "dialectical aptitude" cultivated in only an even more select group of individual listeners, he then pinpoints the movement from a communal to a differentiated model of conceptual transmission. He identifies a disharmony between the message latent in a particular drum "text" (which is pantheistic) and the broad foundation of Akan theology (which is theistic), thereby concluding that "there was no uniformity of thought in the traditional society under discussion," so that even the oral transmission of thought patterns across generations "may be the outcome of an original and nonconforming way of thinking" (11).

One implication of this is that the works included in, especially, the second half of this book are significant to but not necessarily representative of broader African literary production. In terms of their relation to generic trends, they often serve as something like Appiah's "intellectual rebellion" or Wiredu's "nonconforming [ways] of thinking." This is in itself an important statement given the ease with which individual African literary works are frequently seen to speak for larger, highly stratified publics in which literary readerships are small. More pertinent to this book's aims is the fact that, as Appiah's own work demonstrates in its frequent use of literary texts to ground conceptual claims, it is not a far leap to get from this line of thinking about textuality as an epistemological paradigm to the centrality of narrative forms as such. The shared goal of philosophy and the novel is, thus, what he calls "the process of making the implicit explicit," marrying the goal of intelligibility to the possibility of "[proposing and developing] new ways of thinking about the world" (1992, 96). Philosophy in this essential definition is not just the *living-out* or even recording of ideas, but their self-conscious distillation into arguable form. There is an intimate correspondence between an (in)ability to know and an (in)ability to narrate. By turning to African philosophers trained mainly in analytic methodologies as this book's main set of critical interlocutors, I also break with postcolonial and poststructuralist emphases on the problem of language as such—and namely, its communicative failure—through which a more diffuse kind of philosophical interest has often been routed.

To this end, *The African Novel of Ideas* tells a story about how novels from the continent position the act of "doing philosophy" within larger narrative designs. With the term "philosophy," I do not intend to delimit a discipline, or a particular set of standards for systematized thinking. (Put bluntly, I am not myself trying to keep pace here with analytic philosophical methodologies, in which I am not trained.) I intend to treat philosophy, rather, as a textual "character" in its own right, as well as a disciplinary partner: philosophy here denotes an investment in sitting with concepts and breaking them into parts, in awareness of but adjacent to the space of their lived implications. African philosophy is an illuminating partner to the African novel on numerous fronts, not least of which is the fact that the two fields share a number of framing questions. Is the novel or philosophy forever doomed to be a "Western import?" Are they intrinsically liberal, which is to say anti-radical, which is to say unsuited to the political demands of many African contexts because they have inbuilt predilections toward the individual over the collective? What are the merits of indigenizing either one, and what would that look like? (The latter question is a challenge best captured by ongoing popular debates as to whether it makes sense to refer to "African literature" or "African philosophy" at all, if one seeks to ascribe universal significance to them.) The novel and philosophy in their African permutations have both been accused of privileging textuality—and implicitly, modernity—over orality or tradition, a fact that Hountondji, for example, does not deny. Eileen Julien's response to this line of criticism in 1992 still stands: first, the novel in its Bakhtinian theorization bears a strong connection to the polyphony that an oral paradigm permits (9), and second, it is *really* essentialist to suggest that Africa is somehow intrinsically more disposed to oral than textual expression (10). The drive to distinguish "Western" from "native" traditions in both fields betrays a deeper set of conflicts about whether it is possible to find forms that accommodate individual self-determination, abstract thought, *and* a social vision all at once. It is this search, rather than questions of orality versus textuality as such, with which this book is mainly concerned.

As so much postcolonial work emanating from literature departments was busy making heroes and strawmen out of aggregate nouns ("culture," "difference," "subalternity," and the like), African philosophy in the 1980s and '90s was profoundly engaged with more precise terms of analysis that should be of pressing interest to scholars of the novel. First, I intend the reference to novel studies here to invoke its most compelling exegeses of the form's inbuilt principles and capacities. These have found one of their strongest recent expressions, as far as I am concerned, in Thomas

Pavel's book *The Lives of the Novel: A History*, including in his contention that "novels propose substantial hypotheses about human life and imagine fictional worlds governed by them" (17), in an attempt "to understand the relationship between individuals and the ideals and norms meant to guide their lives" (23). I do not think that the rise of globalization has rendered this concern outdated: even if individual subjects' composition has changed or is changing in response to a recent profusion of, for example, rapidly interactive virtual media, the novel's "capacity to stage both the compromise between socialization and individuation, and the interiorization of this contradiction," as Daniel Just puts it, remains compelling (383). In addition to the Beninese Hountondji's formidable output, a cluster of the aforementioned Ghanaian philosophers, including Appiah, Wiredu, and Gyekye, devoted volumes of salutary thinking to the moral status of the individual vis-à-vis the collective amid the global co-optation of both. Wiredu's work finds its touchstones in deriving moral laws from finer points of Akan cosmology, as well as from an indigenously developmentalist notion of personhood; that is, as an "ideal that one may or may not attain in life" (*Person and Community* 10). And while numerous individual African philosophical interventions are discussed elsewhere in *The African Novel of Ideas*, a volume called *Person and Community*, edited by Wiredu and Gyekye, will serve briefly here to characterize African philosophy's relevance to these foundational questions of novel theory.

Following an introduction that remarks on "the practical importance of philosophy" in Ghanaian culture (most famously in Kwame Nkrumah's advanced training in the field in the United States), Wiredu, Gyekye, and others debate the relationship of individualism and communality against a backdrop of global imperialism at the same time as they refuse definition by it (2). Gyekye especially seems to anticipate the current difficulty in imagining a place for individual agency in our social and political setting broadly conceived, with the lives of "neoliberal subjects" determined by an intangible economic order. In the African context, he writes, a longstanding *over*-emphasis on communitarianism poses what we might recognize as a similar challenge of balancing inside-out with outside-in personal formation. A widely attributed African communitarian structure, for Gyekye, "tends to whittle down the moral autonomy of the person," with the end result of "[diminishing] his freedom and capability to choose or question or reevaluate the shared values of the community" (103). As such, Gyekye seeks a model of communitarianism—and by extension, socialism in particular—that reinstates the significance of the individual in order to arrive at a more sustainable form of collective commitment. After working through some arguments in favor of the individual's primacy in forming the community, and then some in favor of the community's primacy in forming the individual, he arrives at a third: defining the mediating term of "autonomy" *not* as "self-completeness," but as the "having of a will, a rational will of one's own" that allows one to evaluate and give feedback on particular traits of the community that has fostered it (Gyekye 113). Gyekye calls this balance a "restricted or moderate communitarianism" (114), which he then also argues would have space for but not fetishize individual rights vis-à-vis a complementary emphasis on duties (117). In effect—and indeed, by turning to the quintessential liberal philosopher John Rawls's work on individual rights defined as a "common asset"! (118)—Gyekye's limited communitarianism is a *liberal communitarianism*. It is the fate of this unintuitive complementarity that this book sets out to trace, first in its possibilities approaching nationhood, and later in its frustration as a global narrative priority.

Book Structure

This book is divided into two halves: part I comprises two chapters on novelists working in anticipation of national independence, and part II comprises two chapters on novelists working right in the belly of the hungry "global literature" beast. My intention is not to uphold a reductive division between "national" and "global" writing, and it will be clear from my analyses in all four chapters that writers working on the cusp of national independence had cosmopolitan commitments, just as recent writers may have national ones. At the same time, it is important not to overcomplicate matters: it is absolutely the case that for J. E. Casely Hayford (chapter 1) and Stanlake Samkange (chapter 2), the nation (respectively, Ghana and Zimbabwe) was the horizon toward which their work looked. Likewise, globality is the default frame for writers in the present and the recent past, including Jennifer Nansubuga Makumbi (chapter 3) and Tendai Huchu and Imraan Coovadia (chapter 4), not least because of the transnational structure of the publishing industry to which they are, for better or worse, beholden. The book's two halves are therefore true to the dominant interpretive scale of the eras they treat, even where they are complicated or resisted. The part titles "National Horizons" and "Global Recessions" should be taken as signposts, not gospels, intended to capture something essential about the power (or lack thereof) of ideas as such on either side of the Big Moment of independence from British imperial rule.

I have noticeably omitted that common historical center as a focus in its own right, drawing it into the book instead through prefatory chapter discussions. The most prominent names in the field are all present, but they are discussed piecemeal, as needed, instead of in chapters of their own. This is for reasons both substantive and pragmatic. The first is that I am hoping to avoid what have become entrenched categories of "transition" followed by encroaching "disillusionment" and prefer to look to works and moments that more forcefully speak to the representational challenges that either precede or follow the heyday of the African nation-state. This is where the question of individualism strikes me as *most* generative, because the nature of the relationship between the part and the whole is in flux. Some books that might seem like natural fits for this analysis are less provocative in this context than the ones I have chosen, precisely because what they represent is not in question. Achebe's bureaucrat-intellectual Obi from *No Longer at Ease* or Soyinka's frustrated scholars and artists from *The Interpreters* are perfect examples of the "missing middle" of this book: they speak powerfully for a generation on the cusp of hope and despair. But they do not participate in foregrounding the individual's relationship to ideas *as such*, an imperative that in some ways ascends in inverse proportion to a tangible sense of belonging to a larger political structure. Just as important, however, are the practical reasons for my choices in this book. Acknowledging the impossibility of doing everything, I have chosen to focus my energies on works that have not received the voluminous critical attention of Achebe, Soyinka, Ngũgĩ, Gordimer, or Coetzee. The works and writers featured in the chapters to come are all sources of profound and largely unrehearsed intellectual challenge, and they are the best examples I have encountered of explicit engagement with demarcated philosophical practice. All of them are worthy of more attention than they have received. For the most part, students and critics are well versed in how African literature bridges the colonial and the postcolonial, and so I have elected to foreground what I see as equally rich cases from slightly further afield.

The four chapters span both publication years, ranging from 1911 to 2014, and national contexts, including Ghana, Zimbabwe, Uganda, and South Africa. This scope is not without risk: *The African Novel of Ideas* is synthetic but not comprehensive. And yet the temporal and geographical variation of its subjects is a key part of its intervention in African literary studies, which tends to favor either a national or global scale. This book has no illusions that it advances an all-encompassing argument and seeks rather to collate situations that are mutually resonant but not identical. In this light, I am drawn to Paul Saint-Amour's notion of "meso-analysis," as he describes it in *Modernism/modernity*: "the scale that mediates between [the] two extremes" of micro and macro ("Medial Humanities"). If the "micro" here would entail charting a particular motif or device across, say, Zimbabwean literature, and the "macro" would be a study of "philosophy and globality" or something along those lines, then *The African Novel of Ideas* unfolds as a medial series of convergences among traditions that evolve along staggered time lines. It would not be defensible to propose a single tradition of African writing, but at the same time it seems cowardly to avoid generalizing about affinities that clearly exist. And so, for example, the year of Ghanaian independence, 1957, is the same as that of the first Shona novel's publication in Zimbabwe (Solomon Mutswairo's *Feso*), before Rhodesia had even come into existence. This means that Casely Hayford in 1911 and Samkange in the 1970s share key concerns about the intellectual's role in advancing the cause of national self-determination. At the same time, Samkange's career overlaps with that of postcolonial writers like Ama Ata Aidoo, drawing into itself both colonial and postcolonial frames of reference. In structuring chapters to have primary arguments and then codas, I have tried to capture both of these correspondences.

The argument beneath the argument, so to speak, of *The African Novel of Ideas* is similarly situated somewhere between observation and polemic. My working hypothesis in beginning this book was that philosophy had once had self-evident prestige in African intellectual life—Nkrumah's aforementioned training is one good example—whereas now it is not uncommon to hear African novelists at book festivals and the like claim to "just be telling stories" or offering up "my truth" as a way of avoiding more penetrating discussion. While there may still be some validity to Appiah's observation, in *In My Father's House*, that "'Philosophy' is the highest-status label of Western humanism" (88), it is undoubtedly also the case that the prestige of "humanism" itself has been dealt decades' worth of blows. Nonetheless, charting the effect of this on the African novel writ large is a very tall order. This book thus works through numerous specific points at which novels by African writers move away from a philosophical orientation and toward what I call an experiential one—something like what Joan W. Scott once described as an "appeal to experience as uncontestable evidence and as an originary point of explanation" (777)—but it stops short of offering a strong, unifying reason for why this occurs. It is certainly my view that the turn to experience as "the origin of knowledge," per Scott, and to the individual subject as "the bedrock of evidence on which explanation is built" marks a diminishment from efforts to see the individual as the threshold of the universal (ibid.). This has been an understandable and even necessary political choice on some writers' part. (A section on *Our Sister Killjoy* in chapter 1 touches on this issue in relation to gender, and in a quite different vein, the same could be said about Marechera's turn toward viscerality in chapter 2.) But the phenomenon of seeing "experience" as the novel's main currency is so widespread, and so multivalent, that I am not prepared to make a grand case for its causality. One easy way to do this would perhaps have been to invoke "the global neoliberal economy" and its self-perpetuation via mass-marketable, atomized forms of subjectivity. I am not, however, convinced that doing so would offer a thick or scalable enough explanation. There *are* material factors that I suspect are at play in the evolution away from seeing the novelized individual as a tool of philosophical generalization, such as the introduction of US-style creative writing programs into African academies. At the end of the day, however, I can only speculate as to how this works.

What I do feel comfortable asserting without qualification is that the "philosophizing individual," where it plays a central role in African novels, is a common representational means that can be seen to reach markedly different ends from the first half of this book to the second. The two authors who feature most prominently in the "National Horizons" chapters—the Gold Coast intellectual Casely Hayford and the Rhodesian-cum-Zimbabwean writer and politician Samkange—both look to philosophy as a force for connecting the reflective individual with a nascent national community. In different ways, they "speak for" at least a certain class of their respective generations. The main character of Casely Hayford's novel *Ethiopia Unbound* is committed to rigorous forms of argument and private reflection because his self-styled identity as a philosopher is what grants him the confidence and presence of mind to navigate the colonial social worlds from which he seeks liberation. In Samkange's case, philosophy picks up where his most successful novel, *The Mourned One*, leaves off to generate an indigenous and yet learnable code of moral and civic conduct. Considered as parts of their larger intellectual projects, the forms of these philosophical novels and of Samkange's novel-adjacent philosophical treatise aim toward hard-earned universality. Philosophical practice is a key part of developing a leadership model that couples individual integrity with a capacity for broad generalization.

In the "Global Recessions" chapters, the most overtly philosophical figures in novels by Jennifer Nansubuga Makumbi (*Kintu*), Tendai Huchu (*The Maestro, the Magistrate, and the Mathematician*), and Imraan

Coovadia (*Tales of the Metric System*) think themselves into oblivion. All three writers cordon off abstract individual thought from multipronged, often frenetic plots of transnational social connectivity. The three main works considered in part II, in other words, depict philosophy as a practice that is ill suited to global structures of representation. Furthermore, unlike the prominent statesmen-writers Casely Hayford and Samkange, the writers featured in part II all publish with small independent presses and thus, to some degree, occupy a niche place in literary fiction. It is worth noting here that these are not isolated instances: numerous other recent small-press African novels depict "deep thinkers" as outright pariahs. These include the Burundian author Roland Rugero's *Baho!* (2012), in which the philosophical main character is a mute hunted down for a crime he did not commit; the South African Unathi Magubeni's debut work *Nwelezelanga* (2016), about a powerful divine messenger who is shunned for being albino; and the Nigerian poet Jumoke Verissimo's debut novel *A Small Silence* (2019), about an aging scholar who literally hides alone in the dark. The final impression is that *something happens* to the place of ideas between the swell toward national independence and the elegies for its lost ideals—something that makes both philosophy and its embodiments seem like oddities instead of aspirations. But if what I have called the individual as the threshold of world-expanding abstraction is marginal to our "global age," this does not mean they can be dismissed. Whether in the streets of Harare, a Kampala home, or a Durban crowd, there has never been a more crucial time to listen.

Chapter Summaries and Conceptual Guide

The chapters in *The African Novel of Ideas* are all written to be independently legible. The novel's negotiation between philosophy and experience as dominant "poles" of expressive meaning is present in each of them, particularly in the codas, which extend each chapter's comparative range within the regional contexts at hand. That said, readers will also benefit from moving through them in order, so that the underlying progression as described in the previous section will be clearer.

The book's first chapter, "*Ethiopia Unbound* as Afro-Comparatist Novel: The Case for Liberated Solitude," centers on the seminal 1911 novel of the Gold Coast writer, lawyer, and statesman J. E. Casely Hayford. Casely Hayford and his intellectual milieu after the short-lived, independent Fante Confederacy (1868–1873) are typically (and sometimes pejoratively) assigned an intermediary historical role as cultural or comprador brokers between native Fante subjects and the English-speaking officials of the British protectorate. *The African Novel of Ideas* instead upholds *Ethiopia Unbound* as a richly *comparative* text, one that studiously negotiates among far-flung civilizations. I demonstrate this by foregrounding the distinctively novelistic properties of Casely Hayford's book—and specifically, its incremental structure—to elaborate a mode of analysis in which concepts become a neutral tool to facilitate different traditions' interaction. Against common readings of the novel's departure from the supposedly Western norm of individual depth, the chapter also argues that Casely Hayford insists on reflective solitude as the route to a comparative cultural sensibility. This takes the form of encounters with a specific divinity (in the form of the *Nyiakropon*, or Fante God); vacillation between solitary reading and forms of public address (speeches, essay fragments, philosophies of education, and so on); performed translation; and a poetics of analogy with other modernities both far and proximate (for example, Greek, Russian, Yoruba, and English). Casely Hayford emerges less as a "middleman" than as a literary contrapuntalist. His method therefore has far-reaching implications for a resurgent critical interest in decolonization, conceived of here in culturally lateralizing rather than recentralizing or "nativist" terms. Crucially, however, the full civilizational equality that *Ethiopia Unbound* enacts is a payoff of the novel's cumulative structure. As a result, I argue, it is precisely the individualizing, developmental properties of the novel—its "liberalism," by some measure—that grant it the power to globally situate Fante intellectual history.

The last third of the first chapter then looks forward to work by Ama Ata Aidoo (*Our Sister Killjoy*) and Ayi Kwei Armah (*Fragments*) as points of transition from a celebratory brand of Fante cosmopolitanism to a more critical one. In the process, it introduces a critical question for the book as a whole and for the novel into the present day: what is the difference, in formal as well as analytic terms, between individuality and subjectivity? While *Ethiopia Unbound* marks space for its main character's subjective experience, the textures of that experience are largely outside the novel's domain. In *Our Sister Killjoy* and *Fragments*, conveying the felt experience of alienation is arguably the central narratological objective: if the dominant form-within-a-form for Casely Hayford is the analogy or perhaps the Socratic dialogue, then for a writer like Ama Ata Aidoo it is the private letter or internal monologue. Thus, a secondary question that I would like chapter 1 to raise for the reader is how a widespread emphasis on subjectivity over other representational modes of individuality has come to have such strong associations with *marginality* and social awareness.

Chapter 2 builds on the comparative dimensions of pre-independence Anglo-Fante forms by turning to pre-independence Zimbabwe, and specifically to the literary and philosophical career of the Shona intellectual Stanlake Samkange in the 1970s. In "Between the House of Stone and a Hard Place: Stanlake Samkange's Philosophical Turn," his novels and philosophical efforts alike reveal a commitment to individual character as the locus of new national institutions. This conduct-based, slowly acquisitional version of national character puts Samkange somewhat at odds with the intellectual momentum of his time, during which a more insurgent liberation politics held sway. As a teacher, the son of a minister, and a secondary-school innovator (he founded one of Zimbabwe's first nonmissionary African high schools), Samkange was also deeply committed to liberal education. This chapter considers his movement between fiction and philosophy as an attempt to reconcile the demands of representing emplaced figures who "do" philosophy, on the one hand, with those of elaborating transcultural philosophical systems, on the other. I look to his novel *The Mourned One* (1975) as a turning point and then move to his little-read treatise *Hunhuism or Ubuntuism: A Zimbabwe Indigenous Religious Philosophy* (1980). My aim is to chronicle Samkange's move from writing novels about historically representative Shona men who fall victim to their times to propounding a linguistically and culturally aggregate philosophical system that will outlive them.

Like the previous chapter on Fante intellectualism, this chapter also ends with discussion of how philosophical civic-mindedness gives way to philosophical ennui in the Zimbabwean novel as it approaches independence, using the examples of Stanley Nyamfukudza's *The Non-Believer's Journey* and Dambudzo Marechera's *Black Sunlight*. Mapping a similar divide to the one between *Ethiopia Unbound*, on the one hand, and *Fragments* and *Our Sister Killjoy*, on the other, it shows how Samkange's measured exposition of Shona individualism gives way to the subjective pangs of Nyamfukudza and Marechera as the most "available" means of representing a self against the backdrop of a changing world order. Chapter 2's time span, however, is much more compressed. Also departing from the model of philosophical individualism expounded narratively by Casely Hayford, Samkange ultimately moves toward philosophy as a *partner* to the novel, rather than as something that the novel itself does. In this sense, he seems to perceive something not as far removed from his more psychologically deft peers as it may seem in regard to the novel's changing fortunes in Africa: that there is room for its nationalist versions at home and for its bold subjectivization as it travels abroad, but increasingly little space for a narrative persona that seeks to hover above the vicissitudes of both.

The third chapter of *The African Novel of Ideas*, on the Ugandan writer Jennifer Nansubuga Makumbi's *Kintu*, moves forward in time to the early twenty-first century, where it starts by outlining some of the key disciplinary debates of the past few decades. "A Forked Path, Forever: *Kintu* between Reason and Rationality" argues that specific terminological disagreements (for example, between singular and multiple modernities) can be mapped as a broader tension between broadening and pluralizing humanistic concepts. This chapter also creates continuity with the endings of the chapters in the first half of the book, which broached the connection between "being philosophical" and impending disillusionment or social alienation (in *Fragments* and *Black Sunlight*, for example). As postcolonialism gradually gives way to the newer terminology of global literature, Makumbi takes stock of her own scale of representation. I argue that *Kintu*'s layered interpretive structure surrounding the possibility of a family curse—and in general, of reading supernatural causation as "true"—stages a distinction between reason and rationality, whose differences I elaborate through like-minded work by the philosopher Emmanuel Chukwudi Eze. Eze, the chapter shows, ties reason to the process of individual will-formation en route to collective intelligibility, which in *Kintu* entails reasonably opting *out* of rational explanation. This distinction comes to a head in one of the novel's key figures, Miisi, a displaced, globally educated, scientific-minded intellectual. I ultimately contend that *Kintu* carries the full heft of African debates about tradition and modernity from preceding decades, so that literature and philosophy again converge around a similar set of meta-epistemological questions.

In chapter 3's coda, I briefly introduce two other works from East Africa in the decade surrounding *Kintu*'s publication. Both Goretti Kyomuhendo's *Waiting* (2007) and Peter Kimani's *Dance of the Jakaranda* (2017), I argue, invoke curses and traditional explanations as social truisms, but not as points of interpretive decision-making. Their respective, albeit very different, efforts at social stock-taking capture another common direction for the African novel in the postnational period: that of localized historical representation that, to one end or another, is its own reward. By "postnational" I mean simply that it is an era in which the nation is often *re*-claimed, and sometimes just taken for granted, but not proleptically hailed into being. Whereas the chapters in the "National Horizons" half of this book include codas about the ascent of subjectivity as the dominant means by which individuality is novelized, already chafing against national narratives, chapter 3's coda suggests that the nation can now be revisited on "softer," more heterogeneous terms. Although there is valuable insight to be gained here, a pointed exploration of individuality falls out of the picture and the novel feels more incidental than essential to the social terrain it presents. The reader is thus left with the question of where the deeply regionally embedded novel could possibly go after *Kintu*.

The book's final chapter before its brief epilogue elaborates the idea of "philosophical suicide," which is lifted from Dostoevsky's novel *Demons* as it is invoked by the contemporary Zimbabwean writer Tendai Huchu. The novels that "Bodies Impolitic: African Deaths of Philosophical Suicide" address go even further than *Kintu* in signaling the social marginality of a self-identified philosophical temperament: it takes up works in which intellection signals not just social illegibility but literal death. The chapter is devoted mainly to two current southern African novelists who foreground the relationship between thinking and dying: Huchu and the South African writer Imraan Coovadia. Each of their most recent novels was published in 2014, and they bear a strong resemblance to one another in their diffuse plot structures, coordination of contemporary nationhood across multiple transnational points, and fatalistic politics. The chapter's first section elaborates suicide as a structural and historical skeleton key to understanding these works' deeper shift toward socially impotent individualism. Huchu's *The Maestro, the Magistrate, and the Mathematician* features a character who dies by self-starvation in an effort to remove himself from a distractingly virtualized and commercialized society, and Coovadia's *Tales of the Metric System* develops one of its plotlines around a fictional version of the South African philosopher Rick Turner. Both books were published in the United States by the same small academic outlet, a sign of their similar positions in a highly stratified African literary marketplace (in which top stars not infrequently sign million-dollar book deals).

I then offer a coda on a third novel from the region, Masande Ntshanga's *The Reactive*. Published in the same year, this novel likewise demands reflection on the relation among self-reflection, self-will, and self-killing through a main character who infects himself with HIV. If the first three chapters' codas suggested varied paths for the novel's development out of a strong philosophical individualism, this last chapter concludes by introducing what amounts to a less explicit version of what occupies its primary texts. This should indicate that the novel is not really *going* anywhere, at least in terms of this book's connecting thread: philosophical individualism cannot quite bridge the gap between the conceptual abstraction that it *can* broach and the abstraction of globality, which it cannot.

Finally, a short epilogue underscores some of the disciplinary challenges lurking behind the book as a whole, before offering some more speculative remarks on the future of both the field and the African novel of ideas as I have described it. What is the fate of the individual in a posthumanistic critical landscape, and how, going forward, might the field of African literature help chart a course toward balance between locatedness and generalization? On what does viewing the African novel as the vanguard of the broader literary world, instead of as its marginal "other," shed new light? I propose that seeing Africa as a point of departure opens up a maximally fraught and therefore globally relevant exploration of the spaces in which ideas might still be salient representational forces in their own right. To close the book and invite further discussion, I suggest that what has long been perceived as a liability by African intellectuals—the denial of the continent's *implicit* claim to universality—might be turned on its head as the basis of a far-reaching call to undertake the profoundest kinds of questioning. In this I return once more to Sekyi-Otu's impassioned case for "the transcendental grounding of an ethical and political project, on condition that this is not confused . . . with a transcendental warrant" (4). By viewing the individual on the brink of abstraction as a defining feature of African literary life, African writers' engagement with a partial universalism becomes the condition of its fulfillment.

PART I

National Horizons

CHAPTER ONE

Ethiopia Unbound as Afro-Comparatist Novel

THE CASE FOR LIBERATED SOLITUDE

In conclusion, universality resides in this decision to bear the burden of the reciprocal relativism of differing cultures, provided only that the colonial status is irrevocably excluded.

—FRANTZ FANON, "RACISM AND CULTURE" (1956)

THE CONVENTIONAL NARRATIVE of the African novel's development begins around the time that colonialism ends, usually dating from the late 1950s. It is often structured around a tension between cultural diffusion and cultural consolidation, which is to say between hybridistic, or cosmopolitan, and more nativist or nationalist ways of defining the form's response to British imperial rule. The nuances and blind spots of these broad-strokes positions have been dissected *ad nauseam*, and it is not my intention to "take a side" again in this chapter. I begin here, rather, to establish a baseline for how an African novelistic genealogy whose terms derive from the independence era circumscribes even critical debate, entrenching truisms that do not hold up in broader historical framings. The familiar opposition of multiplicity and resistance—which has its oft-cited academic corollary in "postcolonial theory" versus more hard-line Afrocentric schools of thought—in fact foregrounds a common critical practice that sees individual subjects in fiction as stand-ins for a social situation. The individual is instrumentalized by the African novel, not *instrumental of* some analytic function within it. At its best, the tendency to read African characters as social microcosms has provided a useful foil to Eurocentric literary standards, often limitedly rooted in psychological depth to demonstrate character development. At its worst, however, it has led to a bias toward seeing African writing as transparently sociological, rather than as depicting a complex negotiation between shaping and being shaped by the world.

To this I now add that intellectual cultivation—the practice of learning and reflecting—is all but entirely squeezed out of the picture of what it is that African novels best showcase to the world. In this chapter, I thus look back to an earlier, often neglected literary context in which individuals' power to craft philosophical arguments was valorized as a key part of anticolonial reform, pushing beyond the implicit assumption that the coherent "liberal self" and the collective goals of liberation were somehow opposed. I turn, specifically, to proto-nationalist Anglo-Fante intellectual life on the Gold Coast (present-day Ghana) at the turn of the twentieth century. The chapter upholds one of its main figures—the pan-Africanist lawyer, politician, and man of letters J. E. Casely Hayford—as exemplary of a literary practice that is at once fiercely liberationist and wedded to individuals' capacity for rational, "objective" exchange across humanistic traditions. His seminal 1911 novel *Ethiopia Unbound* foregrounds a standard of evenhanded *conceptual comparability* rather than just cultural restitution, using a main character who toggles between reflective solitude and a dispassionate mode of public engagement to foster discrete and complementary realms for "felt" experience and intellectual engagement. As a result, the proactive comparison of African and European traditions appears not only as a burden imposed by empire, but as a means of honing an intellectual confidence that thwarts its undue influence. The implications are significant: the African novel and its attendant conceptual traditions, instead of demanding a sometimes patronizing revision of what "counts" as intellectual content (a pervasive kind of "different but equal" approach), are cast as full-fledged philosophical interlocutors. Casely Hayford's explicit intellectualism and emphasis on solitary erudition, coupled with an abiding commitment to race-based institutional reform, allows his novel to straddle investments in lived political dynamics and what Dambudzo Marechera once called the "ideal cosmos" of literature "co-existing with this crude one" (1987/2007, 186).

The following chapter moves through three sections that elaborate comparison as an Afro-originating intellectual model that insists on lateral, conceptually grounded exchange, with the individual philosopher serving as a kind of lever. First, it surveys the rocky relationship between the academic fields of comparative literature and African literary studies, establishing the broader literary discipline's "global turn" as both a challenge and a boon to the comparative enterprise. Both fields, I suggest, have struggled to maintain a clear analytic object as they have shifted away from a delimited textual archive and toward more diffuse concepts of culture and relation. I argue that comparative philosophy—and specifically, comparative Akan-European projects by Kwasi Wiredu and Kwame Anthony Appiah—offers a valuable alternative model that retains the precision of more traditional comparative methodologies (which worked with bounded literary traditions) without sacrificing the imperative to geographically de-hierarchize the field. In the second section, I let this theoretical foundation serve as a space into which *Ethiopia Unbound* and its rich Anglo-Fante intellectual moment retroactively intervene. Finally, I take the measure of better-known, less comparatively inclined works in the later Anglo-Fante tradition against the precedent set by Casely Hayford and his milieu. I contend that intellectualism—elaborated here as a conceptual rather than subjective orientation—evolves from a driving force of Ghanaian novelistic development at the twentieth century's start into depiction as a flatter, subsidiary category of personal experience by the postcolonial era.

Comparison between the Global and the Decolonial

Comparative literature has a troubled reputation for neglecting non-Western traditions.[1] Most narratives of the discipline as it is practiced in English begin just slightly in advance of conventional accounts of postcolonial literature, which is to say, following World War II and anticipating the formal dissolution of the British empire. This coincides, of course, with the ratcheting up of the Cold War, and so "comp lit," as it's known in the American university, becomes a self-conceived bastion of cosmopolitanism against the nationalistic tide. Jonathan Culler offers a summary to this effect in an essay called "Whither Comparative Literature?":

> Comparative literature has been differentiated from other modes of literary study because it did not take it for granted, as did the departments of English, French, Spanish, Italian, Chinese, that a national literature in its historical evolution was the natural and appropriate unit of literary study. Since comparative literature could not avoid, as the national literature departments could, the question of what sorts of units were most pertinent—genres? periods? themes?—comparative literature frequently became the site of literary theory, while national

literature departments often... remained indifferent to the sorts of theory that did not emanate from their own cultural spheres. (85)

I do not intend to offer an exhaustive disciplinary history, but to indicate what is more or less the consensus about comparative literature's identity vis-à-vis other forms of literary study. As others before me have argued, its cosmopolitanism comes into crisis with the shift toward a more geographically expansive postcolonialism-cum-transnationalism located primarily within English departments. This challenge of moving from a well-delineated literary geography—identified for a long time mainly with western European and to some degree with Russian traditions— accompanies a shift away from a well-delineated conception of the literary object, writ large.

In practice, African literary studies and comparative literature have existed largely as separate disciplinary spaces. This is not to suggest that Africanists do not undertake comparative work, but that African literary scholarship has not been chiefly concerned with theorizing comparison, as such, and that comparative theory has not focused much on Africa. In this section, however, I will argue that globality as a "solution" for comparative literature and globality as a "problem" for African literary studies derive from two shared and interlinked challenges: establishing comparability without denying power imbalances, and arriving at a sufficiently stable and thus "comparable" object of analysis. The broader discipline's turn to a global literary paradigm means that would-be comparatists now contend not only with a massive potential archive (quite expressly the whole world) but also with one whose standard of comparability is, paradoxically, either unevenness (à la world systems theory) or mobility/flux. Complicating matters further, the popular solution of a "South-South" comparative framework (that is, one that bypasses the West) goes only partway to signaling a truly de-hierarchized literary field. A fully equalized comparative terrain must at some point be able to account for relations among Western and Southern traditions, and yet this goal comes with considerable baggage vis-à-vis African literary studies especially.[2]

First, I want to pick up with Culler's "Whither Comparative Literature?" as part of a larger set of concerns about what, these days, gets compared. After contemplating the benefits and drawbacks of extending literary study to include all cultural objects in all parts of the world (he is in favor of the latter, but not the former), Culler asks, "What, in this newly globalized space, justifies bringing texts together?" (90). His answer is that comparability is determined by a shared discursive terrain, by which he means "a general field that underwrites comparison," or one text's "relation to others within a cultural space" (92). In other words, comparison requires some kind of bounded cultural context in order to mobilize textual differences within it. Culler rightly notes that comparative literature now makes strong use of "a general postcolonial context within which comparabilities can be generated" (ibid.). Presumably, African literature would fall within this ambit. In fact, however, this vein of what might now be called "global Anglophone" scholarship is in large part at odds with the defining tensions of African literary studies more specifically. The type of scholarship to which Culler refers—he mentions specifically an Anglophone "hypercanon" of "Rushdie, Achebe, Walcott, Coetzee, etc." (90)—might be fine for comparing works whose mutual intelligibility hangs on a relation to Western imperialism. But it cannot quite account for how to compare across African texts and contexts that are strategically self-delimiting or exclusive of the West, as has often been the case.

While it does not merit significant space here, it is important therefore to note that the defining tension within African literature is not between "Eurocentric" and "global," but rather between integrative (or "de-centering") and oppositional (or perhaps "re-centering") objectives for African cultural production. This is best captured in decades of critical controversy over "nativism," which, as Adéléke Adéèkó has usefully described it, functions more successfully as a rhetorical strategy than as a form of genuine cultural reclamation. As Adéèkó suggests, Ngũgĩ's much-discussed "linguistic nativism" (that is, his insistence on Gikuyu-language literary production) rests uneasily with his historical situation. "All that a self-aware nativist critic can do," Adéèkó writes, "is to devise general principles based on an interpretation of second order information," as now-inaccessible precolonial forms are "appropriated for a localist foundation of the emergent post-independence culture" (1998/2007, 236–37). As twenty-first-century literary institutions have rushed to keep pace with the dizzyingly complex, networked condition institutionalized variously as globality, transnationalism, world literature, and the like, the African literary field has spawned ever-new forms of the definitive underlying conflict outlined here. A heated and irresoluble debate over the term "Afropolitanism" is the most prominent example. The novelist Taiye Selasi's now-iconic 2005 essay "Bye-Bye Babar," from the defunct online *The Lip Magazine*, identifies a chic, "scattered tribe of pharmacists, physicists, physicians (and the odd polygamist) [that] has set up camp around the globe," referring in the main to an exodus of educated Africans to European and American cities after the independence era. In attracting the ire of, most famously, fellow writer Binyavanga Wainaina for its valorization of the privileged diaspora over more emplaced and committed continental citizens, Selasi's essay sparks what now seems like a period of profound literary-intellectual déjà vu. As regards African literature's place in the world, then, the discord over Afropolitanism foregrounds a persistent and fundamental division as to whether Africa is best imagined as a site of commerce *with* the West, or one of continued exploitation by it.

The historical topic of nativism thus bleeds into the more contemporary one of cultural essentialism, and in African literary studies one sees in full force the risks of turning from "text" to "culture." Following on Adéẹ̀kọ́'s representative skepticism as to the historical dubiousness of cultural reconstruction (whatever its sometimes worthwhile strategic uses), comparatists have often worried over the practical, methodological implications of the cultural turn. Peter Brooks, for example, critiques what he sees as an unjustified call in the American Comparative Literature Association's 1993 state-of-the-discipline report to turn away from "high literature" in favor of discursive context as stemming from a mistaken view that "the study of literature is an outmoded mandarin practice that had better catch up with the hip world of cultural studies" (99). Moreover, he notes, the report fails to provide "any theory of the practices recommended" in re-forming the discipline as the study of cultural context, risking a replacement of "the study of literature with amateur social history, amateur sociology, and personal ideology" (100). Amid similar fears, Culler's solution is to orient comparative literature to poetics as "a repertoire of possibilities, forms, themes, [and] discursive practices" (95), which is persuasive in accounting for both limitless comparative combinations, in a geographical sense, and necessarily limited comparative endeavors in a more practical one. In this way, his model is an improvement on an ossified postcolonialism that remains tethered to imperial contact as the grounds by which a common field is established. It is easy to see, however, how more economically attuned critiques of comparative literature might find Culler's approach wanting. "Comparative literature has always thought about difference," Haun Saussy writes in his introduction to the volume *Comparative Literature in an Age of Globalization*, "but inequality remains foreign to its usual vocabulary." In a further move toward pitting global economic disparity against comparative literature's worldly self-conception, Saussy continues, "The more cosmopolitan our reach, the more evident the problem" (2006, 28).

The disciplinary debates that Saussy reviews are by now familiar, revolving, as Culler and Brooks likewise suggest, mainly around tensions between formalistic methods of analysis and a "cultural studies" approach to non-Western bodies of work. What is less often observed in the context of connecting African and comparative literary histories is that Saussy, like others who are sympathetic to developing a more inclusive field of academic comparison, sees postcolonial studies as the primary and most useful "other." He cites "much postcolonial scholarship (erroneously categorized as special pleading)" as a body of work that has contended with how "the single [global] economy divides up what it unites" (28). Postcolonialism, in other words, is presented as a productive partner to thinking about the "world system." Saussy extends this line of thinking to his essay in the following state-of-the-discipline report ten years later, published in 2017 as the volume *Futures of Comparative Literature*. He writes there that "the ambition to write literary histories of regions outside of Europe, showing their internal organization and development—which are often instructively different from what is seen in the European example," is one antidote to narratives of capital's global diffusion that have become a rote and accepted form of Western self-critique (26).

What we are left with is a Venn diagram in which African literary studies and comparative literature overlap around the tandem questions of postcolonialism and globalization. And yet this convergence marks a problem space for African literature, and a salvational space for comparison. Whereas postcolonialism has often been seen as a *challenge* to conceptualizing harder-line forms of *de*-coloniality within African literary studies, postcolonialism for comparatists augurs a more general geographical expansionism that in effect becomes a "decolonizing" framework. What's more, seminal debates within the postcolonial field surrounding its diffusive versus agonistic skew—influential work by Neil Lazarus, Peter Hallward, and Vivek Chibber, among others, has mounted strong critiques of mainline postcolonial theory—resound through persistent tensions between world literature and comparative literature.[3] Following this line of thought, postcolonialism is a corrective to comparison rather than its next frontier. Writing in *The Global South* during its first year of publication in 2007, Alfred J. Lopez posits, "The rise of postcolonial studies and related projects has begun to expose [the problem of 'foreignized' subaltern texts] in comparative literature, as the latter has only in the past decade started playing a belated game of inclusive multicultural 'catchup' in an area in which it has effectively been trumped" (2). Lopez thus believes that "the global South signals the death of a certain kind of comparative literature, because it would undermine the originary exclusion upon which the discipline is founded" (5). And while Natalie Melas has painstakingly presented contradictory evidence for comparative literature's less Eurocentric nineteenth-century origins in her monograph *All the Difference in the World*, she also elaborates its racism and overly positivistic methodology.[4] It thus seems fair here to hew to the "myth," as Lopez does, that the discipline originated post–World War II; at the very least, this period marks its rebirth as a field for which cosmopolitanism is a meta-theoretical rather than taxonomizing project.

Whereas comparatists such as Culler and Saussy and, more recently, Shu-Mei Shih in a *PMLA* essay on "World Studies and Relational Comparison" respond to global economic divisions by advocating for more inclusive comparative methodologies, the trend among Marxist-influenced world literature scholars is to see this move as politically flaccid. Consider the following two statements, the first by Shih, and the second from the Warwick Research Collective's 2015 book *Combined and Uneven Development: Towards a New Theory of World-Literature*. "The work of the comparatist thereby partially evens out the terrain of literature across the world," Shih writes, "thus [breaking up] the center-periphery model of world systems theory" (436). Moreover, recalling this chapter's introductory give-and-take between an expanding and contracting scale of African literary study, "a true anti-Eurocentrism should scatter all centers rather than replace one center with another" (435). In contrast, the authors of the Warwick Research Collective (WReC) book begin from the assumption that a literary study should reflect rather than imagine itself as eschewing global economic dynamics. While these scholars also seek departure from a diffusionist model of modernity in favor of a highly varied and yet all-encompassing capitalist system, the WReC deemphasizes method and focuses on "the *literary* registration and encoding of modernity as a social logic" (15). In other words, the members of the WReC are less interested in what we might do with the literature of roughly the past two hundred years and more concerned with what that literature reveals: that the world is a vastly uneven place, and Shih's utopic comparative egalitarianism will not make it any less so.

Following on interventions by Fredric Jameson, Harry Harootunian, and others, which dismiss postcolonial theories of "alternative modernities" as similarly denialist, the logic of the WReC analysis at first glance seems unassailable. If the "unprecedentedness" of the "modern capitalist 'world-system' . . . consists precisely in the fact that it is a *world-system* that is also, uniquely and for the first time, a *world* system" (8)—that is, if capitalism is the system that determines *all* systems—then it follows that all literature somehow registers its dominance. An argument of this scale, however, is doomed to say the same thing over and over: literature shows us only what we already know, the totalizing thrust of which heads off alternative frameworks at the pass. Harootunian perhaps unwittingly acknowledges as much in his like-minded essay "Some Thoughts on Comparability and the Space-Time Problem," asserting that if "the instance of unevenness invariably accompanies the historical spread of capitalism everywhere, it must still continue to occupy a commanding 'space of experience' because it constitutes one of its principal conditions of preproduction" (51). For him, this suggests that a world systems approach to literature must restore emphasis on temporality over what he sees as the faulty postcolonial preference for space, because capitalism manifests in time as an endlessly replaying process rather than a stagnant, achieved, and overturnable state.

The upshot of Harootunian's argument is that global comparison grounded in space "either dramatizes the location of difference or situates place boundedness as an asylum for political and cultural resistance to globalization" (39), wedding an appearance of resistance *to* a Western-originating capitalist modernity to a perpetual definition of the rest of the world vis-à-vis the West. The argument's turns are many, but its final shape looks something like this: comparison gravitates toward space (in that it compares one country or region with another) because it provides a bounded entity for the comparatist to work with. In downplaying time and thus the simultaneous dynamisms of capitalist entrenchment, it denies "a relationship of coevality to precisely those societies targeted for study" (32). Comparison, in short, has often served as an insidious force for instantiating hierarchy even as it claims to dispel it, because "the inevitable impulse to compare," in Harootunian's estimation, has historically been fused with "a strategy to classify and categorize according to criteria based upon geopolitical privilege" (30). His point also relates to the persistent complaint of global scholars working in the comparative domain that "the non-West may be a source of exotic cultural production but cannot be a site of theory" (Krishnaswamy 400). In other words, "global literatures" are adopted as content, never as method.

Here too one can make further connections with another key problem often seen to stem from comparative literature's European and American origins: namely that, at the end of the day, comparison is a function of the *comparatist*. Because "comparative literature ... defines itself by its act" instead of its content, suggests Robert J. C. Young, also in a recent issue of *PMLA*, the "'comparative' is performed by the critic" (683–84). Likewise, Saussy reminds us, "the individual comparatist, engaged on a project, knows or comes to learn quite well what she is doing. But the results of many projects do not add up to a cumulative body of settled law, do not prove for all future comers the 'comparability' of item X and item Y" (2006, 24). Comparative literature's main blessing—its identity as a rich haven for individual critics who feel up to the task of theorizing their own basis for comparative enterprise—is also therefore its curse. Because comparison is something that is *done*, not something, like the world system, that supposedly just *is*, it cannot easily dispense with a strong individualist foundation. When the individuals in question are mostly from the West, it is easy to see how geographical hierarchy would be baked into the discipline.

Perhaps for this reason, the most convincing solutions offered to effectively "decolonize" comparison have moved away from seeing it as the systematized domain of strong, discerning theoreticians, in favor of fundamentally redefining its object of inquiry. Revathi Krishnaswamy, for example, proposes a move away from clearly marked literary and intellectual material, which she associates with national traditions, and toward "regional, subaltern, and popular epistemologies that may be 'emergent' (more informally formulated; less fully systematized) or 'latent' (embryonic; embedded in praxis)" (401). And yet it is hard to feel fully at ease with this direction of thinking, which would seem to entrench yet another division between "major" traditions with systematized thought systems and "minor" ones whose intellectual material is somehow rawer. Young, in his attribution of comparability to the experience of empire, suggests a similar turn away from comparative literature marked as such and toward comparison as an imperial impingement. "Postcolonial authors have always written comparative literature," he writes, "a literature that did not have to wait for the frame of comparative literature to be in dialogue with other literatures. For postcolonial writers had no choice: that work was done by the violent, historical imposition of colonialism, which forced postcolonial society and its literature into comparison in the first place" (688). This is a hard claim to argue with, even should one want to, and yet it risks inscribing a parochial and chronologically abbreviated sense of African intellectual capability. If "comparison" is simply taken to mean "ambivalent cultural contact," then Young's statement rings true of a particular and familiar brand of postcolonial writing. Nonetheless, it is but a short cry from categorically denying the possibility of a full-fledged, systematic, Afro-originating comparative practice.

This is why it will be useful now to turn back to a more distant literary past, specifically to J. E. Casely Hayford's prenationalist Ghana, but also more broadly to the strong Akan tradition of a worldly and evaluative Afrocentrism. In doing so, I aim to show that the perceived liabilities of comparative literature in a global frame—that is, its dependence on bounded analytic entities and its inbuilt critical individualism—are precisely the conditions of its *advantage* as a decolonizing operation in and for the novel. Admittedly, this goes against the grain of some of the best recent thinking on the comparative field. Natalie Melas, for example, has elaborated what she calls "mere" comparison, which bypasses "the positive outcome of producing new categories and measurable increases in knowledge" (2013, 653). She advocates instead for "relationality as such," following Édouard Glissant, by which she means a "comparative condition" that "takes place, as it were, at multiple intersections of differential effects . . . not ultimately reducible or even necessarily related to knowledge or positive certainty" (2013, 654). Melas's argument is subtle and compelling, but it leaves something to be desired in the more active, decidedly knowledge-oriented context of Anglo-Fante anticolonialism. (It is not coincidental that so many past and current debates about decolonization center on university curricula; knowledge is fought for, not sidestepped.) Embracing the role of the strong, cultivated, and in turn cultivating comparatist— the performed, individual act of *making things comparable*—will serve, in Casely Hayford's case, a lateralizing rather than hierarchizing function. In this sense, his brand of decolonizing comparison has more in common with specific comparative philosophical projects than it does with Melas's more abstract contemplations of literary-discursive singularity.

With this in mind, I turn now to two such comparative, decolonial philosophical undertakings by the Akan philosophers Kwasi Wiredu and Kwame Anthony Appiah. Both of their projects get beyond the problem at the heart of this chapter thus far: namely, that neither postcolonialism-cum-globality *nor* the singular simultaneity of the world systems approach quite "solves" the issue of decolonial methodology as concerns literary analysis. Both approaches fall short because neither contends meaningfully with an ongoing search, across the Africanist or comparative domains, for a transposable unit of analysis that can be impersonally evaluated, which is to say one that is not the direct expression of personal experience and thus "true" on that basis alone. In the Africanist domain, Afrocentrism has often fulfilled part of this need for a movable analytic entity: African cultures become bounded objects to be championed and transmitted. Comparative literature, per Culler's concerns, has long trafficked in prefabricated categories of comparability, such as genre or form. For the philosophers in question, comparability is separate from either "culture" or a literary category: it is a quality to be actively cultivated by strategically *un*-coupling concepts from experiential context to give them a decolonizing value all their own.

Wiredu and Appiah both see comparison across Western and African philosophical systems as an essential part of any larger decolonization agenda. Incorporating it entails deliberately bracketing African literary studies' common emphasis on sociocultural power dynamics in favor of proactively modeling a level epistemological playing field; in these influential cases, at least, decolonial philosophy thus liberates itself from the ever-enlarging discursive web with which comparative literature now contends. In a rich essay called "Toward Decolonizing African Philosophy and Religion," which distills his career-long focus on the "particularistic" study of African intellectual traditions, Wiredu proclaims his unit of analysis to be "categories of thought, that is, fundamental concepts by means of which whole ranges of issues are formulated and discussed" (20). Notably eschewing the word "idea" because of its idiosyncratic definition within some strains of English Empiricism, he opts instead for the "concept" as a term that suggests logical movement between a truth and its implications.

Though its Enlightenment specialization is far afield of Wiredu's work, Peter de Bolla's 2013 book *The Architecture of Concepts: The Historical Formation of Human Rights* offers a gloss for "conceptuality" that helps explain Wiredu's use of the term. Concepts, de Bolla writes, "are 'ways of thinking' whose identified or identifiable labels provide in shorthand the names we give to particular routes for thinking such and such, and for getting from one thought to another" (loc. 112). While a concept is culturally particular because it is *expressed* in one language versus another, it does not therefore follow that it is *essentially* a matter of language. (De Bolla expends considerable energy elaborating complex concepts as distinct from words.) In this way, concepts also transcend subjective reference, even as they are employed by individuals: "one must be able to reach for the abstraction 'size,'" de Bolla writes, "without recourse to any specific mental representation" (602).

Concepts, in other words, though enunciated through language, are nonetheless distinctive comparable entities. Again quoting de Bolla, "a concept may be stretched across a number of words, or between words" (476). Wiredu makes this clear in his anti-relativistic orientation toward "independent grounds" of philosophical evaluation, by which he means "considerations that are independent of the peculiarities of the given vernaculars and are, therefore, intelligible to all concerned irrespective of language, race, persuasion, etc." (1998, 25). This creates what may seem like a counterintuitive tension in Wiredu's epistemological project, which values both the full fleshing-out of Akan conceptuality independent of Western philosophical referents *and* their dispassionate comparison. The accompanying vision of decolonization is a universalist one, in the sense that it aims to cultivate a more precise set of tools for discerning culturally specific concepts, and thus where overlaps between them occur. Its guiding principle is not cultural recovery but conceptual enfranchisement: Wiredu's overarching goal, that is, is not to promote undue deference toward any given African thought system, but rather to make African thought systems individually ripe for lateral evaluation vis-à-vis Western and other counterparts. In this line of thinking, an assumption that African philosophy should be treated separately from Western traditions is a simple inversion of a colonial "attitude of racial superiority" (1998, 26), which also moots the intrinsic universal claims of African conceptuality.

A brief example here may clarify how Wiredu positions culturally particular expertise in service of philosophically universalist ends. In essence, he builds from specific Akan cosmological terminology, to its contextualization within Akan grammatical laws, and then toward the conceptual comparabilities (de Bolla's "routes . . . for getting from one thought to another") that they license. While numerous Akan words for what in English would be translated as "God" might correspond to "Creator" (chiefly, the Twi term *Oboade*), Wiredu reasons, based on differences in the verb "to be" between Akan languages and English, that creation implies something fundamentally different to the Akan. Because meaning in Twi or Fante necessarily entails spatial context—that is, "the idea of nothing can only be expressed by some such phrase as *se whee nni ho*, which means something like 'the circumstance of there not being something there'"—the notion of absolute nothingness, and thus an absolute Creator, makes little sense (1998, 29). Instead, Wiredu arrives at a vision of God as one who fashions a world from previously extant but unformed materials, an architect of sorts, to indicate in turn a priority on an *ordering function* rather than a miraculous intervention. As a result, the Akan cosmology emerges in his reading as intrinsically more "logical" than the Judeo-Christian one, unseating deep-seated colonial preconceptions about Africans' incapacity for rational thought. As further evidence of the Akan God's intrinsic rationality, Wiredu turns to the well-known Asante figure of Ananse Kokroko (often called Kweku Ananse), a spider incarnation of God valued for his trickster qualities. "The spider is associated with ingenuity in designing," Wiredu notes, "and therefore the designation is clearly a metaphorical articulation of God as the Great Designer" (1998, 35). In Akan religion, an element of reason thus precedes faith, because if someone or something is responsible for "creating" the universe, it is likely to be a God that possesses such aptitudes.

Crucially, however, Wiredu's end goal is not merely to restore or redeem Akan traditions from unfair Western dismissals, nor is it to chastise or reject a Western reliance on cosmological paradox and mystery. On the contrary, either of these tasks in isolation risks a redoubling of colonial thinking, resting too easy with cultural pride or philosophically unproductive antagonism. The decolonizing thrust of the cosmological comparison in this example is in the act of *engineering cross-civilizational comparability* through sure-footed reduction to the level of concept apart from its linguistic-cum-cultural encasement; concepts are extracted from their lived expression to make them into objects that can then be critically evaluated. Wiredu is forceful in his view that neither the Akan nor the Western Christian cosmology is the "right" one and opts rather to face them off against one another as equals. A broader comparative terrain abets a fuller range of argumentative possibilities, which in turn abets a more informed choice of one's authoritative epistemology. This is where a culturally attuned philosophical methodology does something different toward decolonization from the study of culture as such. Instead of arriving at the anthropological commonplace of a "synthetic" African religious practice—a worldview articulated in sync with how people actually live—Wiredu demands that intellectuals determine *which* conceptual system they are prepared to defend. "The obvious lesson is that African thinkers will have to critically review both the conceptions—of god as *ex nihilo* creator and god as a cosmic architect—and choose one or none, but not both. Otherwise, colonized thinking must be admitted to retain its hold" (1998, 38). Decolonized conceptual comparison is not about what epistemology one chooses to valorize, but about the act of developing an apparatus for educated choice. Nor is it a matter of translation as an end in itself. Epistemological diversification and attention to African languages are means to the end of evaluating the thought systems that are thereby made more widely apprehensible.

One sees a similar methodological reward of comparative evaluation in much of Kwame Anthony Appiah's philosophical work across Akan (namely Asante) and Western traditions. While his 1992 book *In My*

Father's House is probably the most thorough and best-known example, a shorter and usefully distillatory piece on "Akan and Euro-American Concepts of the Person" provides a ready parallel here with Wiredu's stance on decolonized conceptuality. Working with what he calls "theories"—that is, "two ways of thinking that seem to be in competition with one another" (21)—Appiah recodes culturally specific cosmological terms as abstract conceptual variables. As the cultural theorist Mieke Bal suggests, this allows concepts to gain clarity that words cannot: "more than anything," she writes in an essay called "Working with Concepts," "they need to be explicit, clear and defined. In this way everyone can take them up and use them" (19). Wiredu, to recap, first aggregates the Western God and the Akan *Oboade* (or *Nyame*) into the shared concept of a Creator, which he then breaks down into its constituent grammatical implications in order to determine an overarching logic. The concepts of God or *Oboade*, as I have stated, are thus related to but not fully captured by either term; comparison becomes an act not of translation but of *transposition* from the slippery register of words to the more analytically stable one of ideas. Appiah's method goes still further than Wiredu's to divest conceptuality from the vagaries of language, adopting a technique from the British philosopher Frank Ramsey to construct what is effectively a Venn diagram of concepts that do and do not overlap between two theories. In this case, the theories in question represent fundamental conceptions of personhood from one epistemological tradition to another. Culture, like language, is thereby invoked as a proximate but not primary analytic object. Again per Bal, "concepts can become a third partner in the otherwise totally unverifiable and symbiotic interaction between critic and subject" (19). In other words, they form a contestable meeting space for discrepant accounts of the world that does not run the risk of the analytic diffusion feared by, for example, Culler and Brooks. Conceptual claims call attention to cultural context, while at the same time guarding against invalidation purely on the basis of experiences within it.

In Appiah's end result, Akan personhood, presented through its main parts of *sunsum* (something like hereditary will, or personality) and *okra* (something like a divinely given life force, or soul), forces a larger philosophical discussion of the nature of truth. On the one hand, he suggests, a conceptual system might be evaluated on its ability to predict human behavior. On the other, one might find validity in a system's "truth to introspective experience" (2003, 31). Ultimately Appiah concludes that cultural-conceptual comparisons on a grand scale will often be doomed by question begging; an Akan-raised person is more likely to see Akan theories as behaviorally predictive or resonant with introspective experience, and so on. What I want to dwell on here is his alignment, in the first place, of Akan-Western comparison with an end goal of evaluative decision-making. Like Wiredu, Appiah models a multilayered process of individual conceptual interrogation that results in a capacity to make choices beyond restriction to one's culture of origin. "When you are trying to decide whether to adopt a theory, you are asking what grounds you will act on, for what purposes," he concludes (32). At the same time, this capacity to choose one's truth claims on an issue-by-issue basis is not something one can easily opt into. (There is no mere announcing that one has suddenly "found the light" in another belief system, nor room for a cheap act of what might now be called "cultural appropriation.") The point for Appiah in this brief example is, once again, the dynamic act of *forging comparability* itself. Deep epistemological decolonization thus works in tandem with what seems like a profoundly liberal conception of selfhood, bedfellows made less strange by the sheer labor underlying their union.

Returning to the problem of comparison in the literary domain, it is important to emphasize that Wiredu's priority on concepts and Appiah's on theories look toward a more rather than less stable analytic object, whereas logocentric approaches tend to do the opposite. As Simon Gikandi writes in a 2011 chapter on "Contested Grammars: Comparative Literature, Translation, and the Challenge of Locality," opening up the comparative literary field to African traditions often fragilizes rather than affirms the comparative undertaking. "Indeed, if comparative literature departments have appeared eager to embrace the literatures of East Asia ... rather than those of Africa or South Asia, it is because they promised cultural entities that could be disciplined into a unified structure that would then enable West/East comparisons" (258). In a turn to Okot p'Bitek's classic Ugandan long poem *Song of Lawino* and, secondarily, to translation theory, Gikandi then affirms that African literary traditions introduce "source languages that evade the stability that translators and students of comparative literature take for granted" (263). Such demotion of "stability" echoes the turn away from category generation and epistemological clarity that, as noted earlier, Natalie Melas observes. In both cases, African contexts are imagined to trouble dominant comparative methodologies that look toward formal taxonomies or neat historical periodizations; Africa is the thorn in the West's side. There is much value here in terms of auguring a more encompassing suspension of easy-won certainties—the theoretical comparatist's version, perhaps, of what Jeffrey L. Williams in the *Chronicle Review* has called the "new modesty" in literary criticism. Nevertheless, there is also a guarded, obfuscatory quality to this default role, which makes it difficult to envision full-blooded engagement between one set of ideas and another.

Bringing this section full circle, Wiredu's and Appiah's work suggests the importance of the discerning individual mind to the project of geographical de-hierarchization. As I have suggested here, this emphasis flies in the face of comparative literature's embrace of globality as a movement *away* from both the liberal self and a clearly delineated analytic object, marked now as twin dangers of Eurocentrism. It is notable here that Peter de Bolla, a forward-thinking theorist of the European Enlightenment, sees the concept as a means of moving beyond individual minds and toward the "thinking" mechanism of culture. "When concepts are considered as cultural entities," he writes, "it becomes possible to discern how 'ways of thinking something' are not only determined by an agent who thinks" (loc. 693). Kwasi Wiredu provides a stark, even startling contrast to de Bolla's culturalist angle in his take on the common attribution of African thought to proverbs, absent the intellectual work of abstracting their conceptual heft from their collective expression. "It is important, however, to note that a communal philosophy is the result of the pooling together over a considerable length of time the thoughts of individual thinkers," ventures Wiredu. And then, "It goes without saying ... that a communal philosophy is a gathering together of inputs from thinkers who may not have agreed on all points" (1998, 25–26). I do not have a dog in this fight, so to speak, so much as I want to point out the different imperatives of decolonization (or something like it) to which de Bolla responds via Europe and Wiredu via Ghana. Read in tandem, one can see an ultimate goal emerge from opposite ends of the imperial spectrum, which I would venture to summarize as what Wiredu calls "[confrontation] in the spirit of due reflection" (1998, 20). Concepts have an ontology of their own that is fully captured neither by "culture" nor in their wielding by individual thinkers, even as they constitute an analytic object that brings both into vision. On this count, concepts can form a neutral meeting place for a culturally lateralizing methodology, which may not reflect the geopolitical order of things but is, as Wiredu puts it, "the basis of the possibility that we in Africa can learn something from the West and that the West, too, can learn something from us" (1998, 22).

Such determination to go intellectually "all the way"—to refuse limitations of caution, or reclamation, or even a very real geo-economic disempowerment—entails staging a philosophical ideal alongside acknowledgment of its historical occlusion. As I have tried to show in this section, this may take the form of a delicate balance among culture, its indirect expression via concepts, and their comparative evaluation as an expression of individual choice. To lay the last bricks in this groundwork for the section that follows, on J. E. Casely Hayford's early demonstration of precisely such a trade-off, I note a subtle but crucial difference between the comparative as a lived quality or experience and comparison as an intellectual act. The first condition harkens back to Robert J. C. Young's point about the intrinsically comparative nature of postcolonial literature and is easy to associate with a sense of cultural loss or ambivalence inflicted by empire. This point has well-known precedent in Frantz Fanon's *Black Skin, White Masks* from 1952, in which comparison is presented as a racial ontology. "The Negro is comparison," he pronounces. "There is the first truth. He is comparison: that is, he is constantly preoccupied with self-evaluation and with the ego-ideal. Whenever he comes into contact with someone else, the question of value, of merit, arises. The Antilleans have no inherent values of their own, they are always contingent on the presence of the Other" (211). While comparison is allied with evaluation even here, its orientation toward experiences of oppression rather than the liberation of concept gives it a negative valence.

I will thus end this section, instead, with a more recent invocation of the second condition; that is, comparison as a deliberate and decolonizing act. When the Ghanaian scholar Ato Quayson picks up with Fanon's statement in introducing his 2003 book *Calibrations*, he articulates the stakes of this difference in focus: "For unlike what Fanon asserts about the bereft cultural condition of the colonial Antillean (debatable, in my view), for the colonial and postcolonial African, the situation is the direct opposite" (xiv). Quayson, that is, sees his Ghanaian childhood and education as the source of an intellectual edge amid the literary field's globalization, anticipating the shift I've identified here from *living* comparatively to *doing* comparison. To be sure, one may well beget the other, as they do in Quayson's case. But though I am not meaning to present experience and conceptuality as mutually exclusive, I am suggesting that prioritizing one or the other reveals a fundamental difference of underlying inclination. It is the difference, in sum, between seeing the decolonization of comparison as a process of Africa's troubling, problematizing, or complicating role vis-à-vis Western-originating methodologies—as fundamentally a move away from analytic and evaluative clarity—and approaching decolonization as an injunction to expand one's analytic and thus evaluative range.

J. E. Casely Hayford and Philosophy as Historical Redemption

Casely Hayford's roots in Ghana's Fante coastal intellectual tradition—as well as his specifically *novelistic* rather than only political ambitions—add up to what may now seem like the curious aim of both redressing the undue power of European intellectual traditions and seeking earnestly to engage with their merits. *Ethiopia Unbound*, that is to say, can be read as an unheralded work of decolonial literary comparatism: it cultivates an engagement between Fante intellectuals and their Western (as well as other global) counterparts that is truly lateral in nature, owing to a careful trade-off through its main character between historical circumstance and the disembedded conceptual currency of philosophical argument. As I will go on to suggest, Casely Hayford is able to enact this "achieved comparability" by harnessing the distinctively cumulative and thus incremental properties of the novel form. While this does not take shape as individual development in a psychological sense, it does rely on a central individual's intellectual growth to effect movement toward a utopian political vision. After braiding together its emphases on black political enfranchisement and a learned dispassion, or restraint, *Ethiopia Unbound* culminates first in a liberationist analogy between Greek and Fante modernity, and then in a final, proleptic chapter imagining a liberated future Ghana. Comparison and comparability, then, are, respectively, the novel's method and its achievement, or its means and its end; the first is depicted as an argumentative strategy of a distinguished individual mind, and the second as the projective fulfillment of cultural equality in an independent Ghanaian state. Here it is crucial to note, however, that the main character does not *represent* the state so much as facilitate its imagined evolution.

As the African literary historian Stephanie Newell has suggested, Casely Hayford's copious nonfiction writing in the realms of history, law, and educational reform "explores historical events and examines the miniutiae of customary laws as they have evolved over time," even as his novel gestures to "the futuristic level of ideals" (138).[5] By extension, *Ethiopia Unbound* can be understood neither outside its particular Anglo-Fante context nor outside its ordering of formal and rhetorical elements. And yet its reception as novel qua novel has thus far discouraged attention to the dynamic relationship among its pieces, beyond their collective endorsement of a pan-Africanist politics. Its salience on the latter front, in light of Casely Hayford's illustrious political career, makes it easy to overlook the ways in which his turn to fiction distinguishes and mediates between the political and philosophical domains, balancing analytic precision with cultural as well as formal porosity. *Ethiopia Unbound* is a syncretic mix of philosophical treatise, fictional vignettes, political manifesto, and autobiographical history. Quoting Newell once more, "the novel becomes an infinitely expandable rag-bag into which multifarious political and spiritual concerns can be placed" (136). In other words, *Ethiopia Unbound* may seem to present itself more as a historical and ideological hodgepodge than as a text whose analytic labor depends specifically on narrative. Yogita Goyal, in *Romance, Diaspora, and Black Atlantic Literature*, seconds Newell's emphasis on the book's fragmentary design. Calling it an "unstable mix of prescription and prophecy" (109), she notes that though "Hayford's text is insistent that it is a novel rather than a collection of essays," it is nonetheless "difficult to sustain the narrative thread, as the central story of Hayford's thinly veiled alter-ego, Kwamankra, pauses, falters, and soars into several directions at once" (110).

Goyal is not wrong: the novel's central figure, the above-mentioned Kwamankra, fails to serve as a stand-in for the novel's developmental through line. Nor do I mean to downplay the formal freneticism of the text, which is clearly a key part of its lofty ambitions. In fact, however, the book *is* nonetheless also designed to systematically graft a liberal-developmental temperament onto an anticolonial Afrocentric politics. As a Fante intellectual and public servant, Kwamankra typifies what Lionel Trilling in *The Liberal Imagination* describes as the liberal tendency to "organize the elements of life in a rational way" (xx). But whereas Trilling and many after him have grappled with this penchant for order as one of liberalism's flaws or naïvetés in the face of a plural and unequal body politic, Casely Hayford depicts this penchant as the engine of his protagonist's ability to foster a salient sense of racial identity that also percolates in his absence. Kwamankra is in many ways the ideal Kantian Enlightenment figure, with his reverence for the "men of light and leading in Fantiland," a band of educated men who "did not wait for endowments from the rich and philanthropic, or for money-making syndicates to start the work" of improving Gold Coast education (15). Kant's injunction in "What Is Enlightenment?" that man seek thought "free . . . from external guidance" becomes for Casely Hayford a collective racial ethos as he proclaims that "there has never lived a people worth writing about who have not shaped out a destiny for themselves, or carved out their own opportunity" (1). Thinking in terms of the long-standing "action versus contemplation" paradigm revisited recently by Jennifer Summit and Blakey Vermeule in their book by that title, Casely Hayford's interjection of a staunchly individualized mind into a fecund Afro-liberatory context also suggests a liberal selfhood narrativized by other means than psychological texture. Intellection as depicted via character is most often associated, in theories of the novel, with what Nathan Hensley calls the "densely cognitive deliberativeness" (204) or "calm moderation of a hypercognitive disinterest" characteristic of, for example, Henry James (209). But rather than giving form to the Fante intellectual's interiorization of his conceptual terrain—"thinking in motion," per Hensley, via the "vibrating, oscillating, or internally dividing character" of a consciousness in search of equilibrium (204)—*Ethiopia Unbound* marks the demand for private reflection without actually showing it. In this way, it becomes the acknowledged but truly solitary bedrock of an outwardly projected, cross-cultural comparative conceptuality.

Before going further down this road, it is important to provide some intellectual-historical context for what I am describing as a sort of textual meeting place for the lone, dispassionate scholar in his study and the collective endeavor of fashioning an anticolonial state. It seems natural to emphasize the obvious formal syncretism of *Ethiopia Unbound* and to more or less ignore its less pronounced narrative development, because it grafts so easily onto the historically "synthetic" role of Casely Hayford's Fante Gold Coast intellectual class, which emerged from a loose alliance of separate coastal groups that took on official form in the creation of the Fante Confederacy between 1868 and 1874. The impressive network of writers and thinkers incubated by the afterlife of this short-lived endeavor—which also prominently included Kobina Sekyi and John Mensah Sarbah, the latter a cofounder, as was Casely Hayford, of the Aborigines' Rights Protection Society in 1897—offers the clearest precedent for Ghanaian independence and world-revered pan-Africanism under Kwame Nkrumah's leadership in 1957.[6] As a result, the Fante Confederacy is a critical, if underutilized source period for theorizing African literature's later vacillation between hallmark points of specific cultural reclamation (for example, Ngugi's Gikuyu movement) and transcultural African cosmopolitanisms. The Fante elite, to this end, have often been theorized as "middle men" of various sorts, chief representatives of what Kwaku Korang calls "an African intermediary agency" behind the production of "a middle stratum of natives" poised to negotiate between colonial institutions (in this case British) and local ones (37).[7] The difficulty here should at this point be obvious: it was the partly "Westernized" Fante who took the boldest steps toward achieving Ghana's constitutional independence.[8] By working partly within a British-influenced understanding of statehood and education, Fante intellectual leaders during and after the Confederacy mounted an influential bureaucratic affront to imperial control.

Ethiopia Unbound cast in this light, then, is a study in how the two dominant strains by which African literature and literary theory have been incorporated into the larger scholarly field—namely, globality and Africanization—can productively *and* to their fullest development coexist in the same text. In other words, Casely Hayford does not simply compromise between these positions or "work through" their respective complexities; he unreservedly advances both orientations within different formal and epistemological modes of the book. The novel can thus be read within both liberal-progressive and more hard-line political or ideological frameworks, as a parable of racial liberation that is nonetheless sincere in its commitment to a culturally open, intellectually dispassionate, and quietly reflective disposition; it is both radically Afrocentric *and* wedded to a restrained and incremental brand of self-cultivation and social betterment. Following Amanda Anderson's argument in *Bleak Liberalism*, liberalism here can thus "be seen to encompass . . . the psychological, social, and economic barriers to its moral and political ideals," resulting in a prioritization of "the ideal of reflective enlightenment [that] presents itself not as a mere investment in neutrality, principle, or critical distance, but precisely as a kind of existential challenge" (2, 3). This also means that it is a mistake to insist on too firm a distinction between *Ethiopia Unbound*'s experimental form and the liberal-progressive ethos traditionally seen to underlie novelistic convention. The richness and challenge of *Ethiopia Unbound* lies precisely in its capacity to imagine both radical transformation and orderly argumentation, both the practical demands of racial politics and the philosophical expression of transracial ideals.

A few brief and relatively recent critical examples will suffice to illustrate the risks of overpleading *Ethiopia Unbound*'s case for novelistic convention-breaking, to the degree that the form is seen to enforce an unwelcome kind of gradualist ethos. In his reading of a scene in which the main character, Kwamankra, in England as a university student, jokes with an English visitor about the "native" decoration of his home, Mark DiGiacomo insists that the "mélange of both markedly African and ostensibly Western material . . . is emphatically not a paradox for Hayford" (257). This is true, and DiGiacomo's aim is to show that modernity is constitutively rather than just appropriatively African, because the syncretic and fragmentary techniques associated with modernism are as anticolonial in origin as they are a product of Western disillusionment. The self-questioning and disillusionment with "progress" commonly associated with European modernism after World War I—and which often makes its way into modern African literature as a reckoning with how such civilizational disorientation is then *re*-lived by the colonized, fostering a narrative of historical belatedness—is also inverted to show how a fragment might metonymically assume the task of liberating cohesion. The Fantes take on the mantle of "African" to further what Korang calls "the story of an intermediate class, a part" that determines to "include within itself . . . a coherent whole that was imagined as such (a) territorially ('the Gold Coast nation'), (b) interterritorially ('West African nationality'), and (c) continentally and transcontinentally ('Pan-African supranationality')" (51). Casely Hayford's fiction, presumably, thus also bears the meta-synthetic burden of collating these different scales.

Here, though, is where things get trickier. DiGiacomo, like Newell, understandably looks away from what both identify as canonical European narrative conventions in his treatment of *Ethiopia Unbound*, allowing richer appreciation for Casely Hayford's idiosyncratic structure of civilizational in-betweenness and blurred formal lines. For his part, DiGiacomo disassociates the book from a "set of aesthetic criteria that evaluates literary quality by the use of overt experimentation, cosmopolitanism, universality, and an individualistic, interiority-directed approach to character development" (247). Newell similarly seeks a more localized mode of reception, dispensing with twentieth-century Western expectations that a novel, among other traits, demands "continuity of plot, the development and resolution of conflict, fidelity to social realities, psychological interiority in protagonists and a full, empathetic exploration of character" (151). And yet, in terms of how Casely Hayford imagines the ideal relationship of Ghana to Europe in his book, it is crucial that *Ethiopia Unbound* in fact *does* emphasize interiority and developmentalism in its depiction of Kwamankra. We read early on that "he had visited Japan, Germany, and America to study their [educational] methods" before winding up in England, "by [which] time [his] outlook upon life was broadening" (18–19). In light of African literature's recent move toward imagining Europe in a supporting role rather than as either protagonist or antagonist (which I discuss at greater length later in this book), *Ethiopia Unbound* thus seems to do something more like what Wiredu and Appiah suggest: it takes the good from European interlocutors and nurtures strategies to persuasively reject the bad. At the same time, this preference for comparing and contrasting different locales demands that they remain analytically separate, enfolded in an expanded individual mind and not a border-effacing, "fluid" concept of modernity.

What goes missing in readings of how *Ethiopia Unbound* upsets, supposedly, the individualism and continuity that European literary convention overvalues is the fact that Kwamankra is above all a philosopher: he is able to serve as the book's unifying thread only because of his analytic and slightly removed temperament. This is a simple but profound observation, given postcolonial scholars' frequent reliance on a juxtaposition between intellectual dispassion and the lived experience of, particularly, racial disenfranchisement. "In its simplest form, the project of Enlightenment... was conceived as the production and valorization of the subject as autonomous, self-reflective, and un-encumbered by immediate experience," writes Simon Gikandi in his *Slavery and the Culture of Taste* (4). On the contrary, Casely Hayford uses a figure who conforms quite neatly to this description in order to facilitate the book's various formal and ideological syncretisms. Kwamankra modulates his frustration with Europe with reversion to more abstract intellectual terrain, as in the moment during a walk when he confesses to "a sense of the weariness which European civilization had evolved for itself," before immediately noting that "it was of the teaching of the Christian philosophy and its paradoxes that his mind was full" (20). This should not be taken merely as expression of a colonized religious mindset; in fact, it is an immediate reference to an earlier conversation with a close English interlocutor named Whitely, in which Western Christianity is dealt an intellectual blow. The novel opens with an intense conversation between the two men about God's incarnation across the Christian and Akan traditions in which they move from Marcus Aurelius's *Meditations* to Jesus Christ to the etymology of the Fante word *Nyiakropon* (6–11). It is Whitely who veers into the language of "[his] own heart" when he confesses a personal crisis of faith (9), and Kwamankra succeeds in convincing him that Fante grammatical structure is superior to English for linking "the intelligent part of man with the great Intelligence of the universe" (7).

Step by step, across what seem deceptively like discontinuous tidbits, Casely Hayford also alternates between dwelling on Kwamankra as a private, even withdrawn figure and featuring him as a historian-cum-narrator of the "African personality" politics influentially espoused by Edward Blyden, whom Casely Hayford followed for a time while he studied at the famous Fourah Bay College in Sierra Leone. In other words, while Kwamankra is indeed a public vessel for some of the key ideas of this period in African intellectual history (as is often remarked), he is also fictionalized as these ideas' decidedly private and cerebral incubator. The briefly featured metaphysical realm in which Kwamankra at one point encounters his deceased wife and daughter is characterized as a space of deep thought, with "different walks [that] seemed designed with an eye to quiet contemplation" (54). Later, he is annoyed by a disturbance of his writing time, as he is "busy with his scribbling" and "hardly dared interrupt the flow of ideas" (153). Kwamankra's consciousness, however—his *felt subjectivity*—is not at issue. Instead, Casely Hayford foregrounds his preferred and replicable intellectual *mode* of comparison and analogy, as represented through various dialogues across the bounds of race and nationality ("I love to observe without being observed" [22], the character announces). These dimensions of the novel fit less neatly into assessments of African literature than do the ideals of pan-Africanist racial mobilization that are their clearest end result. And yet they are the missing link to understanding Casely Hayford's role as an intellectual who compares, not just a leader who mediates.[9] Instead of just "drawing on the power of romance to synthesize contradictions," per Goyal's description, between Europeanized and "native" Africanity, or between spiritual and material frameworks, *Ethiopia Unbound* advances a comparative *methodology* (123). The book demonstrates how discrete and seemingly incompatible cultural and analytic domains can be put into productive conversation, converging around a strategically disembedded and disembodied performance of neutral conceptual ground. Casely Hayford, thus recast, appears not as a man beset by the historical paradoxes into which he was born, but as one determined to *wield* them toward historical betterment.

The most contentious racial topics in the book are almost always raised through confined, highly structured dialogues among scholars of diverse racial origin, and they are couched in appeals to reason, comparable concepts (on which more shortly), and systematized bodies of knowledge, including constitutional history. "I have never been able to understand the argument in favour of segregation," pipes in a liberal British interlocutor at one point. "In the time of an epidemic, for instance, I can understand why the afflicted, without distinction, should be put away. But in normal times, to be sure, I don't understand the philosophy of the matter" (104). A segregationist magistrate named Bilcox also present in the room counters this case with an appeal to lived experience, or populist common sense: "The question has nothing to do with epidemics," he rejoins. "The man in the street knows that" (ibid.). It is Kwamankra who has the last word, however, when he diverts the exchange back to an abstract explanation that also contains the guiding principle of a de-hierarchized comparative enterprise: "If you took mankind in the aggregate," he argues:

> irrespective of race, and shook them up together, as you would the slips of paper in a jury panel box, you would find after the exercise that the cultured would shake themselves free and come together, and so would the uncouth, the vulgar, and the ignorant; but of course, you would ignore this law of nature, and, with a wave of the hand, confine the races in separate air-tight compartments. Wherefore I preach *reciprocity*. (105)

Racial liberation is expressed via calm learnedness and a baseline principle of exchange, albeit while also putting what may now seem like a naive as well as elitist degree of faith in the power of education.

As I have suggested, Casely Hayford also relies on a strong principle of narrative ordering to create a structure in which public and private—or perhaps better put, the political-historical realm and that of Kwamankra's solitary learning—are shown to mutually reinforce one another without needing to fully converge. First, he introduces the cultural mold into which Kwamankra will be inserted as a dutiful husband and father, namely those same "men of light and leading" who believe that "the salvation of the people [depends] upon education" and the practical development of suitable university-based infrastructure for professional teachers' training (15). He frequently returns, thereafter, to Kwamankra's personal code of conduct as a "learned" man. The merging of his slow, careful habits of mind with more rousing political proclamation allows *Ethiopia Unbound* to overcome the seeming discord between the novel's assertion of a forceful Fante-African politics—it is an open rejoinder to the African "crowd" who "submitted to the worship of the new [white] god, and greedily devoured the good things found upon his altars" (159)—and Kwamankra's intellectual openness to British interlocutors. The enabling touchstone, then, for a lived reality of anticolonial agitation is *precisely* Kwamankra's capacity to harness inward interrogation toward progressive public ends—the novelistic premium on the individual that most readings of *Ethiopia Unbound* seem eager to dismiss as "European." This strong and cumulative association between intellectual dispassion and social progression is especially clear when Whitely, the friend with whom Kwamankra compares the Christian God with the Fante *Nyiakropon* in the novel's first pages, reappears just before the book's midway point. He has now taken up a post as a reverend in the Gold Coast colony, where, absent the influence of Kwamankra's intellectual rigor, his once-searching nature gives way to petty colonial racism. Their expansive back-and-forth from the novel's beginning is thus aligned with antiracist and cross-racial possibility, as Whitely's antiprogressive turn, inversely, is marked by his intellectual debasement in parroting the worst of the colonial crowd.

Kwamankra embodies solitary reflectiveness as a decolonizing force also by way of the capacity it fosters for cultural collation across multiple scales, as he alludes to canonical European texts alongside sundry other civilizational touchstones. References to humanistic traditions beyond his own pile up and grow in force as the novel progresses, and neither Casely Hayford nor his avatar makes any real distinction between intraregional, intracontinental, and transcontinental parallels. In one breath, Kwamankra discusses the "particulars . . . among the Africans, say, the Zulus, the Ashantis, and the Fantis" (108). (The first in this list is a southern African ethnicity, while the latter two are both Akan.) In another, he explains the need for Fante-originating liberation in the Gold Coast using a story about Russians and Turks, followed by a brief history of England's Opium Wars with China (116–17). For the reader, all these threads of reference cumulate into a liberationist imperative that derives from cultural co-exemplarity rather than from either influence or opposition. The Fante intelligentsia, in this vein, are sharply distinguished by their capacity to facilitate such co-exemplarity from an economically or even purely politically (rather than intellectually) motivated elite, of which there are numerous negative examples in the novel. In other words, while it is no doubt true that Kwamankra is an "elitist" figure, this does not imply his automatic association with later, more venal national leaders. *Ethiopia Unbound*'s consistent return to philosophical principles keeps it from slipping into Fanon's infamous "acquisitive, voracious, and ambitious petty caste" from *The Wretched of the Earth* (119). The ideal type that Kwamankra represents, though decidedly urban, eschews the performative populism that Fanon associates with postcolonial party politics.

Instead of appealing to the masses, Kwamankra advances Casely Hayford's equalizing vision through a bilateral comparison between the Fante and English languages as he educates British compatriots in the intricacies of translating between the two. In addition, *Ethiopia Unbound* includes numerous passages in which Fante proverbs and stanzas are translated into English with the intention of convincing non-Fante characters of Akan cosmological virtues, such as in the book's inaugural exchange with Whitely. The ultimate goal is to render Fante traditions more culturally and racially appealing based on their clear merits. At one point, after translating a brief passage announcing *Nyiakropon* (identical to Wiredu's *Oboade* or *Nyame*) as the world's chief moral authority—and retaining the Fante word without italics—Kwamankra notes his discovery in his own spiritual journey that "the teeming multitudes [of the netherworld] represented every kindred, race, people, and nation under the sun. It was a congregation of select souls, men and women who had humbly done their duty, and done it well, in another life" (55–56). Elsewhere, he introduces thoughts on Fante etymology into a philosophical meditation on religion, temporality, and finitude more broadly, creating a fluid commerce between universal truths and the outward presentation of localized language histories (187–88).

The main point to underscore here, in terms of how *Ethiopia Unbound* is structured to advance what I have called a "philosophical temperament" as a racially liberationist asset, is that there is a calculated separation of and conversation between intellectual and experiential epistemological modalities. In other words, Kwamankra's eye toward what he calls "truth as the highest of all virtues, as the apex of character" (119), is not presented through expression of Kwamankra's subjectivity, even as the novel draws attention to his need for interiority. It is, rather, mostly presented through dialogues that stage the formulation of cross-cultural analogies, such as when Kwamankra walks his son through different permutations of the wolf and the lamb story most often attributed to Aesop. This is significant for a novel that deracializes reason, of course, because the lamb's "guilt" lies in his capacity for sound argument against the wolf, who then disregards the lamb's superior logic to justify the crude satisfaction of his hunger. In the first instance of the tale's telling, its origins are left vague as Kwamankra uses it to raise his son's temper. "Coward!" the son is said to cry "excitedly." "Don't I wish I were close enough by with my little pop gun? I should have put a hole through Mr. Wolf right enough" (113). In response, Kwamankra advises him that "we can't always bring to play our pop guns when we may be morally justified in doing so" (113). The next iteration of the wolf and lamb story one chapter later, during a home history lesson, builds on the first to enforce its transposable appeal across vast geographic disparities. "You perceive the application of the story of the wolf and the lamb here, don't you?" enjoins Kwamankra as he relates the dynamics of Russian-Turkish conflict under the rule of Catherine the Great (116–17). For Casely Hayford, the wolf and the lamb tale comes to occupy a place much like that of the "concept" in Wiredu's comparative project: it is a transportable entity of thought that exists, now, not between and across words, but between and across traditions and contexts. It both brings particular cultural knowledge into view *and* denies that it is the end-goal of erudition.

Amid all this movement in *Ethiopia Unbound* across cultural contexts and expository modes, it is nonetheless significant, I again insist, that the book *is* in fact a novel and not simply a disordered collection of stories and ideas. The particular ordering of its elements matters because of its cumulative effect: by the final pages of *Ethiopia Unbound*, it is clear that Kwamankra has successfully bequeathed his values to his son and a new generation of Africans, as Casely Hayford describes a post-imperial world fourteen years into the fictional future of 1925. While Ghana's independence at that time was in reality still another few decades off, the book's culminating structure, over its last four chapters in particular, offers a crowning insight into the payoff of Kwamankra's intellectual habits and, by extension, of the legacy of Fante Confederacy leadership. First, in what would seem in isolation to be a most fitting end to this novel-cum-liberation treatise, linked sections called "Race Emancipation—Particular Considerations: African Nationality" and "Race Emancipation: The Crux of the Matter" espouse a combination of lofty racial metaphysics and nuts-and-bolts plans for educational improvement, including the development of robust African language curricula. Here too, Casely Hayford keeps one eye firmly on the project of knowledge expansion as its own end, even where it may seem contradictorily open to European currents. "How extraordinary would be the spectacle of this huge Ethiopian race," he muses, "having imbibed all that is best in Western culture in the land of their oppressors, yet remaining true to racial instincts and inspiration, customs and institutions, much as did the Israelites of old in captivity!" (173).

On their face, such sentiments might seem like utopian diversion or mere rhetorical flourish, and yet the structure of the novel enfolds them into the definitive reward of an alliance between African decolonization and the capacity for cross-civilizational comparison. The next, penultimate chapter of the book, entitled "A Similitude: The Greek and the Fanti," draws an extended analogy between the locus of Western modernity and Casely Hayford's Fante milieu. It is not a succession story of modernity, however, but a trans-chronological parallelism that organically links Homer to the Gold Coast, and Zeus to *Nyiakropon*. There is no obvious purpose to its inclusion, other than the fact that this comparison seems effectively to license the book's *final* chapter, the salvational "And a Little Child Shall Lead Them," set, as noted, in 1925. In this futuristic finale, Casely Hayford is at last primed to offer an unequivocal moral that *is* the novel of ideas itself. "And herein lay the power of our author," Kwamankra/ Casely Hayford observes of the nineteenth-century Greek-Irish-Japanese writer Lafcadio Hearn, also known as Koizumi Yakumo, whom he has only just introduced. "He treated of the inner things of life. He belonged to that band of men who force their fellow-men to think. They are not always popular; but whether or not, they are the saviours of the race" (211). In its foregrounding of a commitment to private self-cultivation and dispassionate comparison, then, *Ethiopia Unbound* offers a nuanced and underrecognized template for sustained public intellectual leadership.

Flash-Forward: Implications for the Postcolonial Anglo-Fante Novel

I have indicated in this chapter that there is a strong Akan intellectual tradition of using disembedded conceptuality as a bedrock of a decolonized comparative practice. While I have not posited a relationship of influence between Casely Hayford and later Ghanaian philosophers like Kwasi Wiredu and Kwame Anthony Appiah, I have pointed toward a shared methodology whereby an expanded range of culturally specific terms are made universally comparable by their recoding into abstract analytic objects. In this way, "African experience" is invoked as a topic of philosophical inquiry without rendering it beholden *to* the category of experience—rather than argument—for intellectual legitimation. *Ethiopia Unbound* showcases the centrality of reflective individualism to advancing this disaggregating approach: its main character carefully mediates between transposable concepts and particular identities, anchoring his anticolonial politics in the practice of self-cultivation and restraint. This chapter's examples are thus sufficient to suggest a broadly relevant model for comparison's geographical lateralization through strong and conjoined claim to (1) "liberal" selfhood, and (2) a studied distinction between epistemological modes (in this case, conceptual-analytic versus cultural-experiential). In this way, Casely Hayford, placed in the context of similarly minded Akan philosophical undertakings, shows how the novel can be a tool for *incrementally disaggregating* the individual mind from the concepts with which it grapples, with the first wielding the second to model a more egalitarian future.

By the time that Ghanaian writing enters its most internationally renowned post-independence phase—with writers like Ayi Kwei Armah, Ama Ata Aidoo, Kofi Awoonor, and others among the most acclaimed figures in global postcolonial literature—the novel has undergone a dramatic shift in orientation. The *experience of intellectuals*, rather than relating intellection *to* experience, has become its main currency: reflective solitude no longer enables salient mediation among cultures but figures as the mark of a profound and self-limiting cultural alienation. In this brief last section of the chapter, I look to two classic postcolonial novels from within the Anglo-Fante tradition that exemplify this shift in order to suggest the losses entailed in collapsing argument into experience. In Ayi Kwei Armah's *Fragments* (1970) and Ama Ata Aidoo's *Our Sister Killjoy* (1977), two works that foreground the disillusionment wrought by cross-cultural mobility, I read a characteristic flattening of the novel as a form that offers a startling contrast with *Ethiopia Unbound*. The project of conceptual enfranchisement and comparability by which I have linked Casely Hayford to philosophy gives way to a highly subjectivized variant of decolonial narrative, one that devalues narrative's incremental and universalizing properties.

The main point of this concluding section is merely to gesture toward what now seems like a natural departure from *Ethiopia Unbound*'s epistemological versatility, despite the fact that, ostensibly, Ayi Kwei Armah's second novel, *Fragments*, picks up with many of *Ethiopia Unbound*'s main themes: namely, the intellectual's position between Ghanaian and Western societies and the relationship between Akan traditions and multicultural modernity. Its main character, Baako, is a "been-to" who has returned to Accra after a lengthy stay in the United States, now rich with educational credentials but with none of the material wealth his family expects. He has suffered a nervous breakdown while abroad and, the reader soon realizes, is headed toward another upon reentry into what has become a venal and corrupt post-independence order. As Rosemary Colmer notes characteristically in *Kunapipi*, *Fragments* is fundamentally a book about an intellectual who has "recognized the fatal nature of the processes acting upon [him]," but is nonetheless "unable to escape the psychological dissolution which comes with [the] realization of the futility of any gesture in another direction" (77). The critical literature on the novel is full of references to alienation and cultural estrangement, in keeping with Armah's career-long indictment of a Ghana that had succumbed to white, Western values of profit and self-serving individualism. Any thematic continuities with *Ethiopia Unbound* as the seminal Anglo-Fante literary work are belied by Armah's association of intellectualism with a distressing form of loneliness rather than a generative solitude, as well as by his characteristic orientation toward the past at the expense of any viable investment in the future.[10]

More importantly for my contrastive purposes here, Baako is in every respect an impotent figure. The novel opens not with his perspective, but with ruminations on Akan cyclicality by his grandmother, Naana, who has visions of him walking among white people "neither touched nor seen, like a ghost in an overturned world in which all human flesh was white" (11). These visions are communicated to no one but the reader, as Naana confesses that she is now "a person no more, unable to help myself," before offering, "why should my wisest speech not be silence?" (2). The second chapter also unfolds in Baako's absence, chronicling the workday of a Ghana-based Puerto Rican doctor who will later become his lover. Of her adopted nation, Juana thinks, "the sum of her life was only that she was here in another defeated and defeating place" (12). Not a page later, we read that, of her exchange with a nurse, she "sensed the unavoidable estrangement, the politeness of distances created for strangers like herself" (12–13). Right off the bat, then, *Fragments* announces itself as a study in discontinuous experiences of self-isolation, with Naana's invocation of Akan traditions and nonlinear temporality confined to her own mind, and Juana's observations of Accra couched in her bewildered estrangement from it. This also describes the novel's formal design, as it moves from one subjective dead end to another and then, significantly, to a graphic and distressing scene of men killing a rabid dog amid gridlocked traffic (16–20). Juana seems to channel the mood of the book when she ponders, "What meaning could hope have in an environment so completely seized with danger and so many different kinds of loss?" (23). Armah's Accra is a desolate landscape into which Baako can only be inserted; he is a passive figure whose intellectualism is doomed to become a personal quirk instead of a guiding narrative principle.

If Kwamankra and well-meaning British interlocutors like Whitely expand their common ground through conceptual comparison (most notably, of God to *Nyiakropon*)—an abstract meeting point derived *across* cultural terminologies—then Juana and Baako find each other dismayingly orphaned by their respective cultures of origin. Unlike in *Ethiopia Unbound*, there is no intermediary space of intellectual negotiation; the relationship is a more urgent and heavy-handed sort of "meeting of the minds," with Juana a psychiatrist and Baako, eventually, a psychiatric patient. Their first act of sexual congress is similarly immediate and literally adrift, taking place in the ocean with no one else around. In general, the relationship is forged from a visceral and not-quite-articulable sense of loss, a shared traversal of historical memory now made manifest as subjective turmoil. If we take Laura Murphy's reading of *Fragments* at face value in her book *Metaphor and the Slave Trade in West African Literature*, then this extends at the most profound level to Ghana's history of slavery and European exploitation, as this legacy is "elided through the replacement of its previous incarnations with a new Ghanaian institutional power [that replicates], to some extent, the crimes of the past" (113). Curiously, this is a fact that only Baako and Juana in the book seem inclined to acknowledge, as the trauma of slavery is enfolded into their alikeness and thus attraction to one another. Standing at one point within vision of a former trading castle, Juana recalls that she had initially come to Ghana with "a mind . . . prepared to find its own part in a struggle assumed to be going on," before realizing that in fact the country was full of "just the living defeat of whole peoples" (31). Her reference here to her disembodied *mind* rather than herself as the active subject then allows Armah more pointedly to foreclose the possibility of intellectual regeneration, or at the very least, to see the active mind as somehow at odds with the world it is meant to inhabit. Juana comes around to practicing what she calls "Adjustment," or the practice of "adopting a narrower vision every time the full vision threatens danger to the visionary self" (ibid.).

Juana and Baako thus "compare" their experiences of disappointment between themselves, but there is no clear path to this becoming an undertaking that exceeds their relationship. It is not surprising in this light that the critical literature on *Fragments* tends to hew toward explorations of subjectivity (including through trauma theory) rather than what one might call conceptuality. My aim here is simply to point out that *Fragments*' departure from intellectual explication as a viable novelistic aim à la *Ethiopia Unbound* also marks a departure from what may be the definitive attribute of the novel form itself, namely its diachronocity or developmentalism. As Edward Lobb, among others, has noted, Baako's point of view becomes "progressively more unreliable" (30), culminating in his institutionalization and point-blank confession of "I'm crazy" (*Fragments* 190). What is less often remarked on is that his degeneration runs parallel to that of literary institutions *and* of the novel's capacity to model something like "progress," which I intend not just in a historical or institutional sense but in a basic formal one. The novel, after all, ends more or less where it begins: with Baako on the mend from a nervous breakdown in terms of plot and, in terms of narration, with a second monologue about self-expiration by his grandmother Naana.[11] Addressing the Fante "small gods" or *nananom*, she tells them, "You are the end. The beginning.

You who have no end." Then she ends the book: "I am coming" (201).[12] While one could perhaps make a larger point here about Armah's frequent return to the past in contrast with *Ethiopia Unbound*'s reaching into the future—his 1973 work *Two Thousand Seasons* is exemplary on this front, as is his emphasis on Egyptian culture in *Osiris Rising* from 1995—my focus is on the loss of the Anglo-Fante novel as a vehicle for cultural-cum-conceptual comparison. From this vantage, Armah's encasement of Baako's intellectual degeneration within *Fragments*' structural cyclicality is instructive of a larger decoupling of the novel form from the generation of comparable knowledge.

On the point of literary-institutional degradation, Armah quite ruthlessly mocks Ghanaian writers in a banquet scene just past *Fragments*' halfway mark, in which lip service to the revival of "an indigenous literature" (110) is undercut by acknowledgment that "the country's most prestigious [literary] quarterly" is published but every two years (109). On the point of the novel form's growing irrelevance, Baako himself has turned to a disjointed, abstract filmic practice as his expressive mode of choice. "THROUGH REPETITIVE USE OF IMAGE AND SOUND," an all-caps example of his screenplay reads, "IMPRINT IDEA OF VIOLENCE, UNPLEASANT, STRONG, IRRESISTABLE, ATTACKING THE VIEWER, INVADING HIS EYES, ASSAULTING HIS EARS" (145). He explains to his baffled colleagues at Ghana's official state film production outlet that this series of jarring impressions is meant to be "about slavery," and indeed, the "MASSIVE WHITE STRUCTURE OF SLAVE CASTLE" (146) does ultimately appear in the script segment. What I want to draw out here is that what Baako and, clearly, Armah take to be the salient void in Ghanaian cultural-intellectual life (that is, slavery) is conveyed *not* through careful conceptual delineation that merges the historical with the philosophical, but through what is meant to be gut-level impact that merges the historical with the sensory. In this way, Baako's project tracks with Armah's in *Fragments* itself, in the sense that both seek historical redress through conveying the experience of suffering rather than modeling the practice of argument. (While one might "argue," ostensibly, through the presentation of feeling or experience, it is clear that Baako's efforts in the novel are utterly unpersuasive to their audience.) The difference, of course, is that while Baako's creativity within the novel meets with derision, *Fragments* is a key part of an acclaimed literary career.

A second and final brief detour into a similarly revered, "experientially" oriented Anglo-Fante novel that foregrounds cross-cultural engagement brings me full circle back to the first section of this chapter, on the question of what sort of analytic unit and/or formal presentation comparison requires. Ama Ata Aidoo's *Our Sister Killjoy*, first published by Heinemann in 1977, chronicles a young Ghanaian woman's trip to Germany as part of a post-independence exchange program, and it opens with a series of literary fragments comprising single lines, poems, and a short prose reflection. Within this formal mélange is the revealing line, "The academic-pseudo-intellectual version [of a Ghanaian] is even more dangerous, who in the face of reality that is more tangible than the massive walls of the slave forts standing along our beaches still talks of universal truth, universal art, universal literature, and the Gross National Product" (6). It is difficult not to see Casely Hayford's legacy reflected in this description, though there is of course no clear evidence that that is the intention. *Our Sister Killjoy* is in some ways not a successor to but the inverse of *Ethiopia Unbound*, upbraiding its predecessor's arrogant philosophical credentials.

What seems self-evident to this end is the book's distrust of acquired knowledge, which is repeatedly invoked as a distraction from the more visceral truths of subjective experience; "universalism" here is shorthand for a lack of consideration and replication of racist canonical formations, rather than staged as a hard-won philosophical achievement. The main character, Sissie, expresses skepticism toward scholarly enterprise in lockstep with disillusionment toward the West and the Africans who flock to it, whom she refers to as "the recipients of the leftovers of imperial handouts," mocked for taking doctoral degrees in exchange for providing information about "[Their] people / [Their] history] / [Their] mind" (86). Without doubt, Sissie's cynicism has grounding in the systemic inequalities endemic to postcolonial institutions and the trope of the "native informant" enforced thereby. But what interests me here, in terms of the novel's contrast with its early twentieth-century predecessor, is the degree to which the form's construction around what one might call subjectivity as *distinct* from individuality—an interiority narratively performed, rather than privately claimed as a public good—lends itself to a diminution of comparative possibility. Gone is Casely Hayford's range of prototypes for Western interlocutors, alternately censured where appropriate and, elsewhere, convened around more productive processes of debate and analogy. Kwamankra's confident cross-civilizational comparisons are replaced with Sissie's aversion to the same impulse. "We had chiefs like you," a Scottish woman says at one point, "Who fought one another and all, while the Invader marched in." Sissie's response betrays a disjuncture between her experience of and her expression in the moment, as she offers thanks out loud, "but also [feels] strongly that their kindship had better end right there" (91).

As many commentators on *Our Sister Killjoy* have noted, Sissie's almost-erotic relationship with a German housewife becomes the canvas onto which Aidoo projects the impossibility of meaningful intercultural and cross-racial intimacy. Again quoting Murphy and recalling the bond between Juana and Baako in *Fragments*, Sissie "finds that every encounter with love and sexuality is haunted and interrupted by a past that most people prefer to forget" (140). This serves an important purpose in allowing Aidoo to foreground the psychic, internalized ramifications of painful histories, as "Sissie's interiority is the site for [racial] negotiation" (Sterling 137). At the same time, however, it marks a paradoxical diminishment of her status—as an analytic agent, for example—beyond her role as a social-historical overdetermination.

In the furthest possible detour from *Ethiopia Unbound*'s grand finale of civilizational commerce and equalization, *Our Sister Killjoy* concludes with a personal letter from Sissie to her lover, which she ultimately destroys rather than send. I end here not just because the "lost" letter marks the book's conclusion, but also because it relates a series of exchanges between Sissie and diasporic Ghanaian intellectuals that in some ways echoes a Socratic dialogue. Sissie narrates her burgeoning frustration with the Ghanaian expat professionals by whom she's surrounded in Europe—doctors, lawyers, and academics—and who offer measured insights into their choice to help their nation from afar rather than return as a matter of emotional compulsion. What she calls the "perfected versions of [their] loss of perspective" are then associated with the view that "literature, art, culture, all information is universal" (120–21), as opposed to the "secret language" (116) she feels Africans must cultivate. Sissie adopts the role of Socrates in the sense that she performs a *naïveté* at odds with her intellect in order to provoke her interlocutors into self-interrogation. She crucially deviates from Socratic ideals, however, in the fact that morality is unhinged from rather than revealed through the perfection of argument. "I couldn't say anything to that," she remarks of one doctor's explanation for why he has not returned to Ghana. "What could I say? So much of it was true. . . . I was like a stone staring into his animated face" (128). She repeatedly describes being outclassed by her countrymen abroad on the suspect grounds of reasonable debate, to which her response is typically an inward one—for example, "I was going to tell him to go to hell, naturally" (122).

It is not surprising that *Our Sister Killjoy* has become a classic of African feminist fiction, heralded as a record of the almost incommunicable pain and outrage of empire, which defies and exceeds measured analysis. As Cheryl Sterling notes, "the been-to's offer a deliberate, if albeit poorly nuanced contrast to Sissie's enlarged [oppositional] consciousness" (146). Nonetheless, the book might also be read as a record of the trade-offs inherent in the Anglo-Fante novel's naturalization, over the course of the twentieth century, of "consciousness" as the measure of truth in the first place. I am speaking of the jarring gap, represented in this chapter, between *Ethiopia Unbound*'s philosophical temperament as a locus of anticolonial action—a prioritization of concept that lives on not in the novel but in comparative Akan philosophy—and decolonization as expressed through the terrain of a more subjective, visceral experience. Ironically, the liberal-Enlightenment figure of Kwamankra serves as a more agile arbiter of Afrocentrism than does Sissie in her transformative journey toward a status as decolonial literary icon. To begin the story of modern African letters with the era of midcentury independence is thus to entrench a whole host of false assumptions about what anticolonial expression looks like. If, as Frantz Fanon writes in "Racism and Culture," it is the "racist world" that is "passion-charged," then we should hardly wonder at Casely Hayford's insistence on intellectual *dis*-passion as a mode of engagement that assumes civilizational equality in order to demand it.

CHAPTER TWO

Between the House of Stone and a Hard Place

STANLAKE SAMKANGE'S PHILOSOPHICAL TURN

IN 1970, TEN years before Zimbabwean independence, Nadine Gordimer framed the question of how to define "African literature" with a trade-off between local commitments and universal themes. "Must the work deal with situations that couldn't come about in quite the same way anywhere else in the world?" she wondered, or "can it deal with matters that preoccupy people everywhere?" (9). Gordimer determines that African writing favors politics, in terms of both what gets written and by whom. It is, she offers, "essentially a committed literature. Black men have found their voices in the need to protest and demand. African writers have often been and are political leaders and politicians as well" (11–12). As one of her examples, she cites the Zimbabwean writer, educational leader, and nationalist politician Stanlake Samkange, who is best known today for his 1966 novel *On Trial for My Country*. Though Gordimer opines that it is "in some ways a ridiculous book, producing hilarity where it is intended to arouse a sense of social injustice" (22), she grants the appeal of the rich history it takes up. In it, Samkange depicts a legal trial, in the afterlife, of both the colonial magnate Cecil John Rhodes and the Ndebele leader Lobengula, who was tricked into signing his country away to the British in 1888.

I begin with Gordimer's discussion of Samkange because it reflects, by and large, the role to which he has been consigned in African literary history. Even the scholars most deeply engaged with Zimbabwean letters have seen the relationship between Samkange's politics and his writing as straightforward. As "the prototype of African advancement," to use Flora Veit-Wild's words in her seminal account of Zimbabwe's intellectual formation, *Teachers, Preachers, Non-Believers*, Samkange represents a specific, quickly bypassed generation that paved the way for the more momentous developments that followed (66). In more ways than one, he is a belated counterpart to Casely Hayford in the previous chapter: Samkange, per Veit-Wild, is best viewed as a liberal nationalist for whom writing was "not so much a private affair as one with a social and political function," and one who was partial to the "semi-fictional or directly documentary and historical" form to convey commitments to multiracial democracy, progress through education, and institutional reform (17). The expiration of his "type"—erudite, measured, committed to democratic means as much as restitutive ends—may now seem like an inevitable fact of liberation history. His work, therefore, is reduced to an opening pitch for the high-stakes game to come. As with *Ethiopia Unbound*, however, close engagement with Samkange's oeuvre reveals a more intractable and historically transcendent set of problems than a one-to-one correlation between his political and literary careers allows. While Veit-Wild's description is broadly accurate, a few specific and surprising turns in Samkange's work speak to the central concerns of this book: the relationship between the intellectual values of the individual and the strategic imperatives of the collective; the status of ideas as they emerge from and reinflect literary attributes like character and setting; and the interplay of abstract ideals with tangible realities.

Where did Samkange's brand of anticolonial liberal go, this chapter asks, as Africa's literary and intellectual history was rewritten along simpler lines of colonial apologist versus radical liberator? Samkange turned from writing novels to writing philosophy to mark Zimbabwe's independence in 1980, and so this chapter tackles these questions by focusing mainly on the two most pivotal works of this decade of his career: *The Mourned One*, a novel originally published in 1975 (though written in 1969), and *Hunhuism or Ubuntuism*, a philosophical treatise published with his wife Tommie Samkange in 1980. I argue that *The Mourned One* marks a break in Samkange's efforts to represent an ideal of intellectual balance, using historically based characters, as his search for a way to narrativize values such as moderation and civility stalls in the face of his betrayal by their white Rhodesian avatars. In philosophy, he finds a new means of maintaining the primacy of individual *comportment* as a collective concern, harnessing the gap between his intellectual commitments and the disappointments of his social context to chart a new direction in his work. Philosophy, that is, accommodates his investment in a behavioral, deontological view of the individual where the realist novel, in its alternately social and psychic norms of development, starts to falter. He elaborates a moral system that is essentially a de-historicized code of conduct, one that is culturally derived but ultimately learnable, and thus might in theory offer universal guidance.

The chapter that follows makes this case in three parts. The first puts forth the conceptual stakes that Samkange's career foregrounds by elaborating "fairness" as a problem for the postcolonial public sphere, as it abuts exclusionary norms such as neutrality and civility. In the second, I offer a reading of *The Mourned One* in the context of Samkange's work on the brink of Zimbabwean independence, arguing that the novel documents the historical and narrative impasse to which his focus on fairness inevitably leads. Finally, the third section details Samkange and Samkange's *Hunhuism or Ubuntuism* as the culmination of *The Mourned One*'s investments with a brief, explanatory coda discussing other touchstone works from the same year: Dambudzo Marechera's *Black Sunlight* and Stanley Nyamfukudza's *The Non-Believer's Journey*. I propose that while Samkange detours from the novel form in order to uphold what he wishes it could do—namely, depict individual conduct as a source of universal moral value—Marechera and Nyamfukudza differently advance the African novel's broad turn toward a currency of "experience," as I have suggested in the previous chapter.

The Public Intellectual in Late Rhodesia

As critical summaries of Stanlake Samkange's life are quick to point out, he was born into an esteemed intellectual and political family with strong ties to the Methodist Church. (The Methodist mission-school tradition is another biographical point in common with J. E. Casely Hayford.) "The Christian influence was very strong in the families of most early [Zimbabwean] writers," writes Veit-Wild. "Stanlake Samkange's father was educated at Waddilove Institute, the first industrial school for Africans in Southern Rhodesia, was a Methodist minister and leading figure in the early nationalist movement, being a founder and first president of the revived ANC in the late 1940s" (*Teachers* 40).[1] Most significantly for Thompson Samkange's legacy as it resounds through the writing of his son Stanlake, he was named secretary of the Southern Rhodesia Native Missionary Conference, which was founded in 1928 but did not reach its full flowering, politically, until the mid to late 1930s. In this African organization nonetheless beholden to white leadership, the elder Samkange debated many of the issues that would occupy his son's generation, including the role of African languages in educational reform and the balance between racial separatism and cooperation in working toward majority rule.[2] Most significant for my purposes in this chapter, Thompson bequeathed to his son an investment in educational rigor and analytic balance—inculcated especially through Methodist school debate societies—as paths to racial progress. In sum, both Samkanges shared a defining challenge of reconciling an urge to radicalism with more liberal, Christian notions of fair-mindedness and civic conduct, what Veit-Wild calls a "dichotomy between [Stanlake] Samkange's political intentions and his deep-seated inclinations" (*Teachers* 125).

These terms are inherently slippery in the Southern Rhodesian context, and I use them with reservations: by "radicalism" here I mean a willingness to break with white rule by whatever means necessary, and by "liberal" I mean an inclination toward more incremental progress in adherence to principles of due process, reasoned argument, and nonviolence. A quote about Thompson from the Samkange family archive might just as easily be describing Stanlake's own political dealings: "In the end Thompson was more sensible and patient," a close Methodist friend and associate, Esau Nemapare, recalled to the historian Terence Ranger. While Nemapare elected in the 1940s to leave the white-led church fold, the elder Samkange bided his time. "I said it was too much," continued Nemapare. "He stayed in and made his point felt. I could not. I couldn't get on with white people" (84). In his tenure as general secretary of a stricken African National Congress—torn over whether and how to expand from cities into rural "reserves"—the younger Samkange similarly favored a bookish, patient leadership style. Again per Ranger's archival work: "Unlike many of his predecessors in the post, Stanlake was an energetic general secretary. What this meant, however, was not congress activity on the ground but rather a stream of highly intelligent, sophisticated and well-researched memoranda to [the white] government about its Native Policy. Stanlake took the view that Congress needed to be better informed and that it needed to make more impact on officials by means of the expression of balanced criticism rather than blanket condemnation" (144). As illustration of where this tactic either triumphed or erred, depending on one's perspective, Ranger notes that Samkange often received "long and even reasoned responses from government" (ibid.).

It is not surprising, in this light, that the height of Samkange's political and journalistic engagement was during the period of "Federation" (that is, the union as a "dominion," or linked group of semiautonomous colonial states, of Northern Rhodesia, Southern Rhodesia, and Nyasaland, or present-day Zambia, Zimbabwe, and Malawi), and its attendant debates, between 1953 and 1963. As a fairly technical jurisdictional issue, Federation and, relatedly, amalgamation—the merging of these three territories into a single state—offered Samkange a forum in which his scholarly prowess, journalistic interests, and political leadership could fluidly converge. Again drawing on Ranger, in 1949 alone he wrote no fewer than seven articles in the *Bantu Mirror* newspaper detailing the distinction between these two plans. These explications were met, however, with scorn from readers and fellow Congress members, who felt that he was dodging the need to take radical measures against white rule. Ranger concludes that Samkange in this period risked "becoming behind the times" (144) as nationalist sentiments began to take communist shape and the ANC waned in the shadow of newer, more populist organizations, such as the All African Convention. Indeed, Ranger notes, Samkange's suggestion that the Congress retain authority was in one instance met with what now seems like an almost parodical invocation of tensions between democratic and revolutionary outlooks. At a meeting in 1953, "a verbal attack on Stanlake Samkange was greeted by shouts of 'He should be Mau-Maued,'" a reference to the famed and, at that point, current guerrilla insurrection of the Kenya Land and Freedom Army against British power in Kenya (151).

The history of political institutions in this period has been written in detail, and the aim of this brief summary is simply to indicate that calling Samkange either a "nationalist" or a "liberal" does little to recover the live tensions in which his writing was embroiled. Even a glimpse of his career, before he left for the United States in 1965, shows that the real challenge is not to determine whether he represents a "committed" literature, per Gordimer, but to parse the ways in which his literary and affective commitments did or did not seem to line up with his political ones. That Samkange saw his writing as in the service of racial equality is not in question; it is the style and, by extension, the moral fundaments by which his work was guided that make for greater difficulty and lasting interest. "Fairness" and "racial liberation"—be the latter social or psychic—are in no way mutually exclusive goals. And yet, the intellectual and stylistic bent toward one or the other begets very different kinds of written expression. One example of the tense relationship between political-biographical summary and more fine-grained attention to language is Samkange's decision to resign from the liberal-multiracial Central Africa Party (CAP) in 1960 to declare support for Joshua Nkomo's more radical National Democratic

Party (NDP). In retrospect, the significance of this move seems clear: following on a set of Bulawayo riots (named "Zhii") that are now seen as a crucial turning point toward guerrilla tactics on the road to independence, Samkange's switch to the NDP, the predecessor of ZAPU, was an obvious decision for an African nationalist.[3] The terms in which he couched this choice, however, betray a more conflicted, universalist moral sensibility. "Stanlake explained that it was a matter of 'dignity,'" Ranger recounts from the archive, "but that he deeply regretted what was happening. There would now be 'predominantly European parties' confronting the predominantly African NDP, 'a very near thing to a white versus black contest,' which he had for years striven to avert" (190). Samkange, as Veit-Wild notes, is a figure who at various points both channeled ZANU funds through his account, at significant risk (117), and held himself apart from indigenous customs as "an enlightened moderniser" (122). He is thus, ultimately, in search of a written form that can accommodate these contradictory leanings.

As Ranka Primorac offers in her more recent study of Zimbabwean writing, *The Place of Tears*, "there are different kinds of nationalism," and in Zimbabwe, "anti-colonial nationalism has from the outset embodied ideals of freedom, democracy, and equality as well as the restoration of land to [black] people" (4). A treatment of Samkange that does not attend to the ways in which he articulates his positions risks subsuming important alternative sensibilities to the ones that later matured into Mugabeist repression. It is the poignant wavering between liberal values and radical tactics that constitutes Samkange's most provocative contribution to the African literary archive. Indeed, what may seem like basic distinctions to contemporary readers—liberal or left, progressive or conservative—grew so relative, so quickly, during white rule's last gasp in Rhodesia that the dissonance between Samkange's actions and his rhetoric is far more revealing of its political realities. It is entirely possible to evince what we might call a liberal habitus, with its bent toward process and ideals of individual dignity and self-determination, and at the same time participate in advancing an agenda of collective revolt. In moving, as I will later show, between the novel and philosophy as an auxiliary interest to his dialogue between the novel and historical documents, Samkange points beyond an unconvincing and yet persistent juxtaposition of "political" versus "aesthetic" trajectories in African writing. *Hunhuism or Ubuntuism*, in its focus on "the attention one human being gives to another: the kindness, courtesy, consideration and friendliness in the relationship between people" (39), is humanistic without being belletristic, attuned to the fine points of individual conduct without hazarding to portray a representative individual.

Framed in this way, Samkange's work offers an undertapped resource for broad grappling with the challenges of a postcolonial public sphere. His prominent and yet self-alienating place in what would become Zimbabwe gathers key threads of debate about public intellectual comportment, as opposed to simply position-taking, including the balance between dialogue and defiance. In this context, the two most-discussed and, arguably, generative models of public intellectual life are Edward Said's *Representations of the Intellectual* (1994) and, often critically, Jürgen Habermas's discursive public sphere. While neither intervention directly addresses Zimbabwe, the critical dialogue to which they give rise helps crystallize the particular difficulty of Samkange's position. Said, for his part, advocates for what is often summarized as a "speaking truth to power" version of public intellectualism, thus emphasizing individual acumen and accountability. Habermasian public sphere theory, alternatively, describes the shared behavioral norms essential to a robust democracy—namely those of eighteenth-century Britain, which saw the rise of "a relatively homogeneous public composed of private citizens engaged in rational-critical debate" to counterbalance state power (179). Both models are useful as well-known efforts to wed an imperative of oppositional civic engagement to elaboration of a moral-intellectual style, and Samkange embodies elements from each. But they are also revealing in what they cannot address about his role vis-à-vis his Southern Rhodesian public, for which questions of the individual's relation to power grew increasingly muddy.

Consider the following representative statement from *Representations of the Intellectual*:

> The central fact for me is, I think, that the intellectual is an individual endowed with a faculty for representing, embodying, articulating a message, a view, an attitude, philosophy or opinion to, as well as for, a public. And this role has an edge to it, and cannot be played without a sense of being someone whose place it is publicly to raise embarrassing questions, to confront orthodoxy and dogma (rather than to produce them). (11)

In contrast with the conflicted position I have outlined as regards Samkange, Neil Lazarus is able to remark of Said, based on the above, that he "emerges quite unambiguously as a left-wing critical humanist" (2005, 116). In terms of how *Representations of the Intellectual* appears in the broad ambit of postcolonial studies, this is a tough reading to refute. It rests, however, on a number of common and non-universal assumptions about the nature of contextual versus universal principles of action, which offer a provocative disjunction with the choices facing Samkange. As the title of this chapter suggests, Samkange finds himself in neither a fully empowered nor a fully disempowered position: he is betwixt and between different loci of collective empowerment, searching for a moral stance that transcends them both while stopping short of full abstraction from his culture of origin.

Said's description, that is, takes it as given that there is some correspondence between nationalism, nationhood, and power, and that it is against this force that the public intellectual positions himself.[4] The passage that Lazarus cites approvingly as a left-wing credo goes on to define the intellectual as "someone who cannot easily be co-opted by governments or corporations," and who raises uncomfortable questions "on the basis of universal principles: that all human beings are entitled to expect decent standards of behavior concerning freedom and justice from worldly powers or nations" (Said 11). As has been noted many times before, Said's operative definition of intellectual courage is against power, which is assumed to be vested in some kind of governing body, rather than in pursuit of it. This, in turn, leads not only to his second truism about the intellectual's self-definition, which is that it is an often-exilic pursuit, but also to his sense of righteous intellectual bearing. "With regard to the consensus on group or national identity it is the intellectual's task to show how the group is not a natural or god-given entity but is a constructed, manufactured, even in some cases invented object," Said writes later, thus vesting the intellectual with the task of denaturalizing empowered and complacent group identities (33). This role is "dependent on a consciousness that is skeptical, engaged, unremittingly devoted to rational investigation and moral judgment" (20). In sum, Said's social equation consists more or less of a powerful state, minoritized populations within that state, and intellectuals who broker between the two at their own peril.

The Zimbabwean nationalist movement, however, was a highly organized, forceful structure in its own right by the 1970s, when it was not yet officially a "state" but was also far from the markedly "non-state" arena of Habermas's bourgeois coffeehouses and cultural salons. Samkange thus sits awkwardly between two racialized loci of group consolidation—one with power, one in its urgent pursuit—neither of which offers a ready home for the restrained, discussive temperament to which he remains committed. In this way, Samkange can be read as combining a Saidian critical individualism, with its enforcement of equality through clear-eyed opposition, with the anti-individualizing demands of the Habermasian paradigm. As Michael Warner explains in his critique of self-abstraction as the basis of public intellectual engagement, "In the bourgeois public sphere . . . a principle of negativity was axiomatic: the validity of what you say in public bears a negative relation to your person. What you say will carry force not because of who you are but despite who you are" (382). Warner and others have convincingly worked through the limitations of this model, arguing that "the ability to abstract oneself in public discussion has always been an unequally available resource" (ibid.). On the whole, Habermas as a cipher for a socially naive faith in reasoned discussion has thus been cast as irrelevant or downright harmful to the causes of those who are not "implicitly, even explicitly, white, male, literate, and propertied" (ibid.). To put it still more bluntly in Warner's terms, the "very mechanism designed to end domination is a form of domination" (384).

Neither the Saidian focus on individual discernment and justice nor the Habermasian ideal of critical discussion to which anyone, in theory, *might* attain quite capture Stanlake Samkange's commitment to what he calls "socially desirable attitudes," such as fairness and humility (*Hunhuism* 79).[5] Both visions of intellectual conduct, however, contain explanatory elements of Samkange's belief system and paradoxical public role: he is determined to uphold a norm of self-abstracting, rational debate even when he asserts this norm as a self-distinguishing (or even self-sacrificial) act. In this way, his prominent position and increasingly marginal multiracialist values are at odds with each other, which, as I will show in the following two sections, brings about a move from writing historical characters to systematizing "character." At this point, however, I want briefly to mark the inadequacy of existing critical frameworks around terms that are closely related to "rationality" so far as a figure like Samkange is concerned. Rejections of "civility" in particular—a term that Samkange repeatedly valorizes in *Hunhuism or Ubuntuism*—have gained traction in ways that echo critiques of the Habermasian rational subject by Warner and others. Both are seen to demand the public abnegation of certain "marked" kinds of selfhood in the name of a universal code of conduct that is not, in fact, universal, but rather coded in different and exclusionary ways. Erin J. Rand summarizes this shift in a review essay on "Bad Feelings in Public," which surveys a number of books that link the "affective turn" in the humanities to social justice concerns. "Ultimately," Rand writes, the authors in question "illuminate . . . how patrolling the boundaries of affect can have authorizing functions in public discourse," disrupting norms of "rational, unemotional discourse" (174). The problem with civility in this now-common view is not so much with civility as such, but with the ways in which it has been used to enforce the dominance of those for whom being "civil" is easy, because they have little at stake.

In still bolder fashion, a short but highly circulated piece by the cultural theorists Tavia Nyong'o and Kyla Wazana Tompkins in *Social Text*, "Eleven Theses on Civility," pronounces civility to be fundamentally antiprogressive. "Calls for civility seek to evade our calls for change," they write. "The accusation of incivility is a technique of depoliticization aimed at undoing collectivity." Postcolonial subjects in particular are imagined here as buying into civil norms in only a strategic and subversive way, as in Homi Bhabha's well-known concept of "sly civility," which Nyong'o and Tompkins cite. Civility as an affect, then, conceals a rotten moral core, colluding to various degrees with a "racist ontology" and "[negating] the rights of the other to make claims on the space of politics." Perhaps better put, civility is revealed here not as a mere affect—a nonthreatening way of conducting interpersonal relations across social positions—but as a suppression of others' commitments to a more just world. It is a style with antimoral and antisocial implications, an aesthetic that the authors insist is "ultimately invested in the work of defending civilizational racism." When a figure like Samkange roots civility in a distinctly southern African context, then, presenting "politeness, civility and circumlocution" (*Hunhuism* 74) as signal traits of Shona bearing that are, in fact, built into the language itself, one option is to see him as a cultural dinosaur laboring under a false colonial consciousness, bound by his privileged class status to work against the interests of his race. This is a defensible conclusion, following Nyong'o and Tompkins's assertion that "the opposite of civility" is "militancy." It is not, however, a morally sensitive or historically deft one. Samkange's invocation of civility is "anti-militant" precisely in the name of racial renewal, furthered through an affect with a moral bottom line of sustainable communicative attention.[6]

I thus offer a second possibility for reading Samkange's version of civility, which is that it brings a more difficult problem to the fore: what of situations in which an intellectual and moral claim to self-abstraction is a mark not of dominant group belonging, but of minoritization where "dominance" is shifting? Unlike in a white, Western-calibrated context, through which much overly generalized thinking on intellectual bearing has been routed, Samkange's guardedly "liberal" worldview at the time of Zimbabwe's independence was not in a politically empowered position at the local level. In the long transition from an imperial frame to that of a new nation-state, the political valences of his beliefs necessarily mutated. In his case, it is arguable that the dynamics surrounding who was "empowered" and who was not are inscrutable enough to make what may have seemed like an exclusionary norm of performed rationality the only hope for inclusive advancement. Samkange's conflicted assent to the nationalist momentum surrounding the foundation of Nkomo's NDP invites a historical transposition of the Habermasian imperative to rational self-abstraction; Zimbabwe, that is, offers a view from the other side of the social biases that accompanied its emergence. If recast as nostalgia, not for European centuries past, but for what the Zimbabwean writer Stanley Nyamfukudza looks back on as the "new age of enlightenment" that followed his black-led country's founding in 1980, what bases of critique are left (2005, 24)? Samkange's situation presents the ideal of the balanced, fair-minded intellectual as distinct from not just the (white) group that has power, but from the (black) group ascending toward it. His midcentury reservations as outlined earlier seem to anticipate Nyamfukudza's own pronouncement, in 2004, that Zimbabwe under Robert Mugabe's rule lacked a "platform for non-partisan analysis and debate" (24). The country, in Nyamfukudza's estimation, was by that point beholden to an experiential rather than behavioral standard of civic legitimacy (specifically, status as a liberation or Chimurenga war veteran), accompanied by a discursive norm of "strident vituperation" lacking "simple, everyday decency" (ibid.). Though the Habermasian model was understandably criticized in the postcolonial arena for its Eurocentrism and valorization of liberal ideals over illiberal realities, it is its utopianism that seems to have channeled Samkange's (and Nyamfukudza's) formative investments.

This is not because Samkange is not on the side of racial justice, per Nyong'o and Tompkins, but because the self-comportment that racial justice appears, at least to him, to demand feels out of step with what Said calls the "almost athletic rational energy" (23) characteristic of a justice-seeking public intellectual, a trait that is surely on display in Ranger's example of Samkange's point-by-point refutation of white Rhodesian policy. The very notion of statehood, moreover, is in flux: as I have noted, federation, amalgamation, and various nationalisms are all in play as possible ways in which a future Zimbabwe might be structured. It is not possible, therefore, to see the state here as the "fixed point" of power in opposition to which intellectual activity gains its bona fides. The points of ostensible contradiction that Ranger chronicles in *Are We Not Also Men?*—for example, Samkange's simultaneous excitement and disillusionment in witnessing successful West African nationalist movements—look more meaningful in the context of this give-and-take between an insistence on universal principles and what must have felt like an unsettlingly volatile reality. Reflecting on his own dispassionate intellectual posture from the United States in 1965, Samkange suggested a need for reflective distance: "I find it more interesting to concern myself with the doings of Rhodesia seventy years ago than today. I tell my friends that when the news of today is that old, I shall as a student of history be interested in it" (Ranger 203).

I would like now to propose, then, that Samkange's move toward indigenous philosophy with *Hunhuism or Ubuntuism* is in fact a move away from historical experience and toward cultural-cum-moral systematization. Systematization as such—over and above the particular moral system being recorded—suggests a way of splitting the difference between his humanistic values, which demand adherence to "first principles" of fairness and equality in imagining conduct that can apply to all, and the sharp racial differentiation underlying settler colonialism and Zimbabwe's liberation war. His work of "cultural philosophy" so construed marks an abdication of individuality that can be narrativized as experience, at the same time as it doubles down on the moral significance of individual behavior. Per Omedi Ochieng's suggestion, most available models of public intellectualism (including Said's and Habermas's) "[inflate] the agency of those who hail a public into being," overestimating the power of individual conduct to bring about the emergence of shared spaces or imaginaries. (Ochieng looks instead to "the particular historical, ecological, and social structures that allow for certain publics to emerge while making impossible other publics," in which he includes the "vicissitudes of power, chance, and luck" [2016, 111].) Samkange self-abstracts by elaborating a model of moral self-conduct, a poignant turn in his career because it arises from a lack of perceived power. In one view, this marks a still more defanged liberalism than one that "blanches at radical politics because it threatens the politics of civility, incrementalism, and moderation" (Ochieng 2016, 116). In another, it holds open a proverbial space for values that are squeezed out by the world as it is, charging philosophy with the work to which Samkange finds the novel no longer suited.

The Mourned One and the Search for Replicable Selfhood

Samkange's career as a historical novelist is marked by what one might loosely call a liberal orientation toward cross-racial reciprocity, process, and individual integrity, even in its most hard-line anticolonial expressions. In *On Trial for My Country* (1966), his best-known work, both the duped (and last) Ndebele king, Lobengula, and Cecil John Rhodes are given space to literally make a case for their historical transgressions. The demonstration of an "unbiased" intellect, as described in the previous section, is part of both the form and content of the novel on multiple levels. Written correspondence between historical actors, including Lobengula and Queen Victoria, is presented as a story that an old man relates to a young Samkange just outside Bulawayo, Zimbabwe's second-largest city, where he spent the greater part of his childhood. "Thus it was that the old man told me his tale which I will repeat as simply as he told it to me," Samkange's fictional avatar states. "I speak only the words he spoke" (8). Within the narrative thus framed, Lobengula and Rhodes affirm their commitments to dispassionate retelling, with the courtroom setting allowing them an equal hand in establishing the shared truth of their interactions.

This is of central importance, because it creates an impression not of their having experienced history differently, but of Rhodes and Queen Victoria as having outright betrayed what Lobengula understood to be a basic, common set of values. Efforts to take stock of Samkange's oeuvre do it a disservice by categorizing it as either a liberal, colonial apologetics, as Flora Veit-Wild does (*Teachers* 122–27), or, conversely, as "a statement of the fallacies of liberalism" marking a turn to "clearly nationalist statements," as does Terence Ranger (204). While it may seem puzzling that two of the most prolific scholars of Zimbabwean writing would arrive at diametrically opposed readings of his work's significance, it makes sense if we grant Samkange claim to a more encompassing intellectual challenge than either take suggests. With the benefit of hindsight, *On Trial for My Country* sets the tone for a goal whose target is always moving: that of deciphering the relationship between "timeless" liberal commitments and on-the-ground racial progress. Samkange's writing queries not only to what degree one can insulate core beliefs from their decisive political failures, but what sort of expressive shape is adequate to this task.

The choice of what to privilege and, thus, of what to discard—a belief system or its tarnished embodiment—is left provocatively open at every stage of *On Trial for My Country*'s development. When pressed by his Anglican minister father, in the afterlife, as to whether he can "say that in [his] dealings with other men, particularly the Matebele king Lobengula, whose country now bears [his] name, [he] dealt justly and honestly?" (27), the younger Rhodes offers a lengthy response based in the pragmatic imperatives of empire building. "There was little point in sentimentalizing over Lobengula's position and person," he recalls, "no matter how much we sympathized with him, because if the British did not get in first and lay a claim to his rich country, the Portuguese, the Germans, or the Transvaal [South Africa] would have done so" (31). Lobengula, toward the end of the book, replies to the probing of his own father, Mzilikazi, with what ironically sounds like a general formulation of Rhodes's operative principle: namely, tactical reasoning that works in the shadow of apparent virtue. "I thought that if I appealed to the whitemen's sense of justice and fair play," he reveals, "reminding them how good I had been to them since I had never killed or ill-treated a whiteman, they might hear my word and return to their homes" (132). This passage proceeds along a similarly forked path of morality and calculation, with Mzilikazi pressing his son on why, given his history of violent warfare, Lobengula did not want to "spill whitemen's blood." Lobengula replies that he "wanted to be friends with them," but only because he was aware that the Ndebele could "never defeat the whiteman in battle" (133). A disappointed Mzilikazi shames Lobengula for failing to actually make a move toward friendship by becoming a British protectorate, and the son then describes his course of action as follows:

> I knew that if I fought the whitemen I would be beaten. If I sought the whiteman's friendship and protection there would be opposition to me or civil war. So I decided to pretend to the whitemen that if they came into the country I would not fight, and hoped that they would be afraid and not come. When they called my bluff and came I decided first to keep quiet. (134)

Laid out as a deceptively simple, point-by-point historical narration, the bottom line here might seem obvious: Lobengula fails his kingdom, and Rhodes is a deceitful usurper. Both men are guilty, but Rhodes is the guiltier of the two. On closer inspection, however, we see that Samkange is wrestling with a set of questions about the basis for determining right and wrong that cannot be so easily settled. He sets up a situation in which the ultimate grounds on which Lobengula should have acted differently are dual, and in fact contradictory: first, there is the suggestion that he has been morally betrayed, as his offer of a cross-racial friendship of equals is thrown in his face by the seat of the British empire. In this depiction, Rhodes flouts the values inculcated in him by the Church of England. ("Was that not a dishonest and dirty thing for Christian men to do?" [63], says the fictional version of his father about Rhodes's having misrepresented the Rudd Concession to Lobengula, thereby making him complicit in British annexation.) In the second depiction, Rhodes is merely a better strategist, with both men seeking to advance their territorial interests and Christianity a rhetorical-cum-civilizational cover. For Lobengula to maintain his moral high ground—as distinct from his tactical advantage, that is—the liberal system underlying Rhodes's historical armature must to some degree be left intact. This distinction between two possibilities for labeling the bottom line of Samkange's structurally balanced, "reasonably" inflected approach to how history is engaged has been revealingly echoed by the political theorist Seyla Benhabib, writing in the same volume as Warner. For her part, she outlines the discrete but overlapping relationship between the traditional liberal public sphere associated with eighteenth-century England and the "discursive" model now mostly discussed in Habermas's vicinity. Whereas the liberal version values "neutrality" and thus the suppression of fundamentally conflicting visions of what a good life entails, the liberal-adjacent version sees self-abstracting rationality as the key to maintaining open and evaluative discussion about precisely the relative validity of conflicting norms (84–88). In a word, we might say, this model upholds *fairness* rather than neutrality as the goal of a rational, depersonalized civic posture.

Because Samkange employs so many speakers and supposed sources of information in the book's structure—two fathers, two sons, and testimonies and letters from any number of other lesser-ranked imperial emissaries—it is difficult to pin down the tonality of his narrative. At points it is tragic and mournful, and at others almost cheeky and condescending: "Was there no other way out of your dilemma?" Mzilikazi queries his son, who shortly responds, "I did consider marrying the Queen, but even though I hinted at this several times no one followed it up" (134). In either case, the two levels of narrative framing—the retold story and the trial that it depicts—might be aptly described as "neutral," whereas the possibility of determining what moral or religious bottom line is contained therein introduces a related but distinct orientation of "fair." Samkange, for his part, can keep both versions of the "unbiased" ideal in play because Lobengula and Rhodes are legendary historical figures, and he is working in large part with archival documentation. The historical form, that is, relieves him of the pressure to invent a figure to carry the burden of a historical verdict. And were this set of issues of interest only for biographical reasons, it would be easy enough to say that Samkange takes what he needs from the Christian faith in order to reject British empire-building tactics and leave it at that. Given these rich textual ambivalences, however, the book's problems outlast such a quick interpretive fix and lay the seed for their more focused exposition in *The Mourned One* three years later.[7]

When he moves from a dual-protagonist structure in *On Trial for My Country* to a single-protagonist one in the later novel, Samkange ups the ante still further, broaching the possibility that the values to which he is wedded cannot be made historically convincing even as they may remain morally compelling. In *On Trial for My Country*, Lobengula's "realness" permits Samkange to stop short of resolving the question of whether the king's failure was primarily tactical or moral: Samkange positions himself as a mere observer of events as they are retold through multiple layers of mediation. In *The Mourned One*, Samkange assumes the task of building a character to do the observing, thereby seeming to execute his ideal of judiciousness as a matter of "content," or fictional experience, rather than as a matter just of framing or form. In other words, he is venturing deeper into what will come to seem like a discordant relationship between how people are "built," in a fictional sense, and what intellectual investments they advance. As in *On Trial for My Country*, Samkange begins *The Mourned One* with a transparent frame narrative of having been spontaneously gifted with a story: in this case, he claims to have happened in 1960 upon a prison memoir by a now-deceased young man, wrongly hanged for raping a white woman, which had been kept safe by his former cell guard.

The novel proper picks up where its plot terminates in 1935, in a prose whose plaintive quality, at first, stands in contrast to Samkange's immediately preceding profession of tedious scholarly work. "Well, it is all over now," the narrator pronounces. And then, a paragraph later, "But when the death sentence was actually pronounced it was shattering and nerve-wrecking. I was dazed. My senses became numb. I lost all control of my limbs, power of speech and everything. It was as if I were having a bad dream and had become petrified" (1). On the following page, there is a clear shift in intention from evoking an experience to analyzing its implications. The prison notebook reads, "And when I woke up I was refreshed and a man once more. I found my mind clearer than it had been for a long time and my nerves and mind strangely relaxed and calm; such calmness as descends upon a village after an angry whirlwind has swept through" (2). Where the reader is primed for a novel about colonial trauma, she ends up encountering one about victimization as a boon to intellectual distance. "Such calm fell upon me. I could think about fate—my fate; about death—my death; and about life—the life I would soon lose—as if it were not my own" (ibid.).

The thematic crux of *The Mourned One*—the betrayal of mission-educated black Africans by the very white institutions that have raised them—is not difficult to uncover, and Samkange's speaker, named

"Muchemwa," or "he who is cried for" in Shona, gives it pithy formulation as "I was saved to die" (4). It is the following passage that reveals the book's thicker inquiries as I have worked toward them in outlining Samkange's career. Muchemwa ponders, "Can it be that there are other values—ideas, concepts, traditions, personality, religion, civilization—nay, a whole heritage which perhaps, like me, has been saved to die?" (ibid.). Here *The Mourned One* announces itself not simply as a novel of disillusionment with the liberal values of British missionaries, as they are wielded to persecute (and prosecute) African subjects, but as an investigation into whether and by what mechanisms of telling those values may, in part at least, be salvaged. In asking a series of historically specific questions about Muchemwa's racist condemnation—"How does one relate Christianity and civilisation to all this? Is it Christian to hang a man for such a reason? Is that society civilised which has such laws [against miscegenation] and such an attitude to fellow human beings? Is the so-called pagan and primitive society not, in fact, higher and better than this civilisation?" (4–5)—Samkange also raises the more general challenge of whether his way of telling can survive what is being told. The key interpretive question driving *On Trial for My Country*, that of whether Rhodes betrays liberal values or embodies their intrinsic perfidy, now gains an additional level of complication. What of liberalism's merits when it is reclaimed by a person for whom these stakes are literally life or death? How to avoid betraying the already betrayed?

Samkange's investment in narrative fairness is now expressed via a narrator whose omniscience derives from being privy to both strands of his own dual origin. Muchemwa, also named Lazarus Percival Ockenden, or "Ocky," after the white minister who adopts him, has access to both Shona and British institutions and norms. As Mbongeni Malaba suggests, "*The Mourned One* enabled [Samkange] to tease out the various strands of his identity, as both 'a son of the soil' and a representative 'new African' shaped by Christianity and western education" (180). Ocky thus becomes a model of analytic comportment as well as the historical "event" being analyzed: he is form and content alike. The fact that he is able to dispassionately narrate his own autobiography, inclusive of his inception and babyhood, is made possible by the missionary education he receives as a result of being abandoned in accordance with Shona custom. At the same time, however, his narrative facility only serves to confirm his lack of real agency in the world, so that his starting point and end point are different expressions of the same fundamental outsiderness. Muchemwa, we learn, is rescued by a white man who crosses paths with his family when the narrator-as-infant is near death's door from illness and set to be killed by being "put away" in a pot in a river because he is a twin. Even prior to this, there was speculation in his mother's village that he would be cursed at birth by a resentful old woman. "Thus, even before I was born, my life was in danger," Muchemwa-cum-Ocky writes to conclude the novel's second chapter, "and, like today, it was not known whether I would live or die" (11). Contrary to a straightforwardly culturally recuperative reading of Samkange's nationalism, at least as it makes its way into his literary work, Ocky from the book's get-go is critical of both possible paths his life might have taken. Of the (Zezuru) Shona custom of putting twins to death, he writes, "what was abnormal was evil, and therefore had to be destroyed" (16). This implicit condemnation of his originary community applies just as fully to the white milieu in which he ends up, so that the novel cultivates a peculiarly static quality. Indeed, its third chapter ends almost identically to the second, which in turn echoes the first: "Thus, even at the time I was born, my position was much as it is today. I was to be deliberately put to death" (17).

For this reason, *The Mourned One* could be and has been read as a "failed" novel, promising character development where it offers only a thematic stutter.[8] Ranka Primorac offers a more generous reading when she describes it as a "colonial-native inversion" of the biographical novel in its Bakhtinian definition, which depends on the typicality of its main character's life progression as it is established over the course of generations. A typical unfolding, in Ocky's case, is impossible, because he is fated to "a life of anxiety in an unjustly dual moral system. In his role as the narrator, he therefore positions himself in an in-between discursive space, allowing his own voice to be 'contaminated' by echoes of both the 'traditional' African and the missionary discourses with which it is in dialogue" (61). I agree with Primorac that Samkange's strategy of permitting *The Mourned One* to serve as a "moral evaluation of missionary discourse" is deliberate (ibid.). Crucially, however, I do not see Ocky as exemplary of a "neither/nor" position, but rather of a "both/and" one. In other words, the significant trait of his narration is not that he is denied full access to both the Shona and missionary worlds, but that he is able to penetrate each of them with encompassing and exacting precision. The foregone conclusion of his condemnation at the hands of Shona elders and the white legal system alike is tied to his knowing too much. As Malaba rightly points out, "both cultures are seen as imperfect," though both strive, at their best, "for 'humaneness'" (180). The problem for Ocky is that his understanding of each of his worlds is comprehensive and systematic: he does not see them as simply *what they are*, but as a frustrating interplay, as if watched from afar, of their respective virtues and failings.

As *The Mourned One* goes on to show, however, Ocky's narrative facility, in its breadth and tonal remove, also teeters on the edge of historical discrediting. His mode of balanced, omniscient telling moves toward its fullest expression as the novel literally approaches the Waddilove Institution, the prestigious, real-life Methodist high school that Samkange himself attended. At this point Ocky even demonstrates retrospective access to his peers' minds, albeit in a curiously non-intrusive way; for example: "Their minds, for the first time, drifted back to the people who had accompanied them" (66). This line and the chapter in which it appears are devoted to the journey of two of Ocky's school peers, Gore and Kahari, as they make their way toward Waddilove. It is the most spatially descriptive section of the novel, providing a rich, detailed view of Southern Rhodesia's racial geography. Over the course of several weeks, the two boys walk the reader through the onerous task of getting school supplies at the one store in a twenty-mile radius (58); their community-wide farewell (60); and their eighteen-mile walk to the closest town and train station, during which they "knew all the streams and rivers they had to cross" (61). Upon arrival there, Samkange spends three pages chronicling the boys' interaction with white railway personnel, as they are "served through a hatch about a foot square," which was "usually closed until the white man inside took it in his head to open it and serve Africans" (62). The ordeal of buying tickets is among the most vivid in the book: "Finally, one of the boys knocked gently at the wooden shutter of the hatch. In a minute the shutter flew open and out came a string of the most sonorous, unprintable, vulgar swearwords in kitchen Kaffir [a debased white version of Shona] the boys had ever heard" (ibid.). Such vividly racist interaction continues through the train ride itself. The overarching effect, as indicated with these excerpts, is that the novel's setting gets the most "real" as it builds toward the space of Samkange's intellectual ideal. Waddilove, in all its multiracial erudition, appears on the horizon as either an island refuge or a lie.

Formally, Samkange seems determined that it should be both. Ocky's uniquely omniscient role grants him the ability to record the many settings and experiences that detract from Waddilove's primacy. The supporting figures whose lives he channels either reveal an alternative Shona community or imply the hypocrisy of what James Graham, in his book *Land and Nationalism in Fictions from Southern Africa*, calls the school's representation as an "ideal landscape of hybridised Afro-European modernity" (23). At no point, however, does *The Mourned One* narratologically *invest* in the experiences its narrator describes. Ocky "abstracts" himself, to use the Habermasian vocabulary, from the long road to Waddilove in a literal sense, maintaining an omniscient distance from others' fraught journey from village to town. The novel thus only partly adheres to what Robert Muponde, in *Some Kinds of Childhood*, refers to as a "nationalist journey motif" that entails leaving home and then returning with greater commitment to its anticolonial bulwarking (55). While it is true that it contains many of the key tropes associated with nationalist coming-of-age narratives—Muponde even includes Samkange on his list of "ideologues of black nationalism" (4)—at no point does it relinquish its claim to a balanced, removed narrative sensibility. The various African settings being marshaled in support of a nationalist politics in the 1960s (the time of the book's writing) are portrayed with a similar impartiality, appearing as parts of a rounded historical awareness rather than as singular, ideologized commitments. Samkange, we might say, is searching for a critical posture more than a culturally situated politics.

On the one hand, there is the heated urban environment of the city, and specifically Bulawayo; here the strongest sentiments are reserved mostly for minor characters' speeches. (A "big, fat fellow with a deep baritone voice," for example, is picked up *in medias res* shouting, "But the white man does not want us to be workers. He wants us to be his tools" [121], before quickly being dropped again [120–21].) On the other hand, there is the welcoming communal environment of Ocky's home village, where he feels "the inexplicable, serene tranquility" (96) of communal Shona life. This too is presented as an ebullient but short-lived "vacation" (106), followed closely by a critical description of rural gender norms. As Graham pronounces, Waddilove does indeed serve in many ways as the political and moral center of the novel (23): it is described as "a small but beautiful place" (29). Graham explains this fact in historically specific terms, casting *The Mourned One* as Samkange's act of mourning for "the demise of the religiously inflected, liberal and multi-racial politics of an earlier generation of African nationalists in the context of a seismic shift towards a more radical nationalist ideology" (21). While I do not disagree, I have tried, in this chapter, to suggest that there is something still more at stake, namely, a mode of intellectual comportment that can maintain an encompassing and, if necessary, self-abnegating critical posture. In response to persistent questioning by other students about his identity, Ocky narrates, "I confess these questions embarrassed me because, up to this time, I had never given much thought to who I was" (90). Since "who he is" is then related to "where he is from" by virtue of language (Ocky bemoans that he "spoke

English before [he] could utter a word of Shona" [ibid.]), Samkange offers Ocky an easy path to a galvanizing plot line of cultural reclamation. But *The Mourned One* is not this—it pulls back each time it approaches anything like full-throated cultural or political endorsement. Instead, it offers a multiply framed plot structure rife with checks and balances. While I do not agree with Jonathan Culler's much-cited rejection of "omniscience" as a narrative descriptor (Ocky is privy to others' thoughts but also to his own knowledge gaps, which makes Culler's "telepathy" an incomplete substitute), his discussion of it is useful in this context. Echoing Samkange's self-description after his move to the United States, he invites the labeling of a would-be omniscient narrator as a historian "who can investigate and capaciously survey" (2004, 31).

Cast in this light, Waddilove is significant not so much because it produces a specific class of "Europeanized" midcentury Zimbabwean leaders (which it no doubt does), but because it provides an education that, perhaps inadvertently, encourages taking stock of the Waddilove legacy itself along with everything else. Its signal activities as described in the novel are debating and team athletics, which, on their face, are quintessentially British colonial pursuits. But it is precisely the supposed "neutrality" of the debate nights—during which diametrically opposed positions are entertained in close succession (72)—that Samkange repurposes as the characteristic "fairness" of his narrative voice in its revelation of colonial injustice. To reiterate, I mean this distinction to invoke that between suppressing the assertion of a moral norm and asserting one. "Neutrality," per Benhabib, performs balance for practical reasons and to maintain a status quo. "Fairness," for Samkange, sees measured process as essential to any worthwhile and even dramatic social change. *The Mourned One*, in this spirit, neither valorizes nor discards the mission school experience. Instead, it presents two coexisting (rather than contradictory) facts: in the "real" terms of Southern Rhodesia's racial geography, Waddilove's liberalism *is* a lie. In terms of the capacity for self-abstraction its key activities inculcate, its emphasis on intellectual vigor over introspection nonetheless plants the seed of a culturally fungible moral standard. To be "fair" to his boarding school, Samkange takes its best—a learnable habit of attempting to view things from all sides—while acknowledging the untenable landscape in which it is enmeshed. Waddilove provides him with a *way* to be, through which he then cautiously works toward an answer to the more delicate question of who.

The Mourned One, then, ultimately serves to extricate a measured, universally applicable mode of intellectual inquiry from the missionary-colonial project to which Samkange, following in his father Thompson's footsteps, to some degree remains beholden. Its main character "self-abstracts" in a way that permits selective reclamation of the African cultural context. Across multiple settings—from a rural village to a white-administered rail station, to a multiracial boarding school and, finally, to a deeply unjust court of law—the novel unfolds through an omniscient, cataloging sensibility. A moral value of fairness is decoupled from its personal and institutional betrayals, paradoxically creating a bottom line where liberalism is measured by how one is, rather than by what one claims to believe. While "the missionary" teaches Ocky that "all men are equal and important in the sight of God" and that "colour means nothing," he "forgets that Christianity must not only be practised but must be seen to be practised every minute of the hour, every hour of the day, every day of the week, every week of the year and every year of the lifetime" (145). In effect, Samkange keeps behavior and belief on separate planes in order to demand just conduct, which in turn has the effect of salvaging liberalism from the ill purposes to which it has historically been put.

Conversely, daily practices of fairness and dignity are imbued with moral seriousness regardless of whether or not they are outwardly proclaimed as such. Shona culture, in Ocky's final estimation, upholds a universal morality for which a primary standard of comportment—of affective means rather than political ends—is simply assumed. "For instance," he explains to his long-lost twin brother when the latter visits him on death row, "see an old woman walking over there, she may be dirty and poor, or she may be rich and clean; you will greet her and accord her the respect due to, first, a human being, second, an old person ... and third, a woman" (ibid.). At the same time, at crucial points in the novel, including his brush with death at birth and his trip "home" while a student at Waddilove, the narrator foregrounds what he perceives as the moral flaws and irrationalities of Shona culture. Muchemwa-cum-Ocky thus acts as a fictionalized avatar for Samkange's broad faith in intellectualism as Southern Rhodesian politics grow more racially bifurcated. "Education will ultimately enable us to meet the white man on his own ground and topple him from his pedestal" (146), Ocky avers on the book's penultimate page. The investments ideally bequeathed by education can be summarized as, first, openness to measured evaluation of everything and thus to a universal possibility of redemption; and second, rather than *either* a strategic or essential standard of value, a procedural standard that allows key ideas of morality to remain constant across culturally variable contexts. Having made these points, however, *The Mourned One* is held back from their full expression by the racism of its time. In its stunted narrative development, coupled with a systematic yet never totalizing view of cross-cultural mobility, the book chomps at the bit of the history it knows so well. It chomps at the bit of all history, in fact, observing it in service of an aim at once grander and more emplaced.

Hunhuism or Ubuntuism: *Philosophy as Way of Life*

Samkange and his co-author, his American wife Tommie, begin *Hunhuism or Ubuntuism* with what amounts to another multilevel frame device. In its two-page preface, Stanlake describes his rejection of Western-originating Socialism and Marxism in favor of a Shona moral system called "hunhuism." He enjoins fellow Zimbabwean intellectuals to make it "our business to distil this philosophy and set it out for the whole world to see" (9). Keeping pace with Ocky's documentation of both the richness and liabilities of Shona culture in *The Mourned One*, the Samkanges add that "it is not our claim that everything Africans evolved under hunhuism or ubuntuism is superior to anything evolved elsewhere." Instead, they insist, "We must develop the perspicacity to discern what must be preserved and what must be eschewed in both hunhuism and Western culture" (10). The "we" here is specifically "the majority that will soon rule Zimbabwe" (14), but it also extends, by design, to a wider theoretical readership. The book's authorship and title are transcultural and transnational: "ubuntuism" is the Zulu- and Ndebele-language version of the Shona hunhuism, and the book's first chapter explicitly notes that there is "a sense in which we are all Africans: black, white and brown" (ibid.). The relevant point here is that the work is set up to facilitate movement from immediate context to a broader public; as the preface states, the intention is to put forth "the wisdom of centuries" as it will "stand the test of time and space" (10). In effect, the work offers guidelines for its own reading as a means of connecting Zimbabwe's independence to a universally replicable way of being.

Hunhuism or Ubuntuism accomplishes this through a narrative strategy of "zooming out" in time and space, which allows for both cultural specificity and narrative flow without demanding the individualized interaction of setting and character that a realist novel does. The Samkanges begin the book's first non-introductory chapter with a vivid yet vast description of its privileged locale: "Between the waters of the mighty Zambezi, in the north, and the languid Limpopo river, in the south, lies a land which is bounded in the east by the coastal waters of the Indian Ocean. Today, a large portion of this land is called Rhodesia, and its coastal trip is part of Moçambique" (15). Zimbabwe, in this way, lays claim to epic grandeur and an unusual degree of situatedness at the same time, a complementarity made still clearer in the next paragraph's parallel between the date of its first habitation and the birth of Christ (ibid.). As the Samkanges walk the reader through the Mwene Mutapa and Rozwi empires that once occupied this magisterial, evolving space and through its agricultural advancement in the nineteenth century, the country's present racial geography comes into focus as but a blip on the civilizational radar.[9] If Zimbabwe is established as an indisputably fertile cultural landscape best viewed on a scale of "deep time," it is also one whose intellectual contributions require an unusual amount of context, at least as far as philosophy is concerned, to be brought to full fruition. Samkange thus "experientalizes" philosophy even as he opts for philosophy over a more experiential kind of narrative, demanding that the reader extract an intellectual modality from a real place.

With *On Trial for My Country* and *The Mourned One* fresh in mind, it is as if Stanlake Samkange has made his way from the historical novel genre (with its characters granted by life), through a more "abstracted," fictionalized avatar in Muchemwa-cum-Ocky (a combination of autobiography and historical distillation) to finally arrive here at a fully generalized mode of exposition. "Hunhuism or ubuntuism is, therefore, a philosophy that is the experience of thirty-five thousand years of living in Africa," the Samkanges write. "It is a philosophy that sets a premium on human relations. In a world increasingly dominated by machines and with personal relationships becoming ever more mechanical, Africa's major contribution in the world today may well be her sense of *hunhu* or *ubuntu* which her people have developed over the centuries" (34). And yet to deindividualize hunhuism in this way is not the same thing as to *disembody* it, in the sense that customary behavior is essential to the moral value that Samkange assigns the broader question of comportment. On the following page, he offers an account of hunhuism in the flesh, recalling an episode in the early 1950s when two young Shona men refused payment for getting his stuck car out of a ditch. Their refusal, a local elder reminds them, should be dictated by a distant family (what Samkange calls "tribal") relation, on account of which accepting compensation "hahungave hunhu ihwo hwo" (would not be humanness) (35). The ordering of elements here is significant. Samkange begins with an implication—at once moral and historical—and only then summons the example. Philosophy thus performs—or, more aptly, is defined *as*—an explanatory function that is distinct from the cultural codes it observes. As a result, *Hunhuism or*

Ubuntuism marshals a sense of cultural embeddedness that avoids the trap of so-called ethnophilosophy, which, as Mudimbe succinctly puts it, is often seen to mistake "a language *of* experience" for "a language *about* experience" (146).

Instead of seeing Shona particularity as an antidote to speciously generalized first principles, thus consigning African philosophy to a "critical reading of the Western experience" that is "simultaneously a way of 'inventing' a foreign tradition" (171)—to quote, again, Mudimbe—the Samkanges see Zimbabwean codes of conduct as intrinsically morally valuable and thus ripe for explication as a replicable way of living. *Hunhuism or Ubuntuism* particularizes in the name of hard-won generalization: a preexisting language of experience ("we act in this way for this reason") is grafted to a language about it ("here is why this way of doing things should matter"). In asserting philosophical truths alongside anecdotal description, the Samkanges encourage a moral bottom line of how, rather than who (in terms of interiority or essence) or what (as a social identifier), one is. In this sense, *Hunhuism or Ubuntuism* aligns with *The Mourned One*. It finds an ideal of intellectual comportment through Shona culture and elaborates Shona culture through an ideal of comportment, but unlike the novel, the philosophical work does not venture to concoct a representative figure for either. There is no Socrates here, self-reflexively conversing as the fleshly embodiment of his epoch, no Shona man who teaches; instead, there is the authors' gentle observation of what there is to learn. In the figures of the young men rescuing Stanlake Samkange's car from a ditch, Samkange offers the reader an unknowing model of the values he then translates—in and as his body of work—into an at-once intellectual and moral disposition of "kindness, courtesy, consideration and friendliness in the relationship between people" (39). But philosophy need not broach the question of whether such comportment seems historically useful or likely. It only aims to ascertain whether or not, in ideal circumstances, it feels right.

Ironically, though hunhuism is not defined negatively in a broad intellectual sense (that is, it is not for the most part asserted to escape or negate Western values), Samkange notes that it is typically identified in its context of origin by absence and not fulfillment. "It is a peculiarity of the concept of hunhuism that it is more discernible when described in terms of what it is not than what it is," he writes. "'*Hausi hunhu ihwo hwo* (That is not hunhuism),' we are often told, usually as a reprimand. The positive side: '*uhwu ndihwo hunhu chaihwo* (This is real hunhuism),' is rarely pointed out" (40). Implicitly, then, humanity is by default aligned with fairness and generosity, making Samkange's insistence on such norms when it does not seem politically sensible an act of hunhu in its own right. In recoding Samkange's simultaneous disenchantment with British hypocrisy *and* dismay at the nascent country's bifurcation along race lines, this identification by lack is also linked to Zimbabwe's racial demographics. In citing the Shona phrase "Hona munhu uyo ari kufamba no murungu" (there is a person [*munhu*] walking with a white man) (38) as a common reaction to seeing a white and black man approaching together, Samkange shows that Europeans are not seen by default to exhibit hunhu. And yet, neither are Africans granted automatic claim to it.

As Ruby Magosvongwe writes, "A good/virtuous person (*munhu chaiye*) embraces and observes the duties and responsibilities that uphold peace, justice, freedom, and stability for society's greater good, while those who shun such social responsibility are usually deemed bad and/or useless people (*munhu pasina*) or senseless and insensitive—*munhu asina musoro/rombe*" (159). Thus, hunhuism is a choice: it is made by the act of its explication into a system of "attributes," to use Magosvongwe's word, that can thereby be transmitted. It is a moral code that some are born into but that one who is not can adopt, a ritualized and yet *rational* process of becoming best summarized as a "covenant with the land" reinforced by a series of rites from birth to death (160). Hunhuism's definition as an affect or disposition that a person may or may not fulfill, best captured in the Shona word *tsika* (culturedness), thus suggests a continual possibility of redemption. Hunhuism as an *idea*, that is, points to an ongoing aspiration toward a developmental *ideal* that is at once social and individual: it is an "education that is intended to develop the whole person" (161), or, as Patrick Sibanda puts it, a call to behave as "a good citizen who is able to act upon both his/her rational consciousness and according to the expectations of the society" (27). Negotiating between rational decision-making and social harmony also affects institutional function. "In passing final judgement," according to the Samkanges, "the African court will take into consideration an element which a Western court would consider quite extraneous and irrelevant, and that is whether the judgment or sentence reconciles the parties to the dispute" (44), because they have to go on living together. In behaving with hunhu (which is to say, with an eye to civility and reciprocity), individuals thus offer a model for institutional decision-making. The individual as the primary unit of analysis—a fundamentally liberal approach, though rightly criticized when unhinged from larger systems of oppression—carries within it a blueprint for the self-bracketing moral logic of society as a whole. In this case, an African court of law exists to maintain not only procedural correctness but also sincere moral conciliation. It exemplifies not liberal "neutrality," but what we might more thoughtfully call a collective moderating temperament that in its own right keeps liberalism's flaws in check.

Furthermore, there is a central paradox in play that echoes that of the willful self-abstraction I described, via debates about Habermas, in the first section of this chapter, whereby one achieves fully fledged intellectual participation by opting into self-erasure. The ready association of self-abstraction with the normative status of Western and, implicitly, white men looks less obvious in the Zimbabwean frame. Codes of respect conveyed by greeting are important, the Samkanges write, because "there is a tendency among the Shonas to concede their higher status" (72), so that "not being arrogant, pompous or puffed up when one meets or deals with other people, is a characteristic of a true Mashona gentleman or lady" (73). There is no doubt an element of status here, inherent in *who* self-effaces appropriately. And yet in reclaiming self-*un*-marking as a point of cultural restitution, the Samkanges force confrontation, in a fashion similar to the novels in the last section, with what one really indicts when rejecting liberal norms such as "civility." Is the problem with a fungible situational effect (with a bent toward "moral harmony" itself, that is) or with the racial power dynamics of its historical enforcement? While hunhuism thus cast is in some sense conservative in its insistence on social propriety, the mechanism of earning social status through humility suggests an egalitarian possibility as well. Through learned practices of deferential greeting, one both announces oneself as discriminating and moves incrementally toward a nondiscriminatory network of relations. "Furthermore," the Samkanges continue, "all this enables us to claim relationship with just about anyone and have that claim allowed. . . . There is no Mashona who cannot show himself to have a *hukama* (relationship) with whomever he chooses; and that relationship will rarely be disclaimed or disallowed" (73). Self-definition and self-restraint go hand in hand.

To have hunhu, then, is to demonstrate moral maturity by asserting a priority on moderate behavior and to act out an ideal of fairness and reciprocity regardless of whether it can be contextually motivated. It is, quoting Oswell Hapanyengwi-Chemhuru and Ngoni Makuvaza, a decision to cultivate dialogue as a means of "inculcating respect for others as much as we would like them to respect us" (11), on a par with the golden rule. Hunhuism thus emerges as a deontological belief system in the sense that its demands exist apart from those of situational consequence, but its elaboration, by Samkange and others, has often been put to contextually specific ends. Given this long-standing interplay between cultural specification and transcontextual significance, it is not surprising that hunhuism is frequently discussed in the context of Zimbabwean education reform. It is marshaled as a homegrown norm of liberal comportment that counters both its duplicitous British incarnation and what is perceived, by Samkange and others, as an overly mechanistic and imported socialism introduced in its aftermath. Whether through an ongoing claim to land access or reinstatement of a hunhuist idea of social consensus-building into Zimbabwean schooling, as Samkange saw himself doing with the founding of Nyatsime College in Chitungwiza (based loosely on Booker T. Washington's Tuskegee Institute), it dictates a rational choice to exceed what might seem like rational calculation. As summarized by Joseph Slaughter, ubuntu entails "a set of social duties that are necessarily attached to any rights an individual might enjoy" (2016, 206). Acting with hunhu is its own reward, because hunhuist principles cut grooves for a world of habitual decency.

The problem, as I have suggested, is that hunhuism for Samkange is not quite *representable* in novel form during Zimbabwe's extended liberatory moment, because, on the simplest level, it is nowhere to be found in its full, lived expression. *The Mourned One* cannot quite maintain the communitarian exuberance of Shona village "tradition" in the shadow of its own injustices (Muchemwa *and* Ocky, so to speak, are "saved to die"), and the civility ostensibly on offer at Waddilove gives way to the racial betrayal at the book's core. In structural terms, the challenge of expressing hunhu, as per Samkange's understanding of it, is that it demands a separate methodological, negotiatory space, akin to that of conceptuality in the previous chapter. *Hunhuism or Ubuntuism* is notably subtitled *A Zimbabwe Indigenous Political Philosophy*, and the political dimension takes shape as a set of concrete policy prescriptions for the new majority government (laid out in chapters entitled, for example, "Foreign Policy," "Thou Shalt Not Kill," and the like). Chapter 10, "Public, Corporate, and Private Property," is a microcosm for Samkange's larger goal of moderating between individual and collective commitments. Whereas numerous other expositers of ubuntu foreground its communality, Samkange systematizes a tripartite understanding of property.[10] "To say that all property must belong to the state or must be held communally is, therefore, as much to run counter to hunhuism or ubuntuism as to say that all property must be held only by individuals," the book offers. In fact, as exemplified in a story that the Samkanges excerpt about understandings of theft under Lobengula's reign, "our heritage accommodates all three categories of ownership—public, corporate and individual or private" (64). The behavioristic, mediating *functionality* of hunhu emphasized in the book is enforced in other ways too. Samkange advises that the new government would do well to employ *ngangas* (divine seers and healers, often spelled *n'anga*) to help prevent murder, not because he believes in the efficacy of traditional faith practices, though he may well, but because enough people *do* believe in *ngangas*' power that fear of their ability to discern guilt can be mobilized as incentive to act in hunhuist ways (53–54). Samkange thus gestures toward ontological questions—do spirits (*ngozi*) and seers exist?—without needing to develop or resolve them beyond the codes of conduct they facilitate.

One could certainly quibble with how the book selects the historical evidence from which it draws general claims, and debates about ubuntu continue apace in academic philosophy. The argument I am making is not that Samkange is "right" about hunhu's meaning or implications, but that he uses philosophy to fill gaps in what the realist novel and, by extension, a historically oriented narrative can do in his place and time. His triply differentiated model of property ownership counters a too-easy binary of Western individualism versus African communalism, but it also demonstrates how philosophy itself performs a moderating, mediating function. Hunhuism here occupies the space of a culturally rooted best practice that need not (though it may) correspond to how anyone actually lives: philosophy assumes the task that Muchemwa/Ocky can embody but not fulfill. A human protagonist, that is, whether reality-based or fictional, cannot attain to the level of abstraction that a philosophical system can and must. Ocky is essentially martyred to the conjoined cause of narrative omniscience and an untenable posture of intellectual fair-mindedness. Philosophy then steps in to advance Samkange's literary ambitions where literature falls short: it looks to the past to instantiate values for the future, bypassing the polarizations of the present.

Coda: Samkange's Literary Surrounds

The moderating function of philosophy in general and the self-moderation of Samkange's hunhuism in particular converge in a representational mode that is *individualized* but not *subjectivized*. In other words, his novels do not operate based on a principle of history being made internal to individual characters' minds, even as they work in conjunction with his philosophy to maintain a priority on *individual character* as such. This grants Samkange's behavioral and affective code, which I have summarized as one of "fairness," the capacity for replication. As a result, the movement from the self to the collective appears as an act of differentiated generalization rather than opposition. To put this distinction in literary-historical context, it will be useful to turn briefly to two other Zimbabwean novels published in 1980. If the novel form on the whole is most memorably harnessed, at this juncture, to explore and critique the nationalist energies that fueled the Chimurenga War, it also entails a retreat from the complementarity of embodied experience and abstract ideas. In different ways, both Dambudzo Marechera's *Black Sunlight* (the follow-up work to his classic *House of Hunger*) and Stanley Nyamfukudza's *The Non-Believer's Journey* refuse the demand for radical collectivity by resisting generalization of their main characters' experiences. While I make no grand claims about causality, there is a similarity here between the novel's evolution in the Zimbabwean (and specifically Anglo-Shona) tradition and the Ghanaian one described in the previous chapter.

When the prolific Shona scholar George Kahari, in 1990, attempts to taxonomize Zimbabwe's literary work leading up to independence, he points to the need to account for this difference between exterior and interior approaches to representing individuality *without* neatly assigning the first a "social" and the second a "subjective" orientation. As the two main categories of pre-independence novel, he offers "Novels of Political Protest" and "Novels Portraying Spiritual Bankruptcy," with Samkange's *On Trial for My Country, The Mourned One,* and *Year of the Uprising* (1978) as examples of the former. Post-independence novels are divided into "Novel on a Historical Figure" (including only James Langa's *Shaka*), "Novels Portraying Spiritual Bankruptcy" (*Black Sunlight* and *The Non-Believer's Journey*), and "War of Liberation Novels." In both *Black Sunlight* and *The Non-Believer's Journey*, the "spiritual bankruptcy" of this heading refers to the lone-wolf status and self-destructive habits of main characters who are not veterans of the Liberation War (Second Chimurenga), during a period when this status becomes a litmus test for national belonging. As Muponde and Primorac note in their 2005 volume *Versions of Zimbabwe*, the early 1980s saw swift rejection by Zimbabwean critics of overly artful, private, and socially disinvested writing.[11] As a result, they argue, Zimbabwean literature, in searching for a means of transcending policed divisions between social "commitment" and its absence, "challenged the discourses of Zimbabwean nationalism long before its historiography did so" (xvi–xvii).

In this sense, Samkange, Marechera, and Nyamfukudza in fact *share* a resistance to nationalist consolidation despite the contrasting retrospective positionings of their work, including by Kahari. *The Mourned One*, I have shown, far exceeds "political protest" in its central concerns and challenges. How, then, does Samkange come to occupy such a divergent role from that assigned to Marechera and Nyamfukudza in so many accounts of Zimbabwean literary history? One answer might be found in his reluctance to equate the moral status of individuality with a psychic one; he represents comportment without interiority. I will return to this point shortly. In a broader viewer of African (and specifically, southern African) literary criticism, an outwardly descriptive rather than subjective means of depicting the individual is associated with protest fiction in an aesthetically *and* politically impoverishing way. The best-known articulation of this view is in the title essay of Njabulo Ndebele's wildly influential collection *Rediscovery of the Ordinary*, first published in 1991, in which he elaborates a notion of "spectacular" fiction, citing the South African writer Alex La Guma as his chief example. Writing of this kind prioritizes "the exteriority of everything," Ndebele writes. "What matters is what is seen. Thinking is secondary to seeing. Subtlety is secondary to obviousness" (46). While often crudely interpreted as endorsing an opposition between aesthetics and politics, what Ndebele really conveys here is a distinction between work that is oriented chiefly to an effect on its reader (La Guma, for instance, means to inspire indignation that can be mobilized) and work that is more concerned with "complexity" (50), defined as *motivation* rather than cause and effect. Inwardness, then, becomes a key ingredient of successful struggle, not its opposite; literature provides "an occasion within which vistas of inner capacity are opened up" so that a *class*—and this is crucial—of individuals develops "as complete a knowledge of themselves and the objective situation as possible" (58). On its surface, and as concerns a good many writers under white minority rule in southern Africa, this fluid movement from an expanded individual consciousness to an expanded collective one makes sense.

Because such expansion of the collective consciousness via the individual gives way, in Zimbabwe, to what many of its outstanding writers perceive as a too militantly enforced group identity, it also seems natural that writers such as Nyamfukudza and Marechera would wish to disaggregate the individual mind from group subsumption. Nyamfukudza does so by depicting an English teacher who chooses a life of debased sensory pleasure over one of "joining up" to fight white minority rule. *The Non-Believer's Journey* opens with this character, Sam, vomiting up the previous night's escapades, as "grimy, smoke-stained walls set the tone" for his life of drinking, smoking, and partying (4). A fixture of black nightlife in Harare, he has just received word from his home village that an uncle has been killed by "The Boys," as Zimbabwean insurgents are referred to in the book. On a meandering late-night walk also clearly meant to orient the reader to the country's social and political dynamics, Sam recalls "the political violence of the early 1960s, when they had skipped school to join the gangs of thugs going on the rampage. They stoned cars, houses, schools, beerhalls, government buildings, and joined in beatings of whose reasons and purposes they had, then, had no understanding." His memories here coincide precisely with Samkange's period of growing reservations about political tactics, so that the young Sam becomes a fictional bête noire to the real-life Stanlake. The older (if not entirely mature) Sam, however, echoes Samkange's concerns about the internal power dynamics of radical politics. "He knew well enough now how some of the men currently claiming the leadership had clawed their way to influence," he thinks. "Scattered amid the rubble and ashes of property belonging to genuine traitors and collaborators had been much that had belonged to business, career, tribal and even life rivals" (15). From this angle, *The Non-Believer's Journey* rescripts the central problem of Samkange's *The Mourned One*: how is one to *be* in what feels like an impossible situation?

With no clear safe harbor in view, Nyamfukudza's protagonist looks out just for himself. Sam sees blatant racism on one side of him, and a dangerous group dynamic on the other. His journey from Harare back home for his uncle's funeral tracks this refusal to sacrifice present gratifications—both righteous and not—in the name of a future cause. First, on the bus to the town of Mrewa, he fails to show obeisance to the Rhodesian soldiers who stop them to check passengers' documentation and flex their (literal and proverbial) muscles. Sam talks back to one of his interrogators, which leads to an indignant search of the whole bus's baggage and, unexpectedly, the escape of a passenger at the back of the group. The passenger who runs off is labeled a terrorist and promptly hunted down with trucks, guns, and a helicopter, leaving Sam to take the blame for having escalated the situation in the first place. "You shouldn't have caused all that trouble for him, whatever it is you said which made the soldier angry," an old man chides. "You shouldn't have answered back, that man was probably carrying things for 'The Boys'" (36). Sam is described as "astounded" by this suggestion that his behavior should be dictated by the mere indirect *possibility* that he might somehow hinder the struggle. And while his stubbornness vis-à-vis the Rhodesian forces might seem forgivable to many readers, it is quickly placed in the context of a more encompassing apathy toward others' fate. In Mrewa, he seduces a hardworking childhood friend into sex after giving her too much to drink. "You can't think of responsibilities all the time," he urges her, claiming that "nobody expects you to. Even with this bloody war going on around us, people dying day and night" (50).

As it meanders toward its oddly anticlimactic finale, *The Non-Believer's Journey* seems to suggest that a meaningful life is found by conforming one's behavior to some sort of larger code. At the same time, it offers its main character no clear alternative to his cynicism. In a heated exchange with an elder relation who asks, "Do you seriously suggest that people can believe in nothing but money, jobs and the next meal?" Sam rejects both Christianity and ancestral religion as "a deliberate, cynical decision to get at people's hearts through their strongest, most enduring beliefs" (92). He is only confirmed in his jaundiced view of the world by tales of "The Boys" acting as a neat counterforce to Rhodesian power, as they single out for harassment anyone thought not to be contributing money and provisions to their fight. The overarching effect of Sam's character, then, is twofold. First, he embodies the bad faith and futility of asserting a claim to individual choice in the middle of a polarized situation. Second, he marks a narrative effort to do just that, associating strong subjectivity inevitably with death. Sam meets his at the hands of one of "The Boys" whose authority, yet again, he declines to accept. Taken from his father's house in the middle of the night, Sam is made reluctantly to join in singing patriotic songs in the woods. "He felt a horrible sense of dread, like a man gradually losing control of his bodily functions and fearfully, despairingly, awaiting the ultimate humiliation of shitting himself in public" (105), Nyamfukudza writes. When Sam then assaults one of the leaders who demands that he find and deliver supplies, this leader responds by calling Sam a "fucking coward" and spitting in his face before dealing him a fatal stomp with his boot (111–12). Unlike in *The Mourned One*, a novel whose protagonist might also be said to "expire" in the face of competing demands for collective affiliation, Sam has not provided any extractable way of being. There is neither a positive nor a negative lesson to be found in his death: his corpse is unceremoniously picked up and carried home, with the Chimurenga soldiers as indifferent to it as most readers will be.

As Samkange tries to articulate a behavioral mode that has meaning beyond its immediate circumstances, Nyamfukudza explores the stubborn appeal of claiming a life of meaninglessness for oneself. This is a selfhood that requires a clear line between Sam and everyone else, and that snuffs itself out rather than seek generalization. While *The Non-Believer's Journey* does not delve deeply into its main character's mind, it does suggest that he acts to preserve a subjective space of anger, desire, and impulse, and that this drives outward comportment instead of comportment constituting the main site at which "individuality" is manifest in the text. It is not a far leap from Nyamfukudza's novel, in this sense, to Dambudzo Marechera's more famous work set during the same moment in Zimbabwean literary history, *The House of Hunger*, which is well known for laying the colonized psyche bare in all its trauma and tribulations. Marechera—who to this day inspires what the Zimbabwean writer Memory Chirere has called "Marechera mania" among frustrated teenagers—makes a strong case for reading the destructive effects on and in an addled mind of feeling historically "locked in." At one point in his 1978 novella, the young male narrator stands on a hill overlooking his township with a character named Immaculate, his brother's abused lover. "She made me want to dream," he writes of his simultaneous attraction to and loathing for her; she "made me believe in visions, in hope. But the rock and grit of the earth denied this" (12). This is, from one vantage, an obvious moment of reality-induced contradiction, with the narrator entertaining a range of possibilities at the same time as he stamps them out because of the time and place in which he lives. As Annie Gagiano has written, "Fragmentation may be thought of as [*The House of Hunger*'s] major theme—the disruption of human potential characteristic of so many African societies . . . in the latter part of the millennium and beyond."

From another point of view, however, Marechera innovates precisely on these grounds of history's subjective *registration* by means other than representation. His literary avatars' minds are shaped by the bind in which he exists—unable to hope, and unable to give up hoping, defiant of postcolony and metropole alike—at the same time as they reject its determination. As Ato Quayson has argued, the turn to a (loosely) psychoanalytic model has been especially necessary and yet also unusually tricky as concerns African writing. "It seems patently necessary in the face of this threat of abrogation [in favor of nation, ethnic group, or kin] to restore the individual to history," he writes. "But how is this to be done without allowing the individual to devour his or her own history and to emerge as the titan to whom all discourse is obliged to make obeisance?" (2004, 758). As part of what he refers to as a "symbolization compulsion"—in short, a textual overabundance of metaphorization where it does not seem to advance plot or character development—Quayson then notes that "the world seems to lose its polar articulations and is unified in the emotion it reflects" (762). In even the brief passage from *The House of Hunger* just quoted here, Marechera fits Quayson's extended description to a T. The text evinces an "intensification of the perceptual sensorium" (766) through an interplay of polarities, serving not "as the mark of abundance," but as a sign of "emotional isolation and lack" (764). But I would push the idea of symbolization compulsion still further. While Marechera's work does indeed exemplify the transformation of worldly lack into psychic profusion, this "conversion" is also the mechanism by which his characters' subjectivity is cut off from larger significance. By this I do not mean that Marechera is not a major literary figure; on the contrary, his poignant and self-consuming obsession with subjective experience is far more emblematic of the novel's future, in Zimbabwe and elsewhere, than is Samkange's effort to sustain his moral commitment to a replicable, moderate, and moderating kind of individuality. I am suggesting, simply, that Marechera's "psychic turn" is an all-or-nothing gambit, with the mind turning inward on itself.

I would like to conclude this chapter with a few key passages from *Black Sunlight* that more boldly draw out the contrast with Samkange in representations of individualism via intellectual comportment. Marechera's avatar in his 1980 novel, a photographer named Christian, narrates life as disconnected observations through his lens, while spinning webs of rich vocabulary and condensing his worldly experience into an internal jumble. "Europe was in my head, crammed together with Africa, Asia and America," he thinks. "Squashed and jammed together in my dustbin head. There is no rubbish dump big enough to relieve me of my load. Swinging upside down, threatening to burst the thin roof of my brains" (3–4). It is not just the amped-up intermingling of the real and the figural that sets him at a remove from the various friends and lovers with whom he interacts, but a resistance to acquired knowledge. Christian draws a hard line between inside and outside, regardless of whether the "outside" comprises social groups or depersonalized information. "I was hot with resentment and pain," he recalls of his youth. "So this was school. From all sides my head was being jammed with facts. With ideas" (17). It is difficult to know how much to make of any given formal choice in what is, as others have noted, a somewhat haphazard-feeling text. Per the novelist-critic Helon Habila, *Black Sunlight* "reflects Marechera's growing paranoia" as he sank deeper into drinking and depression while he was composing and revising it, and his already-difficult style "becomes here even more obscurantist and autobiographical." Still, the ordering of this segment seems important. Christian first introduces his own discomfort; only then does he note that he is actually at school; and lastly, he identifies the source of his torment, not as a teacher or fellow students, but as *ideas* themselves. Speaking later of the "facts" he was meant to learn, he states that "it was days before [he] could scrub them out and let the dirty water gurgle out of the sink" (18). The passage does not make literal sense, nor is it meant to: the notable achievement here is to make depersonified knowledge seem like a contaminant.

On this point, Marechera's work from the year of Zimbabwean independence seems best to illuminate the contrastive stakes of Samkange's work and to articulate more richly Nyamfukudza's conjuncture of self-will and self-expiration. Though it is true, per Habila, that "the story line totally disappears to be replaced by long political and philosophical discourses on history and power and anarchism and race," *Black Sunlight* never fuses an *idea of* individuality with the individual at the center of his text. It is not, in other words, a book in which any one person's comportment has implications for individual conduct generally. Marechera's main character grabs at different intellectualized versions of a psyche laid bare—from Fanon to Darwin, and in one case literally ("Rousseau's naked man vainly fleeing ... from a pouncing leopard")—but arrives ultimately at a void of even self-knowledge (109). Christian's intellectual modus operandi is anti-expository and indeed, almost anti-analytic, entailing frantic cycling through and expulsion of "knowledge" conceived of as something that has life beyond its momentary and contingent habitation. Recalling a relationship in which the parties "grew to know less and less of each other," he then ends the book with the stark line, "And the mirror reveals me, a naked and vulnerable fact" (117). This, then, is the full and simultaneous inversion of *The Mourned One*'s self-abstracting, learnable mode of individual comportment as the outer limit of what the novel can demonstrate at Zimbabwe's birth. For Samkange, philosophy picks up where his fiction leaves off. Marechera's work, here in brief counterpoint, suggests both the vibrancy and the loss that attends the eclipse of *how* one should be by the more gripping narrative paradigm of who.

PART II

Global Recessions

CHAPTER THREE

A Forked Path, Forever

KINTU BETWEEN REASON AND RATIONALITY

AFRICAN LITERATURE CAN be linked to a broader set of global humanistic concerns by its mapping as a set of cognate debates over whether to expand or pluralize Enlightenment concepts. Prominent examples of this tension are singular versus multiple modernities; universality versus vernacular universalisms; and what to do with reason/rationality (whose pluralized form is more elusive). To some degree, the African denotation itself might be said to have split across similar lines. A much-discussed turn to "Afropolitanism" after 2005 met with resistance from a resurgent pan-Africanist position, seeming to pit multiplicity against solidarity.[1] As defenses and counterdefenses of such paired terms accrete, however, a clear sense of their normative stakes recedes. Readers are left struggling to navigate between two expressions of Africa's place in the world that both seem progressive in their own way: one suggests that pluralizing what should be self-evident claims—to being modern, or universal—substitutes relativistic "difference" for Africans' full-fledged humanity. The other rejects singular nouns that have long been used to humanize some and not others, seeking to build more inclusive terms of critical exchange.

Perhaps no work of fiction has captured this impasse better than the Ugandan writer Jennifer Nansubuga Makumbi's *Kintu*, first published in 2014 but completed between 2004 and 2011. Though praised most often for its epic scope as a historical novel, *Kintu* at its core is a book about whether and how reason can accommodate cultural plurality. By this I do not mean just that it reflects the syncretic state of African cultures in the twenty-first century—what some have called the "post-post-colonial" era—but rather that it grafts fundamental questions of how to interpret onto timely epistemological conflicts as to *what* one is interpreting in the first place. *Kintu* asks whether different ways of knowing demand different conceptions of reason; or, whether a broader application of reason than has traditionally been allowed may even render reason an outdated tool of intercultural understanding. It does this by creating a world in which signal events, their causation in doubt, are read tenably either as products of a multigenerational curse or as epiphenomena of mental health struggles. *Kintu* keeps the possibility of the curse explanation in play for some characters at the same time as it depicts its rational rejection by others, effectively having its cake and eating it too. An a priori kind of reason thus intersects with a "local" one, both of them not only evidence-based but based on the same evidence.

What is at stake here, ultimately, is the connection between an ability to reason—based on the laws of modern rationality or traditional belief in a curse, but not both—and the ability to exert agency in a culturally mixed-up setting. *Kintu* thus remains invested in an interpretive standard of reasonableness while at the same time allowing characters who favor a supernatural reading of the book's events to appear more reasonable than a key figure, Miisi, who rejects such a reading in favor of a "rational" explanation. In keeping with the opening paragraph of this chapter, we might say that *Kintu* depicts pluralized ways of *reasoning* as a means of renewing the universal significance of reason to human experience. The self-enfranchising act of reasoning, defined here as maximal responsiveness to available evidence, is mainly depicted via characters who give over to the logic of the curse. Miisi, for his part, winds up as the least viable self by internalizing traditional *and* modern beliefs: he fails to follow his own powers of reason through to the point of their decisive reevaluation. Because he is also the book's lone intellectual in terms of formal training and self-conception, Miisi's final descent into madness casts doubt on the capacity of the individual mind to harbor the full interpretive conditions of a "global African" setting. In other words, his commitment to what he sees as the neutral evaluation of different knowledge systems—the very expansiveness of his range of cultural access—becomes a liability when faced with evidence that this stance may itself be unreasonable.

Like those before it, this chapter develops across three sections, moving from a conceptual framework, through a reading of the central work, and finally to a shorter conclusion that contemplates texts from a similar time and place with different approaches to shared concerns. In the first section, I situate *Kintu* in the context of African literature as it relates to broader debates in the African(ist) humanities, specifically those concerned with the place of reason and rationality in a self-consciously global context. The section builds toward work by the philosopher Emmanuel Chukwudi Eze, which, as the most robust version of a reason at once situationally embedded and universally attuned, helps to draw out *Kintu*'s likeminded accomplishments. The second section argues that *Kintu* evolves through a motif of "twinning," using an explicit theme of twins to hook on to the problem of a twinned interpretive design. Neither a psychoanalytic nor a historical heuristic, I contend, can quite encompass the challenge such twinning poses to Makumbi's reader, to whom the novel's seminal events appear structurally but *not* epistemologically determinative.

In the final estimation, *Kintu* underscores the centrality of nimbly evaluating evidence to meaningful individual development, including in relation to community. It stops short, however, of making a transposable normative recommendation as to how: contextualized responsiveness matters more than epistemological bottom lines. The interpretive duality that underscores this message also fuels two related depictions of how cultural syncretism acts on individual lives. The first represents self-actualizing individual *responses* to a split possibility for "reasonable" interpretation, while the second represents the disabling and passive individual *internalization* of it. *Kintu* thereby advances a meaningful difference between individuation and subjectivization as narrative strategies, prioritizing local effect over representationality. To conclude, I briefly discuss two novels from East Africa published in the span of a decade that feature curses to historical but not philosophical effect. Goretti Kyomuhendo's *Waiting* (2007) and Peter Kimani's *Dance of the Jakaranda* (2017), I suggest, entertain supernatural causation at the level of reference but not of epistemological choice-making. They thus shed light on *Kintu*'s trade-offs between reason and record, national certainties and globalized doubt.

"The Great Ugandan Novel" as Periodizing Device

In African literature circles, *Kintu*'s origins have become almost legendary. Published first by Kenya's Kwani Trust in 2014 and then by Transit Books of Oakland, California, in 2017, the novel was begun more than ten years earlier while Makumbi was a doctoral student in the United Kingdom. Much has been made of her difficulty finding a publisher, which she attributes to the book's non-adherence to key expectations for African writing. Rich with local references, *Kintu* spans six sections and four centuries, from the eighteenth to the twenty-first, as it follows the descendants of its foundational figure, Kintu Kidda. (In the Buganda kingdom's mythology, "Kintu" is the first man on earth; the name was then taken by their first *kabaka*, or king, in the fourteenth century.) What it does *not* do—not explicitly, at least—is parse the relationship between Africa and the West. "The reality is that Europe is absent in the novel," Makumbi admitted to the Kenyan literature scholar Aaron Bady in 2014; that hindered its uptake, she felt, because "post-coloniality sells" (Bady, "Post-coloniality"). Makumbi does not deny Europe's influence on present-day Uganda, but neither does she feel compelled, as her literary forebears did, to make it a central topic of concern.

In declining to thematize Western cultural and economic influence even as a means of redress, Makumbi by her own admission strives toward something unprecedented in postcolonial writing and criticism. Dating back at least to Achebe's *Things Fall Apart* and its inauguration of the African Writers Series in 1962, African literature and its critical apparatus have moved contentiously and definitively between paradigms of subversion and resistance, often mapping onto cultural versus economic critical orientations. Achebe, whose critique of Europe is nested in near-constant reference to its intellectual traditions, becomes broadly representative of a twentieth-century emphasis on "writing back" to empire.[2] Roughly bookended by such iconic classroom texts as Jean Rhys's *Wide Sargasso Sea* (1966) and J. M. Coetzee's *Foe* (1986), this formative movement was characterized by a foregone intermingling of literary sensibilities between colonizer and colonized, with a methodological corollary in the hybridistic interests of "postcolonial theory."

If the mainline of that field welded the insights of poststructuralism to a concern with the cultural output of formerly colonized peoples—via epistemological "decentering," linguistic constructivism, and skepticism toward the universal claims of Western philosophy—there was an equally formative counterforce that emphasized struggle over what it perceived as obfuscatory complexity. In this book's first chapter, for example, I referred to Neil Lazarus's definitive *The Postcolonial Unconscious* in this light. Ngũgĩ wa Thiong'o also adhered to a firmer division between African and European traditions. "From the point of view of alienation," he writes famously in *Decolonising the Mind*:

> that is of seeing oneself from outside oneself as if one was another self, it does not matter that the imported literature carried the great humanist tradition of the best in Shakespeare, Goethe, Balzac, Gorky, Brecht, Sholokhov, Dickens. The location of this great mirror of imagination

was necessarily Europe and its history and culture and the rest of the universe was seen from that centre. (17–18)

I do not intend to relitigate these debates, which, looking back, often seem to be of greater historical than ongoing hermeneutic interest. I gesture to them here to accomplish two, more immediate tasks. The first is to indicate that *Kintu* represents something genuinely momentous in the corpus of "modern" (which is to say independence- and post-independence-era) African literature: colonization is not its organizing principle. As Bady suggests, "The point is not that colonialism didn't happen, or was inconsequential; the point is that colonialism wasn't the only thing of consequence that did" (Bady, "Story"). Second, I want to argue that Makumbi does something more to this end than depict histories that have been previously underrepresented in literary fiction, which is the dominant goal of many peer texts. Asked in the *Johannesburg Review of Books* about her own work's place in the "new wave of African historical fiction," for example, among which *Kintu* is frequently included, the Ghana-born Ayesha Harrunah Attah responds, "As a writer, there's so much I don't know about myself and where my people come from, that writing historical fiction is a way of fighting that rootlessness and searching for what we lost when we suffered invasions on every front: physical, religious, cultural, and so on" (Malec). As important as such work is, *Kintu* has still bigger fish to fry. It does not register Europe's presence at the level of theme or even ultimately of history, as in, for example, Eileen Julien's influential formulation of the "extroverted African novel," which represents global circulation to register "the formidable imbalances and inequities that characterize Africa's place in the world" (696). Nor does it turn to pre-colonial African history in order to expand or enflesh the African historical record (even though it does this too). Instead, it takes the main thing that Europe is seen to have inflicted on its colonies—a reason/rationality that is partial, flawed, and standardized along racist lines—and examines it at the level of first principles.

Kintu thus exceeds any working definition of the historical novel, even as it is easily absorbed by this label given its grand multigenerational structure and the recent surge of interest in the historical genre in the African literary context.[3] It is not persuasive in depicting social transformation, à la the genre's Lukacsian version with its "imperishable basis of future human development" (29) in the French Revolution. In *Kintu*, the question of whether there *has* been deep sociological change remains open, as its plot emphasizes continuity more than "progress." Its first main character, the eighteenth-century ruler Kintu Kidda, believes that he is plagued by a curse after he accidentally kills his adopted son. At least some of the book's successive characters (discussed in the next section) believe in the same curse, based on the same sorts of signs: madness, the haunting of a living twin by a dead one, and premature death. The book's main achievement is thus meta-interpretive rather than meta-historical: its central challenge of discerning *which reading* the events in its plot support moves through time but is not fundamentally altered by it. At the same time, *Kintu* is not "metafictional" along the lines of Linda Hutcheon's definition of "historiographic metafiction"; its defining preoccupation is less with "a past that can only be known from its texts, its traces," than with two competing versions of what kind of explanation a particular past demands (4). The novel, in other words, is not about "[mocking] any notion of either single origin or simple causality" (12), but about trying to *pin causality down* in a culturally pluralistic landscape that makes it especially difficult to do so.

Though it contains familiar markers of historical fiction, including what Alexander Manshel has described on the website Post45 as "the prestige of historicity" invoked by using particular places and dates in section headings, it is thus more meaningful to say that *Kintu* suggests a distinction between the historical novel and the philosophical one. If historical fiction tracks certain events to show why and to whom they mattered, and historiographic metafiction asks what it means to narrate an "event" at all, then philosophical fiction on the order of *Kintu* evaluates how best to make meaning from one's relation *to* events. The role of rationality in what is sometimes a tense relationship between African literature's historicity and its ability to make universal claims is of paramount concern here. In asking its readers whether it is tenable to read *Kintu* as the story of a curse—through a plot that accumulates family hardships that may or may not be attributable to it—the novel asks whether it is possible to make an evidence-based choice against rationality. Complicating this determination is the fact that *Kintu* is a novel and not a philosophical treatise as such: readers contemplate the nature of reason alongside characters who do so as well, based on invented and selective textual evidence. That it is specifically the possibility of a *curse* on which readers must weigh in (and more precisely, a curse as the source of mental illness) seems to present a standoff between scientific and supernatural ways of accounting for the world. To some degree it does: the novel partakes in a long tradition of troubling the tradition-modernity dyad. What *Kintu* does best, however, is give narrative shape to a distinction between rationality and reason, based on the proposed "philosophical novel" criterion of a foremost concern with making meaning from one's relation to worldly events.

Before taking the measure of this difference, I would like to turn now to some background discussion of how the conjoined version of reason/rationality has figured in African literary studies. This will facilitate a smooth passage toward a more supple formulation of reason as the pursuit of meaning through the development of will, in work by Eze in particular. First, it will be useful to have a basic working definition of the "Enlightenment values" that have driven much justifiable but frequently reductive debate in the field. Justin E. H. Smith offers as good a recent summary as any in his book *Irrationality: A History of the Dark Side of Reason*. He writes that what has become known in aggregate as "Enlightenment philosophy" stipulates, "first, that each of us is endowed with the faculty of reason, capable of knowing ourselves and our place in the natural and social worlds; second, that the best organization of society is the one that enables us to freely use our reason in order both to thrive as individuals and to contribute in our own way to the good of society" (8). To see humans as rational thus entails thinking that we are capable of responding to the world in ways that increase knowledge of it and ourselves, and that we generally act in our interest to further this goal. As African philosophers have long noted, however, universal human reason as a theoretical postulate has been partner to dehumanizing realities. The usual starting points for a critique of this nature are Kant and Hume, on whose racism there is ample scholarly work.[4] And as Kwame Anthony Appiah writes recently in the *New York Review of Books*, the eighteenth century's "systematic forays into physical anthropology and human classification laid the foundation for the noxious race science that emerged in the nineteenth century." His summary of the Enlightenment's reception by postcolonial scholars then pinpoints the putative gap between grand ideals and their perverse application. "A heedless sense of universalism," he continues, "might encourage the thought that the more advanced civilizations were merely lifting up those more backward when they conquered and colonized them" (2019).

To be sure, such civilizational prejudice has often been on flagrant display in Western relations with Africa. But as Appiah goes on to suggest in his review of Smith's book, many of the scholars engaged in this critique have also "shared a larger worry about 'rationalism' itself," a fear that "light is destined to generate shadows." The postliberal turn in post–Cold War thought, then, has seen the self-conscious reckoning with global plurality as an impetus to get beyond the valorization of reason. This position typically stems from some version of the argument that reason's individualistic and, often, masculinist bias is intrinsically Eurocentric, not just misapplied and thus outdated on both moral and political grounds. Appiah in this context cites the English political philosopher John Gray, whose 1995 classic *Enlightenment's Wake* elaborates a "view of political life as being permanently intractable to rational reconstruction" (13), discarding "the liberal individualist fiction of the disembodied or unsituated human subject" (24).[5] It is fair to say that a postliberal persuasion also dominated the most fertile decades of postcolonial studies in the 1990s and early 2000s, in era-defining books like Gayatri Spivak's *A Critique of Postcolonial Reason* (1999) and Dipesh Chakrabarty's *Provincializing Europe* (2000). The latter is particularly germane to discussion of *Kintu* and its curse: Chakrabarty remarks on how "reason becomes elitist whenever we allow unreason and superstition to stand in for backwardness, that is to say, when reason colludes with the logic of historicist thought" (238). "Reason" appears in such critiques as a historical specter and ideological cipher, part of a capacious unseating of entrenched civilizational-cum-political hierarchies. It is more a *figure* than a verb.

This is also where "critical theory" and "philosophy" meaningfully diverge, and where, I believe, the latter may now be the more illuminating partner to African literature. During the same years that Africa gained metonymic prominence within Western-originating postcolonial criticism—outside its traditional, differently fraught homes of anthropology and area studies—African philosophers were thinking through the problem of reason in more locally trenchant ways. I have already discussed work on this topic by Kwasi Wiredu, Kwame Appiah, and Kwame Gyekye, among others, in the introduction and first chapter of this book. But it is a farther-reaching undertaking. The South African philosopher Mogobe Ramose, for example, states outright that "the struggle for reason—who is and who is not a rational animal—is the foundation of racism" (3). And yet Ramose advocates on this basis for an extension of reason beyond its traditional exemplars to grant African thought a rightful status as philosophical. He suggests that this process will overcome Western insistence "on the identification of reason with absolute obedience to the convention to rely on the authority of references" (8). In effect, Ramose accuses Western philosophy of having failed at its own game, owing to its inbuilt ethnocentric bias. At the same time, he resists merely imputing the same trait of reason to Africans if the goal is to make location seem insignificant by absorbing "African philosophy" into a geographically unmarked discipline. "To discover familiarity... is not the same thing as to affirm identity" (7),

Ramose remarks, indicating that part of philosophy's task now is uncovering *how* reason operates from place to place.

As many before me have discussed in detail, there is a disharmony here between postcolonial scholarship that includes Africa among its interests, on the one hand, and specifically African/ist scholarship on the other. A broadly postcolonial approach tends to unmask reason's biases—be they "merely" historical or constitutive—and to indicate the need to pluralize or reject it. Approaches that are invested in particular African traditions, meanwhile, have often aspired to show just what reason *looks like* outside a Eurocentric frame. (Kwasi Wiredu's work as referenced in this book's chapter on Casely Hayford is a prime example.) Writing in 2006, Paul Tiyambe Zeleza describes a similar impasse in the discipline of history: "Because [postmodernism, poststructuralism, and postcolonialism] suggest the pluralities but repudiate some of the practices of history, they are both welcomed and rejected by many African historians, who believe that it is possible to formulate historiographies that are not Eurocentric, to write history . . . that focuses on varieties of human experiences and connections and tells stories of change without presenting linear tales of progress" (114). It is not incidental that Zeleza makes recourse to the idea of narrative here. His preference for an emplaced as opposed to a metacritical methodology, though admittedly a tricky line to mark, is also a point on which the novel and philosophy seem to have a natural affinity. Adopting the Africanist philosopher Bruce Janz's description from a piece on "The Geography of African Philosophy," we might also say that a novel of ideas like *Kintu* seeks "the local or fine-grained spaces in which concepts find their vitality" (162) across different scales of representation. Shifting critical gears from one task to the other involves, at some point, deciding just to take it for granted that Africans have reason. If the bugbear of reason's historical malformation along race lines is allowed to recede, presaging *Kintu*'s treatment of colonial history, then "Africa" assumes philosophical texture instead of just polemical significance.

This is readily done, in theory, but it is also the point at which the limits of rationality vis-à-vis supernatural causation come back into view. Chakrabarty speaks for many proponents of a "multiple modernities" framework when he criticizes the association of traditional belief systems with backwardness or a life lived somehow outside of history. The anthropologists Jean and John Comaroff ably advanced this line of thinking as far back as 1993, in their influential volume *Modernity and Its Malcontents*. Blurring what was at that point a better-entrenched disciplinary and cultural line dividing the secular from the ritualistic, the Comaroffs wrote that "modernity... has its own magicalities, its own enchantments" (xiv), and they sought to trouble the long-standing view that ritual "conjures up the very inverse of practical reason" (xv). A tremendous amount of innovative, sophisticated Africanist work emerged from this change of course, and fruitful connections, among history and the social sciences in particular, were built. At the same time, it is easy to see how the descriptive orientation of anthropology would offer a more readily available means for reconciling modernity and traditional faith practices than does the normative bent of philosophy. The Comaroffs tellingly conflate the terms "reason" and "rationality" (for example, on page xv of *Modernity and Its Malcontents*), which is not a problem in that they *have* often been used and are frequently perceived as interchangeable. An anthropological answer to the question of whether modernity can accommodate "global" religions is, simply, that it does.

On the other hand, a philosophical discussion of the same problem should concern itself with contradiction even where it is overcome in lived experience. Kwame Anthony Appiah's "Old Gods, New Worlds" chapter of his likewise influential book *In My Father's House* (published around the same time as *Modernity and Its Malcontents*) drills down into modernity's constituent tenets, testing each of them as they relate to a sustained belief in unseen spirits, in this case in an Asante cultural context. "Rationality," he writes, "is best conceived of as an ideal, both in the sense that it is something worth aiming for and in the sense that it is something we are incapable of realizing" (116). Per Appiah, rationality is related to the ideal of truth in the sense that rationality is practice-based while truth is fixed or objective. In this way, "rationality in belief consists in being disposed so to react to evidence and reflection that you change your beliefs in ways that make it more likely that they are true" (ibid.). To follow the turns of his argument, however, exercising one's rationality to arrive at reasonable conclusions does not *necessarily* result in arriving at a "true" understanding of the world. The ends to which rationality is put are dependent on the context and scale of one's encounter with evidence. A belief in spirits is not unreasonable if "again and again... the traditional view is likely to be confirmed" by outward displays, including trance-states, recovery from illness after traditional medicines have been administered, and death "from the action of inimical spirits" (118). Appiah is thus able to grant traditionally minded Africans claim to rationality (a principle of truth-finding) and reason (acting based on that principle) at the same time as he maintains that their causal explanations are inaccurate. He allows for a distinction here between beliefs that are reasonable and those that are true, also permitting the possibility of their *epistemological*, as opposed to just cultural, syncretism because both are arrived at by rational means.[6]

I believe that *Kintu* asks something slightly different of its reader, which is a willingness to interpret *as if* a belief in supernatural causation might be not just reasonable but true. In some sense, this ups the stakes: characters at an individual level are not able to content themselves with "syncretizing" traditional and rational-scientific worldviews, even as that is the broad cultural setting of their depiction. This is, again, a place where, though the novel maps the same terrain as a philosophical mode of inquiry, it can dispense with philosophy's firmer argumentative standards. Making sense of *Kintu* as a philosophical exercise on this order requires veering slightly off course from thinking about the world "as it is" vis-à-vis figures who really inhabit it (and the different kinds and amounts of information available to them). Instead, the book choreographs different degrees of access for characters and readers to a range of possibilities for reading the same evidence. All the while, however, it remains self-enclosed in design: the book's historical scope allows the distant past within it to serve as a simultaneously external and internal point of reference. Interpretive resolution for characters occurs within a fictional world whose boundaries are far-reaching but still demarcated, so that their convictions about what is "true" can hold without our needing to decide whether curses exist in Uganda or anywhere else. Reason, rationality, and what Appiah calls truth can thus be modeled as a system of relationships without being tested. For this reason, and as a last step in building the conceptual apparatus that will anchor the next section of this chapter, it will be more useful to dispense with a grounding in objective or scientific fact.

So far, I have suggested two ways of formulating the relationship of reason/rationality to truth. First, there is the use of rational faculties to devise reasonable conclusions that are then modified as necessary to discern empirical truth. Then there is a gap between a conjoined reason/rationality and what *feels* like truth: this possibility is evident in Appiah's examples of where perceived evidence for unseen spirits may be reasonable but is nonetheless ultimately inaccurate. In the paragraphs that follow, I want to flesh out a distinction between reason and rationality in a way that can help negotiate between characters' readings of evidentiary events, on the one hand, and on the other, how *Kintu* as a whole takes up the problem of "doubled" evidence as its conceptual core. Another way of putting this is that there is a ground level on which characters exercise reason, and then there is the meta-analytic structure of the book in which characters can be observed to reason differently from one another. The reader is then privy to all of the text's events without needing to come to a determinate conclusion about what sort of causal explanation they indicate. Reason is variable and dynamic, and rationality (the set of tenets undergirding acts of reason) looks something like a capacity to collate different reasonable conclusions. Reason *does* and rationality *is*, with the first supporting the second. And as discussion of philosophy entails discussion of philosophers, contemplating reason entails contemplating who is reasoning, and where.

In his 2008 magnum opus *On Reason: Rationality in a World of Cultural Conflict and Racism*, Emmanuel Chukwudi Eze devises a relevant means of getting from plural contexts for reason—"Rationality . . . is best appreciated from multiple points of view" (xiii)—to a universal conception of how reason works by welding philosophical history to an African setting. He does so through an interest in the cultivation of individual will, thereby refusing to relegate Enlightenment principles to besmirched Enlightenment histories. Eze contends that to universalize reason entails pluralizing it at the most fundamental level of individual encounter with worldly surrounds, so that extreme localization becomes the vehicle for sweeping epistemological reforms. At the same time he insists, like Wiredu elsewhere in this book, that a philosophy based in African experience does not mean, by default, that experience itself is a philosophical framework. "I start," he writes, "with the justifiable premise that reason is not a thing, that is, it is not a self-subsisting object, substance, or essence among other self-subsisting objects, substances, and essences—but rather a field of mental acts in perception, understanding, and explanation, including the frameworks of comprehension and justification of the horizons of the field itself" (xvii). Eze thus gives the dynamism of reason a highly figural objective shape. He intends to "guide the reader to see in one's own mind's eye what the formal contours of the productive work of reasoning look like," in order to "reconstitute in one's own mind what one rationally believes must be the criteria for determining what should count and should not count as adequate or ideal grounds for a claim that one has a reason for doing or thinking something" (ibid.). Reason is an intrinsic pairing of observing and evaluating on what grounds one observes. The more "evidence" one accumulates—which is to say, the more one lives analytically in the world—the more fine-tuned do one's powers of reason become.

On Reason is a long, dense book to which I will not do justice here, so I will dive right into its mainstream of connection between individuality and cultural emplacement. What Eze calls "the everyday" throughout the text is not a tool to pluralize reason for pluralization's sake; his is not a project of "democratizing" philosophy simply because that is a good thing to do. The main contribution of his philosophy, rather, is painstakingly to demonstrate *why* reason's locational pluralization allows for the enhancement (rather than subversion) of individuality. A moving passage from the book's first chapter bears quoting at length to this end:

> Thought is the need for language. We can therefore establish an intimate and absolute conceptual relation not simply between thought, word, and world but also between language and freedom of thought. The breach in tongue is therefore the origins of freedom, whereas freedom is the work of—the working-out of—the need for tongue, the need for speech, and the coming to voice. For all this, the best definition of thought is: That which spontaneously composes itself as, in itself, an object of work: the work of freedom of "mind," namely, the freedom of a voice, the freedom self, the freedoms of cultures, and the freedom of the world. As we called the spontaneity of this work freedom, then, we can say that it is only in the history of the work that thought becomes manifest as universal language—the language of freedom as expression of mind. (9)

To be reasonable, for Eze, is to bring one's mind into being, an assertion of freedom that may or may not correspond to "freedom" in a grander and more easily problematized historical or political sense. Thinking about one's experience is in itself an act of reason, provided that the categories through which one thinks are clarified and made open to responsive revision. Reason, then, inheres in the process of ordering one's thoughts, marked, whatever the broader circumstances, as "this idea of experience as the contingent intellectual and practical organizational triumph of this part of my existence over the diversity in the realities of thought and of the world" (16). One might well exercise "everyday" reason quite literally every day, as culture becomes not a determinant of individual behavior but, rather, the cumulative product of humans' unavoidable movement between "independence and belonging" (147).

Moreover, reason at this "ordinary," everyday, and so locationally particularized level catalyzes a drive to generalization. At their farthest reaches, the concepts by which experience is transformed into thought can then expand into universal truths. "The missing link between the universal and the particular," Eze writes, "is necessarily in the concept, and specifically within the processes of conceptual generalization. After all, what are grounds for generalization if not the will to systematize?" And a bit later: "everyday reasoning requires the individual to engage in processes of subsuming diversity and difference under actual and possible unities of general experience. Rationality cannot be distinguished from these processes" (20). One might just as well describe rationality in Eze's philosophy *as* a process: one that sees experience as the wellspring of individual will, and will, in turn, as the path to *de*-individuation, in the sense that it is defined as a means of generating a broad conceptual vocabulary. African settings enrich philosophy, writ large not by introducing a communal counterpoint to reductive liberal formulae (the unsituated mind and the like), but by demanding that key philosophical terms be more encompassingly, situationally dependent. Communality is no doubt a part of this, but more important is the interplay among the self, its surroundings, and the abstractions generated thereby. Undergirding this revision is an emphasis on will as a conjuncture of marginalized places and universalizing force, rather than casting will *as* a canonical instrument of marginalization. Reason is something to do and then *re*-do, not a static trait to attain.

It is along these lines of sketching a map for the world's broadening via sharpened individual minds that Bruce Janz's layered review of *On Reason* offers a bridge (of my making, not his) connecting Eze's work and *Kintu*. Eze only sometimes takes pains to distinguish between rationality and reason, but Janz ventures a firmer account of how their interaction drives the book's argument. The distinction, he suggests, is that "reason is a process and an activity, while rationality is a property of the person, one that expresses itself through (at least) the processes of reason" (296). The closest analogy he can find is that between knowing a language and merely using one—that is, between grasping an underlying system and an act of memorization. This is important because it raises the question of how to determine ultimate understanding—coded, in this example, as "rationality"—based on external evidence or "reason," a question that then roughly translates into that of how to distinguish agency from mimicry. As Janz acknowledges, this is no easy task: languages can be partly known and/or used intelligibly often enough to make them operative *without* being able to verify that they are truly "understood." It is also unclear to what degree "real" knowledge of a single language, once granted, implies understanding of a broader conception of language as such. These problems, in turn, force consideration of whether discrete instances of reason in fact indicate the singular notion of rationality that is supposed to be fueling them. At the risk of sounding glib, it is a bit of a "chicken-or-the-egg" problem—or, perhaps more elegantly, a problem of the one versus the many. If plural demonstrations of reason are possible—there are many languages, after all—does it not follow that at some point rationality must be conceived of as plural too?

In keeping with Janz's reading of Eze, and also returning to this chapter's framing quandary of whether to pluralize, expand, or outright refuse Enlightenment concepts, this all matters a great deal because of the long history of Africans being allowed reason but *not* rationality. Lambasting the racist colonial way of thinking, Janz describes it as a conviction that, "like animals, [Africans] could be trained" (or, "like computers, they could be programmed"), but that they "did not, and could not, possess rationality" (301). It is possible then to pluralize reason without pluralizing rationality, both in this pejorative sense and, conceivably, in an inclusively universalizing one. Most important here, however, is Janz's third, definitive layer of insight into Eze's intellectual project: that concerning pluralization of the *routes* by which reason and rationality meet. Eze, in this vein, "wants to move the problem of rationality away from the question of how we might recognize it (and who is equipped to recognize it), and toward the question of how its development and capacities are irreducibly in debt to particularity, or as [Eze] puts it, diversity. But he does not want to tie this diversity primarily to cultural factors" (303). Instead of seeing reason as the worldly application of an abstract rationality, Janz sees Eze as positing a creative, improvisational view of reason that, over time, "produces rationality" (305). In this way of thinking, any particular way of using reason in response to experiencing the world could be a way to participate in the creation of a universal rationality. With reason, again, defined as the meeting place of thinking and evaluation of one's thoughts in order to articulate "the requirements of a place" (307), we see the universal derived from a global that is in turn derived from the local. Quoting Janz a final time: "The key is not to identify who is and who is not rational (everyone is), but rather to see what new concepts might be made available under emergent practiced expressions of rationality" (ibid.).

To summarize: Eze's thought and Janz's elaborations on it help to universalize rationality by grounding it in endlessly plural processes of everyday reasoning, rather than by pluralizing rationality itself. The destination stays the same, but it is supplied by many more tributaries. Place is indispensable to reason because, per Appiah's argument as described earlier, place is the context in which people respond to events outside of themselves. "Place" in this sense is nearly synonymous with what I have referred to as "evidence," which is to say the events that inspire reflection and, crucially, interrogation of the terms by which that reflection is routed. Reason becomes the connecting thread between a non-normative observation that people respond differently to different kinds of evidence, on one end, and on the other, an insistence on philosophical rationality as grounded in conceptual evaluation, revision, and choice-making—in short, between a variable *way* of thinking and an invariable essence of what it means to think. In this formulation, rationality is universal in that any one way of reasoning has the intrinsic capacity to rise first into individual mind-making, or will, and then into a shared conceptual vocabulary as elected and generalized by that will. In a passionate footnote, Eze writes that "the religious, aesthetic, and moral investments we thus make in material or immaterial cultures and traditions are warranted only because we see in them sources or evidence of morally transcendent values such as freedom and agency" (280). It is obviously not the case that the historical playing field has made the equal enfranchisement of philosophical experience likely or even possible, but Eze wants us to get the reasons we fight for cultural recognition right.

This insistence on the communally meaningful and yet individually will-defining stakes of pluralized reason, I will show, resonates throughout *Kintu*. Eze's argument is also distinctive in the context of theorizing a novel, because it suggests the necessarily diachronic nature of the connection between reason and rationality. Reason comes first, which is to say that *experience* does, developing over time into a data set from which individuals can generalize to form larger conceptual communities (with "culture" standing in for wide agreement on which operative concepts work best). This quality of gaining meaning only over time makes "ordinary reason" a strikingly apt partner for a *narrative* philosophical work, which is ultimately what *Kintu* is. Rather than attempt to arrive at an a priori definition of rationality based in a sense of what a rational conclusion can or cannot be and only then testing reason against it, *On Reason* zeroes in on rationality as the cumulative product of meaning-making choices about what sorts of terms best account for one's experiences. Like a novel that entertains the idea of a curse as a reasonable explanation for successive life mishaps, Eze's philosophy privileges how one gets to truth over pinning truth down, inverting and subverting received knowledge as needed to make the act of reasoning live up to its tarnished name. The way in which *Kintu* performs such philosophical revision—and in particular, the distinction the novel enforces between reasonable *individuation* and a deadened rationality's *subjectivization*—will be the subject of the next section.

Reading Kintu's *Twins: Individuation versus Subjectivization*

Kintu's outsized splash on the African publishing scene owes much to the fact that it forsakes the clichés about transnational mobility that were dominant for a time. Nearly all its characters across a 250-year span are firmly rooted in Uganda, oriented, as Bwesigye Bwa Mwesigire writes, not to the geographical range of Afropolitanism but to bringing "the past into the present" in order to "put them into conversation" (110). Even the sole figure who ventures abroad for his education—Miisi, the humanistic scholar—ultimately returns home, so that his time in Russia and England is made meaningful within the frame of present-day Kampala. In my earlier comparison of Appiah's work with Eze's, I showed how the latter declines to rule out the possibility that traditional belief systems are rational by describing rationality as a cumulative entity. *Kintu*'s constrained setting in effect lets it similarly off the hook for needing to render a verdict about what is or is not rational given a *world* totality of evidence. More simply put, the fact that *Kintu* is *not* a global novel in terms of its plot allows it to create a more pronounced collision between traditional and "global" ways of viewing the same events, with reason and rationality up for grabs. This is useful because it draws the reader's attention to the process of interpretation itself. Instead of inviting conclusions as to whether a curse-based explanation is *ultimately* rational, the novel demands contemplation of characters' more immediate responsiveness to their surroundings. Reason, as in Eze's philosophy, can then be defined by what it *does*, and namely by its capacity to sharpen individual will and collective intelligibility at the same time.

A bit of plot summary is in order here to clarify *Kintu*'s stakes. The novel's foundational event takes place not at its formal beginning, which is a prologue set in Kampala in 2004, but in the first of its six books, "Kintu Kidda," whose events take place in 1750. As the *ppookino* or governor of Buddu Province (located in the Central Region of present-day Uganda), Kintu is exhausted by Buganda kingdom politics and the sexual demands of his many marriages. Among his wives are two identical twins, Nnakato and Babirye, the first of whom he married from love and the second out of customary obligation. There are hints of Eze's interpretive conundrum as to whether reason makes or simply demonstrates rationality right from the introduction to Kintu's life, apparent in his difficulty determining whether to apply or invert a customary principle. "Tradition claimed that identical twins were one soul who, failing to resolve the primal conflict in the self, split—and two people were born," Makumbi explains. "The older twin, Babirye for girls, was supposedly the original soul. Nnakato, the younger twin, was the copy, the mutineer. But Kintu could not see how this could be true of his wives. For him, Nnakato was the original" (17). As such, he marries her first "against counsel, against custom" (19). This deviation from the norm while still upholding its overarching framework echoes throughout the book, as does a guiding question: does Kintu anticipate tradition's irrelevance to modern ways of thinking, or is he ushering in a curse that warns precisely against its defiance? Already, Makumbi sets up a layered set of interpretive "doubles," using Kintu's dealings with actual twins to foreground a structural ambivalence surrounding Kintu himself.

Into the large primary family that he heads with Nnakato, built of four new sets of twins born to Babirye, Kintu adopts a Tutsi son named Kalema from a wandering widower, Ntwire. In addition to introducing an ethnically foreign dimension into Kintu's household, Kalema also brings a problematic association with individualism that compounds what is already on display in Kintu's own life choices. Ntwire, "unlike the Tutsis who found their way to the capital and who assumed Ganda names on arrival and married Ganda spouses, . . . stood aloof" (35). Selected by his adoptive father to take part in a journey to visit the *kabaka*, or ruler of all Buganda, it is Kalema's fate that ultimately seals Kintu's. After Kalema dares to drink from Kintu's gourd, against customary taboo, "Kintu's backhand crashed into Kalema's jaw" as the son "looked up at his father, surprised," with eyes that "kept rising as if the slap had come from the sky" (39). The ensuing events are quick and dramatic, leaving Kalema's ultimate cause of death unclear. Though he crashes into a rock as he tries to stand, there is a sense that the slap itself causes an unlikely degree of injury. "He started to blink rapidly and then sank to the ground" (ibid.), Makumbi writes before the second collision. And then, afterward, "the force of his thrashing flipped him, turning him onto his back" (ibid.). It seems implausible that the force of a disciplinary slap, even coming from a grown man, would be sufficient to end in Kalema's writhing "like a caterpillar whose hairs were set on fire" (ibid.) and then his rapid death. ("We all slap our children. They don't drop dead" [40] suggests another member of Kintu's party.) The reader, then, is put in the position of having to contemplate immediate versus ultimate cause of death: is it simply human error, or is there already a larger, supernatural force in play? And thus, implicitly, Makumbi also introduces a deeper question about what *sorts* of causation we are willing to entertain as possible.

Kintu handles Kalema's death poorly, neglecting to oversee his son's burial to ensure that it is held to customary standards and then concealing the death from his family, including Ntwire, once he is back home. In Kintu's version of events, this deception leads to Kalema's appearance as a restless ghost: "But I am frightened," he tells Kintu, "I want to come home" (63). The aggrieved leader visits a traditional healer of high repute, and for a while the trouble seems to subside; Kalema does not return. In ten years' time, however, Kintu's most beloved family members begin dying. His only son with Nnakato (Baale) grows paralyzed and then expires from a mysterious facial affliction that starts out as a pimple. Then Nnakato hangs herself in despair. The salient point to derive from all this is that *Kintu* the novel is set up as a battle for causal determinacy amid evidential indeterminacy, a collision to which only the reader is privy. Upon Baale's death, Kintu is certain that "Ntwire had struck. It took him by surprise yet it was no surprise" (90). At the same time, he is confused about the ostensibly basic fact of which twin is which. "Who are you?" he asks the surviving Babirye. "I mean, who, which one of you twins was buried?" (93). While Babirye considers taking the opportunity to trick Kintu and improve her own standing, Kintu lacks access to both her thought process and the certainty it yields to the reader as to which twin remains. At this key juncture, Kintu disappears, trailed only by hearsay that he is alone in a cave haunted by his dead loved ones. Rumors of his sighting include the information that "his mind was in disorder" (ibid.), introducing the additionally complicating possibility that the curse he imagines is itself the product of psychic distress.

How, in all this, is one to determine what caused what, or *who* caused what, or which explanations should precede or preclude any other? Is it enough to say that Kintu's fatal slap results in both his mental traumatization and the supernatural punishment of Ntwire's curse, or does the curse demand recognition as the *source* of the madness that follows? And if the latter, does this not indicate a larger realm of supernatural causation, perhaps even suggesting that Kintu has been a pawn all the while? Conversely, can the scientific paradigm of "mental health," which will be elaborated later in the novel among Kintu's descendants, permit the possibility of a curse at all without its becoming code for social stigmatization? I could go on. The underlying problem that unites the two modes of explanation for Kintu's erratic behavior and disappearance—his curse-begot madness, or his madness-birthed delusion of a curse—is that of will, or rather its absence. This is true on two levels. First, *neither* type of causation offers space for Kintu to choose how to respond. Second, Kintu himself is not aware that there is an interpretive choice to be made at all; as far as he is concerned, the curse simply is. The reader occupies a different position in that, while the text provides no means of ultimately determining whether or not it *is* depicting a curse, it at least allows us to weigh multiple causal options. Book 1 of *Kintu*, then, most obviously sets the stage for a thematic and even dictional juxtaposition of tradition and modernity. (Discussion of Kintu's sex life in 1750, for example, rings as decidedly contemporary.) Less obviously, it also establishes a gap between the range of interpretive options available to its characters and those available to its reader, which in turn yields a tension between a focus on response—to a slap, to a death, to a curse—and one on *responsiveness*. The latter trait, evaluative and dynamic where the former term is automated and self-evident, might be recoded here as reason.

When the novel jumps to book 2, "Suubi Nnakintu," set in Kampala in 2004, the main event on this second, structural-hermeneutic plane is a closing of the epistemological gap between the reader and the main character. Suubi, Kintu's descendant (though unbeknownst to her), inhabits a world in which both traditional and rational-scientific explanations are on offer, perhaps syncretically in a far-reaching anthropological sense, but often in opposition to one another on the level of individual lives. Kintu's story is also now packaged precisely *as* a story, marked by italics, that Suubi's grandmother recounts to her as a child (104–7). In fact, the tale of the erstwhile pookino, who Suubi is told *"is still roaming the world"* (106) in order to protect his children from Ntwire, becomes all that she recalls from her early years. "It felt as though someone had come with a broom, swept away all her childhood recollections, but missed her grandmother's voice" (107). Formally, Makumbi here partakes in a long tradition of what Emmanuel Obiechina calls the "story-within-the-story" technique by which orality is introduced into the African novel to mark the form's collective consciousness or "populist impulse" (124, 125). Following Eileen Julien in *African Novels and the Question of Orality*, this repackaging also serves as a reminder of the interpretive complexity that has been effaced. The collapse of Kintu's multifaceted realist narrative into this new oral form risks its becoming "an overworked, and therefore devalued, sign made to stand virtually alone as a measure of authenticity in contexts where little else seems to emanate from traditional culture" (21).

I suggest, instead, that Makumbi's isolation of the Kintu legend from the larger context of Suubi's life is a key strategy here because it fosters narrative and thematic continuity without encouraging evidentiary bias.

In other words, it is as if the interpretive design of the book has now shifted up a gear in complexity: Suubi's life presents the same fundamental conflict as Kintu's did, in the sense that it lends itself to both supernatural and psychological explanations. (Makumbi suggests by Suubi's memory loss that she has undergone some kind of trauma, even though she has yet to clue the reader into the details of her impoverished childhood and later adoption.) Unlike Kintu, however, Suubi herself grows aware of both kinds of causal possibility as book 2 develops, where her story quite literally contains and then builds on his. In effect, Suubi's plot evolves to mimic the reader's experience of book 1: she responds to the mishaps that befall her in a way that heightens her sense of there being more than one way of accounting for them. In the process, the reader attends to *how* she responds—to the persuasiveness of her responses in making sense of the evidence before her—instead of noticing which worldview her responses end up advancing. Her gradual acclimation to a curse-based account of her own life thus does much more than channel collective consciousness, as the "oralized" version of the Kintu myth indeed does in parallel. Makumbi actually carves space for an individualized opting *into* a traditional belief system, precisely because the motivation for doing so—the events, as it were, that make the curse seem like a reasonable explanation—is held apart by her memory loss from these beliefs' naturalized transmission. The Kintu *myth* is static, but the interpretive dilemma surrounding Kintu's life persists.

There is now room in the novel for a character to evaluate and *elect* her terms of causal explanation, so that the default cultural syncretism of the "global" era by and into which *Kintu* is produced serves as an instrument of willed epistemological narrowing. In this way, reason as it is bound to the cultivation of individual will, as per Eze's formulation, can still circle back around to a sense of "traditional" cultural belonging. "The basis of this dual allegiance to freedom and to culture is more obvious if one considers the differences between freedom and liberty," Eze explains. Drawing on practices of Sumerian apprenticeship, he then argues that "going home is a right to freedom because home is that community where one belongs by right. Freedom in this ancient sense is a freedom to community, a right of belonging" (147), whereas *liberty* has historically connoted "individuality, autonomy, initiative, agency, even a dignified aloneness" (148). These values are not mutually exclusive—in fact, Eze writes that they "need each other" in a mode of "conflicted inseparability" (148)—but neither is their balancing straightforward. We might thus see *Kintu*'s philosophical work as that of slowly working through the optimal relationship between freedom and liberty. It does this by inculcating an "everyday reason," or the revision of one's operative concepts based on responsiveness to immediately available evidence, that is facilitated by the novel's bracketing off from any setting in which the conflict between tradition and modernity seems materially consequential.

In Suubi's plotline, this optimizing space grows up around encounters with yet another of the book's identical twins, first presented through a flashback upon her curbside reappearance. "This was the second attack," we read, after Suubi's heart is described as having "flipped and then shattered" upon sensing the dark presence of someone named Ssanyu.

> The first happened eight years ago on the morning after Suubi's graduation. She had lain half-awake in bed when a sensation of being "locked"—she could not open her eyes or move or scream—came over her. Yet she could see a young woman standing above her bed looking down at her. The woman looked exactly like Suubi only she was so emaciated that it was surprising she could stand at all. (108–9)

Over time, Suubi concludes that the specter must have "been a bad dream" (109), and so she is horrified by Ssanyu's new intrusion. This time, the dark figure also comes bearing a message. She commands Suubi to tell her boyfriend, Opolot, "the truth" (110) of who she really is, but Suubi has no awareness of what that truth is. In the background of this scene of two women's confrontation—one of them living, one of them dead—we hear a familiar suggestion of mental illness. This time, however, it is one to which Suubi herself is privy: "She distantly heard [a] woman say, 'She's short-circuited that one,' but Suubi ignored her" (ibid.).

Kintu, I again contend, uses the figure of Ssanyu to enact the formation of what strongly resembles Eze's "everyday reason" through the reinstatement of supernatural belief as an interpretive challenge rather than a normative command. Suubi does not just reason differently from Kintu Kidda in book 1; she also weighs different ways of reasoning against one another. The book reveals that, indeed, she did have an identical twin who died shortly after their birth, along with their mother. Suubi was then abandoned to a violent, neglectful aunt who lived in a single filthy room, before later being abducted, quite possibly sexually assaulted, and finally adopted by a wealthy family whom she had been meant to serve. All the while, Makumbi guides the reader away from a psychological explanation for Ssanyu's appearance at the same time as she seems to be scripting it. (Ssanyu's "predecessor" twin, Kintu's unloved wife Babirye from book 1, appears in Suubi's childhood in a protective role, warning the abusive aunt through Suubi that she'll "cripple [her] hands" (121) if she makes to strike the child again.) This is not because the novel has any evident stake in denying that mental health is a real thing in the real world, but because a psychological explanation does not present a way of accounting for "stacked" interpretive junctures within the text. By "stacked" I mean the novel's careful layering of textual evidence in order to increase characters' capacity to act reasonably between 1750 and 2004, even as the epistemological options do not change. (They remain "curse" and "madness," reconfigured as mental illness.)

If reason is not so much a matter of what one concludes but *how* one "makes one's mind" through the process of evaluating experience and then determining which concepts work best for its generalization, then a psychological means of accounting for Ssanyu fails to offer Suubi the option of a reasonable response. In this sense, it is no more supple a heuristic than is Kintu's fatalism about Ntwire's curse in book 1. Suubi's initial, default conclusion that Ssanyu is just a bad dream is made doubtful by Ssanyu's reappearance while she is not in bed. More significant, however, is the fact that even a higher-order psychological explanation falls short within the novel's evidentiary design. It would be easy to view Ssanyu as a Freudian doppelgänger, for instance: she might be explained away as a psychic projection born of the classic "urge towards defence which has caused the ego to project that material outward as something foreign to itself," embodying an uncanniness or spectral familiarity that "can only come from the fact of the 'double' being a creation dating back to a very early mental stage, long since surmounted—a stage, incidentally, at which it wore a more friendly aspect" (Freud, 235). The novel's stacked design, however, makes this reading less tenable. While Ssanyu could conceivably be a doppelgänger strictly within Suubi's story, the buried, originary trauma of which she serves as the "involuntary repetition" (236) is not as clear within the book's larger structure. If the originary event—an essential part of the Freudian model—is taken as the 1750 plot of book 1, then the originary event *itself* is causally ambivalent. To be clear, I am not arguing that mental illness, and specifically trauma, has no explanatory force in Suubi's section. I am pointing out that it is not self-evident that it is *more* explanatory than the curse, and that attributing causation to the latter structurally undermines the power of the psychological explanation. The cumulative effect of the book is to make the curse seem more explanatorily compelling the more layers of it one considers.

As I have indicated, this is also an interpretive dilemma that Suubi herself faces. After the conclusion of her eponymous section, she reappears in book 6, "The Homecoming," which gathers all of *Kintu*'s main characters together at a clan reunion-cum-summoning of ancestral spirits. The Kintu descendants evince different degrees of skepticism about the process. Pressed by one of them, local councilors confess "that none of them had actually ever sighted Nnakato the spirit themselves" (375). The group is also populated, however, by those who have come around to believing in spirits for what we might call "reasonable" reasons, which is to say responsive rather than received reasons. Among them is the medium brought in to lead the ritual proceedings, who acknowledges that he's "never converted actually [to belief in ancestors]." Instead, he remarks that after having been on antidepressants to address recurring headaches and hallucinations, he "had a violent episode and my father asked me to lie in the shrine to rest. Twenty-four hours later, I woke up exhausted. Only I did not wake up, I had been up all night hosting all sorts. It took me a week to recover from the exhaustion but the headaches and hallucinations never returned" (385). For her part, Suubi arrives at the proceedings in a matter-of-fact state of mind. "I am neither Christian nor atheist," she proclaims. "I am just plain," she says, then quickly adds, "These things have no place in the modern world" (389). Nonetheless, she agrees to perform what is customarily expected of her, conversing with relatives and contributing a dollop of mud to the wall of a shrine.

It is important to note here that Suubi comes to the clan gathering with a philosophical disposition, in the clichéd, self-relativizing sense, as she positions her own struggles within a broader view of the world's chaoticness. "Nature is as ugly as it is beautiful," she says. "People drop dead, people kill each other, people go hungry: you don't dwell, you just exist. But then this other world comes along and gives you ideas. You start to think, *hmm, I am not right, it's not fair*. Things you would never have said before. Soon you start to blame everything on a curse" (392). She views modern life instead through the lens of "options" (393), this new, spiritual domain being but one of many, and an overly restrictive one at that. In the ensuing medium-led ceremony, however, Suubi faints, after which we are told, "The woman's body, swinging or rotating, picked up momentum and started hopping about on her hands" (399). She then breaks a number of bones in the commotion and, as in childhood, speaks in a voice "as thin as a child's" that claims it is "Babirye, her twin" (ibid.). Suubi's life is supposedly saved when her twin—referred to alternately as Babirye and Ssanyu, the first a generic name and the second a personal one—is bound in a stick that is then presented to Suubi. And *here*, she finally makes a considered, affirmative choice that resolves her problems once and for all: Suubi elects to wear her twin carved into jewelry for the rest of her life (437), literally reuniting what she once referred to as the "pieces" of herself within the frame of her individuality (392).

A few things happen here that demand elaboration before I pivot to the figure of Miisi, the self-proclaimed rational intellectual who heads the gathering of Kintu descendants. First, Suubi evolves from embodying a position more aligned with "liberty" in Eze's description (especially what he calls its "dignified aloneness") to choosing a worldview that seems to advance "freedom." In electing to wear the spirit of her stick-bound twin for as long as she lives, she concretely marks herself as constrained by an inherited belief system. This also means that in exercising reason in her responsiveness to the evidence on display, she paradoxically moves from a wider to a narrower range of interpretive possibilities. Second, Suubi comes around to believing in the curse based on the perceived reality of its effects. While all of them might in theory be explained by the psychic toll of her originary trauma, what Suubi experiences at the clan gathering is powerful enough that this no longer persuades her. In addition, humans' deep propensity to seek freedom through acts of reasoning as Eze propounds in *On Reason* entails an expression of will. Sticking with a more passive, received adherence to psychological causality would not offer Suubi the room for self-making *and* collective intelligibility that giving over to the curse does, at least in her immediate context.

Finally, Suubi's extreme physical reaction during the ancestor-conjuring ceremony becomes evidence not only for her own belief in the curse, but for others'. While it does not seem like a good use of space to review every character's trajectory in the same depth with which I treat Suubi's, the most telling example of this is Isaac Newton Kintu, the protagonist and namesake of book 4. Similarly neglected as a child, and at a turning point in his life (he is convinced that he has HIV after his wife dies, but refuses to look at his test results), watching Suubi's ordeal prompts him to think, "This is real" (401). It is ultimately owing to the intensity of the clan gathering that he views his HIV results and then resolves to live a more responsible life with his young son upon seeing that they are in fact negative. In both Suubi's and Isaac's lives, then, ritual practices surrounding invisible spirits provide the means by which individual will emerges alongside collective intelligibility. The evidence for their turn to the curse is as real, in both cases, as its effects, even as the paths connecting their shared experience and resultant shared causal identification vary.

As in Eze's work, there is also an indispensable diachronic element here: Isaac's turning point is meaningful only as a response to Suubi's, and

Suubi's, in turn, serves to actualize the latent thread of cross-generational connection. In both cases, multiple kinds of epistemological ambivalence are resolved. Wolfgang Iser, in a salient exposition of the pastoral mode, once argued that doubling "brings to light fundamental conditions of literary fictionality" by establishing "a frame that allows the continued presence of what has been exceeded" (44). From this vantage, *Kintu* incorporates the "exceeded" world into later characters' lives in the form of the Kintu legend as it appears in an oral story form. It then reverses tack ("unexceeds" it) as the story in a sense comes true of its own, non-allegorical accord. I will push Iser's work just slightly further here, despite *Kintu*'s different generic identity, because it so ably accounts for the significance of doubling in a structural but not psychological sense. *Kintu* as a whole stages what Iser calls "the simultaneity of the mutually exclusive" (55) in its pairing of an unquestioned traditional belief system with an equally presumptuous modern one. Much as Kintu's story in book 1 fails to serve as an originary event in Freudian terms, since it is in its own right subject to a split interpretation, Iser writes that a "lack of any transcendental reference and the impossibility of any overarching third dimension show literary fictionality to be marked by an ineradicable duality, and indeed this is the source of its operational power" (80). This is, I think, absolutely descriptive of *Kintu* from the reader's perspective: we have no clear metaphysic within which to distinguish ultimate right from wrong, or truth from belief.

Iser's reading falls short, however, as a tool for helping to make sense of Makumbi's novel with regard to the implications of macro-interpretive doubling for character. In a way that is perhaps indicative of his critical era, Iser links his theory of genre to a theory of the human subject. "In overstepping all boundaries," he posits, "fictionality becomes the epitome of inner-worldly totality, since it provides the paradoxical (and perhaps, for this very reason, desirable) opportunity for human beings simultaneously to be in the midst of life and to overstep it. This simultaneity of two mutually exclusive conditions ... enables human beings to experience their inherent split" (83). This is quite different from the relationship between *Kintu* as a work and the characters it creates: Suubi and Isaac evolve as willful individuals precisely by *not* reflecting the split explanatory possibility of their world as it appears to the reader. Indeed, part of the dissonance that Suubi must overcome in order to achieve self-realization is attributable to the fact that her perspective more closely tracks that of the reader than does Kintu Kidda's. While both Suubi's and Isaac's plotlines are nicely wrapped up to end the novel by removing their doubts about the curse's explanatory validity, a reader is likely to be left with lingering questions. Only one character, Miisi, maintains the doubled knowledge that Iser sees as marking "inner-worldly totality," and in his case, it is a mark of subjective *in*-capacity.

As the Western-trained arbiter of epistemic decolonization in the era of postcolonial studies' emergence, Miisi (short for Misirayimu) occupies what can sometimes seem like a transparent position in *Kintu*. In the first pages of book 5—as one of his children, unbeknownst to him, lies dead just miles away—we read that "nature played out a drama so bizarre that Miisi's wife and sister looked to the supernatural. But not Miisi. . . . He was rational. There had to be a logical explanation" (310). The drama, Makumbi then writes, is the arrival of a massive swarm of bees at Miisi's home. It moves as one into his guest room, and though Miisi looks "all around to see the reason for the bees' behavior" (311), he remains at a loss. The significance of his bafflement soon becomes clear: despite all his foreign education, Miisi is powerless to explain pivotal moments in his family's life. He is, after all, the sole figure in the novel to have had access to not just one sort of foreign schooling but three. He was raised in a Catholic seminary, partly by a group of Irish priests; he later went on scholarship to Moscow for a master's degree, as did many educated Ugandans in the 1960s and '70s; and finally, he moved to Britain in 1972 to avoid being killed by Idi Amin back home (341). There, much to his surprise, Miisi is accepted to a doctoral program in sociology at Cambridge, where he decides to study "child worship in African communities" through Chinua Achebe's *Things Fall Apart* (342). Upon returning home to Uganda's premier university, Makerere, after his disappointing time in a racist England, Miisi has begun performing "authentic" African identity. His countrymen are bemused as he becomes a walking series of intellectual clichés, "[sucking] their teeth in contempt" (346) when they realize that his doctorate is of the useless, bookish variety.

There are hints throughout Miisi's penultimate section of the novel that his avowed rationality does not express itself in what this chapter proposes is a reasonable way. In response to a feeling of racial alienation while abroad, "he and his friends constructed their own narratives of *we, they, us*, and *them*. In these narratives, Miisi concentrated on those things that made black more human, wholesome and natural than white. Once he had convinced himself of this, it was not hard to find evidence in the everyday manners, actions, tendencies and behavior of Europeans" (344–45). The racial dynamics of this passage aside, Makumbi clearly marks a shift in interpretive direction here from responsiveness to evidence to its foreordainment: belief yields events, rather than events prompting a reexamination of beliefs. Miisi's commitment to scientific rationality comes across as similarly tendentious, part of a smug refusal to see local experience—or really, experience at all—as epistemologically meaningful. "As for the family curse," we read, "Miisi argued that it was a documented fact that in Buganda mental health problems such as depression, schizophrenia and psychosis ran not only in families but in clans" (380). Even given a reader who is inclined to see Miisi's position as "true," per Appiah's discussion of rationality, Makumbi signals that he hews to it for unreasonable reasons. Even after agreeing to serve as Kintu family head in advance of the clan gathering, his outlook is anthropological. He describes it as "a chance . . . to observe and study traditional spirituality" (367), thereby quarantining supernatural causality outside the possibility of truth. Miisi, for his part, sees his self-professed atheism as protection against foreign educational norms: ironically, the Irish priests who helped raise him *did* believe in the Kintu curse! But his is a reactionary and not a responsive rationality—or in the terms built up thus far, a rationality that is unhitched from a scalable and will-making reasoning process.

Miisi's deficiencies matter a lot to *Kintu*'s larger intellectual stakes, because he is the closest thing the book offers to an individual representative of *Kintu*'s post-post-colonial context. Only Miisi has seen the world on both sides of its Cold War divide, and only Miisi claims his Ganda identity as a result of having witnessed the shortcomings of a global one. He "comes home" in a literal sense, fueled by problems of scale in geographical rather than evidentiary terms. If, as I have stated, place is relevant to philosophy because it *is* in some sense the evidence that drives how one reasons, then for Miisi only *other places* serve this function. This is to say that the expanded scale of his educational background trumps the constrained one of either the bees' appearance or the clan gathering, so that evidence provided by the clan context (and deemed as such by other characters) is predetermined to conform with evaluative norms developed elsewhere. Interestingly, Miisi comments on this cultural mixing-and-matching within the novel in an editorial piece for the local paper called "*Africanstein*," which he translates into Luganda as "*Ekisode.*" "*We cannot go back to the operating table and ask for the African limbs*," it concludes. "*Africa must learn to walk on European legs and work with European arms*," he maintains, and will evolve into something "*neither African nor European*" (337). In her review essay on *Kintu* in the *New York Review of Books*, Namwali Serpell sees Miisi's text as part of a larger pattern of split identifications, by which Africa finds its way to the universal "in the philosophical sense rather than the platitudinous one." She includes a useful reminder of *Kintu*'s duality right down to its title, which refers both to a specific character and to Bugandan cosmology's first man.

There is a missing link here, however, in what is nonetheless an essential first step in reading *Kintu* in a philosophical vein. Serpell argues that achieving universal personhood is attained by "holding all these divisions together, gently," and that this is "radical because it rejects a long philosophical tradition of considering 'humanity' as a matter of self-containment and integrity, of what the human *excludes*." Because Makumbi sets this intervention in Uganda, Serpell's take in a major international publication suggests a fluid and overdue intermingling of global and universalist critical frameworks. A deeper look at Miisi nonetheless makes this less persuasive. While it is certainly true that *Kintu* as a whole seeks universal significance by its sustained contemplation of the relationship between knowledge and experience, it is not the case that it does so by upending individual integrity in favor of the sutured subject, who is able to "just be," as Serpell puts it. The only figure who really exists on the cusp of various epistemologies—that is, without pushing toward some resolution—is Miisi. And Miisi, rationalist intellectual though he is, winds up bearing the full brunt of *both* the curse and his inability to articulate its explanatory legitimacy. A plurality of cultural traces and exposures does not therefore translate into epistemological *or* identitarian versatility. Instead, it stymies both.

The very last subsection of the novel depicts Miisi in a "disturbed state" (439), sleeping outside, foraging for food, and rambling that "he is the lamb, the chosen one" (441). He is filthy, his hair matted, as he parades around in a Western waistcoat over his traditional *kanzu*. While his relatives see this as clear evidence of Miisi's having returned to Kintu Kidda's lost state from book 1, this is not a recognition in which he shares. "The realization that her father hovers in the middle world between sanity and insanity is hard to take" (442), we read of his most successful (and surviving) child. In effect, then, Miisi's plotline demonstrates the dissolution of reason in its conjoined form of local responsiveness, self-evaluation, and willed generalization of elected concepts into shared intelligibility. It also marks a split between the development of the novel qua novel (because other characters recognize Miisi's insanity as a thematic culmination) and the regression of a key figure within it. Miisi *does* in this way reprise Kintu Kidda's seminal role, in that his acknowledged scope of interpretive possibility is less than the reader's.

As a final note to this effect, it is revealing that Miisi's conscious mind never merges with the line of significance suggested by his dreams, which recur through his section marked in italics, as was the story of Kintu passed down to Suubi by her grandmother. Though "Miisi knew that this relentless return to his childhood in dreams signified something disturbing," he avers that "he never revisited the dreams when he woke up" (312). While a more responsive mode of reasoning might view even the "irrational" domain of dreams as objects for reflection, Miisi sees their harrowing depictions of his mother as things to keep separate from his intellectual pursuits. In this case, the dreams offer undigested insight into Miisi's family history as it pertains to its handling of the Kintu curse. As with all of the curse's manifestations in the novel, the evidence for its power might be alternately read as evidence for a passed-down history of mental illness. (Miisi's father, Makumbi reveals, sacrificed his older brother in an effort to break the curse.) The relevant fact is that Kintu does not recognize dreams *as* evidence of any sort, and so he makes no effort to make sense of them, even as the reader is clearly called on to do just that. "Anyone can separate myth from fact" (326), he maintains in a political discussion among some friends, echoing Wole Ogundele's designation of devices such as mythic flashbacks in African novels as tools of historical "evasion."[7] More to the point, the alternative epistemological register of the dreams goes narratively unfulfilled. This stands in sharp contrast to the oral Kintu legend from Suubi's section, whose meaning is then played out in her plot as she slowly comes around to heeding his warnings on her own terms.

To conclude, I argue that Miisi *is*, in some sense, the global novel's avatar within *Kintu*'s world. Having tasted something close to the full range of epistemological options on offer to an educated Ugandan man in the late twentieth century, he synthesizes his experiences into a reenergized claim on African selfhood. In Miisi and his allegorical Africanstein, Makumbi brings colonial, Cold War, and postcolonial histories back to the hills of Kampala. The rationality fueling this syncretism, however—in Miisi's professed commitment to an evidence-based reading of the world that holds steady from one locale to the next—combusts in the face of a demand for responsiveness to different kinds of evidence. Ironically, what should be a "universal" language of rational analysis becomes the wedge between embedded reasoning and its conceptual generalization by way of Eze's evaluative "will" and so serves as a blunt instrument instead of a fungible path. *Kintu*'s defiance of postcolonialism and Afropolitanism in favor of more local kinds of meaning thus points to an uncomfortable disjuncture between the philosophical novel and the place of the reflective individual within it. To advance the book's development into universal import, self-sustaining characters reason their way into a constraining system of belief. (Suubi and Isaac might model Eze's "everyday reason" in coming around to the curse, but their trajectory is also toward the impossibility of its narrative repetition. They opt into something that does not easily bear opting out of.) Meanwhile, the lone figure to openly advocate for a practice of cross-cultural movement through discussive, meta-evaluative norms is scripted into psychic oblivion. Makumbi's magisterial achievement is to have built a novel of ideas that morphs into a parable for our age: rationality will get you nowhere good.

Curses as History in Recent East African Fiction

At some risk of anticlimax, it will be helpful to work briefly through some alternative ways of representing curses in fiction from East Africa in the decade surrounding *Kintu*'s publication. The comparison is significant because I have upheld *Kintu* as marking a turning point in African writing broadly, but also because this turning point is tied to its philosophical challenge more than to its historical scope. At the same time, the historical novel is a much hotter topic in the field, so the distinction merits additional consideration. The first work I will turn to here is Goretti Kyomuhendo's 2007 novel *Waiting: A Novel of Uganda at War*, which works well to shed light on *Kintu*, not least because Kyomuhendo and Makumbi have been in productive conversation about the state of literary writing in Uganda. As a novel that personalizes the retreat of Idi Amin's soldiers after his defeat in 1979, *Waiting* also employs one of *Kintu*'s main tactics of sidelining major events in order to focus on the level of the family.

In a 2018 *Wasafiri* interview with Makumbi, Kyomuhendo offered a reading of *Kintu* as symbolic of "a reawakening of national identity," and as an "icon that legitimises Ugandan cultural heritage" (39). The exchange that follows from this strikes similar notes of privileging a Ugandan and, secondarily, African readership over the typical "world fiction" reader used as code for a Western one. Makumbi said that she was "shocked" by how this decision "affected [her] story," in the sense that she was "not just writing about Uganda" but "*to* Uganda" in terms of style and tone (40). She took pains in the interview to clarify that she did not seek to exclude any reader, but instead sought merely to unseat the assumed cultural or national representationality of her characters. "Why is it," she wondered, "that when the west writes violence it's imaginative/literary; when Africa writes it then Africans are violent?" (41). Such resistance to easy metonymizing of the individual with the social makes sense in light of the reading of *Kintu* this chapter presents. While Suubi and Isaac, among others, might be said to model a *way* of reasoning based on their experiences of a distinctly Ugandan setting, the particulars of their lives do not stand for any larger group. The Kintu clan is an exceptional bunch, as the sordid realities of their affairs diverge from modern norms to live out epistemological quandaries first presented in a mythological register. The only one who seems to "represent" a larger social situation is Miisi, and he is rendered incapable of meaningful development by this fact.

Where *Kintu* derives its philosophical heft from a cumulative, layered structure, *Waiting* skillfully locates its most meaningful statements outside the flow of time. By this I do not mean that nothing happens, or that African cultures are somehow "timeless," but that understanding the novel is not essentially dependent on its diachronicity. The intimate village setup of *Waiting* takes historical vectors into itself, with the book configured centripetally instead of as a collation of different scales (for example, global, national, local). It begins with an unpaginated note of explicit connection between characters it will soon visit and the pivotal year of its setting for Ugandan history, when "Ugandan exiles and the Tanzanian Army, known simply as 'the Liberators,' combined to oust Uganda's dictator-ruler, Idi Amin, whose murderous regime has exterminated half a million people through state-sponsored violence." From the momentous scale of this preface to the first page of the narrative proper, Kyomuhendo reduces her frame to simply "Saturday evening" as a family jokes and prepares food (3). Their collective introduction, though narrated technically in the first person, is rendered mostly through dialogue. After a section break, the narrator, a teenage girl named Alinda, takes on a more distinctive presence as her actions are described separately from those of her family members. All the same, their rush to move from their house and out into the more protected bush as night falls, to avoid Amin's fleeing troops, feels like a process so rehearsed that it could be this day, a month later, or the one before. Expressions of fear are interspersed with descriptions of familiar surroundings and, most notable here, casual digressions into myth. "Is it true Sun made Moon pregnant," Alinda asks her neighbor Nyinabarango, "and denied responsibility when the child was born?" (8). The older woman casually answers yes, and then moves on to another subject.

There is, of course, a long tradition of historical events intermingling with mythological or supernatural registers in the African novel. In Ogundele's estimation, this has even resulted in "the displacement of history by myth in the postcolonial African novel in English" (125). Books such as Amos Tutuola's *The Palm-Wine Drinkard* (1952) and Yambo Ouologuem's *Bound to Violence* (*Le Devoir de violence*, 1968) are often cited as seminal examples of this trait. Obiechina, for his part, looks to *Things Fall Apart* to make a similar point, noting that it typifies the "use of narrative proverbs in the structuring of the action of the novel" as "a major constructional strategy in the expression of the oral traditional impulse in the lives of the characters and in defining their vernacular sensibility" (128). *Waiting* is a different case, since it neither depicts mythology as reality nor integrates the proverb mentioned earlier into the novel's deeper structure. The reason for its inclusion seems to be precisely the fleeting, casual nature of supernatural beliefs in the mundane interactions of its characters, with supernatural causality presented at the level of dialogue but not through an "enchanted" plot. In other words, mythology does not pose an explicit epistemological challenge as it does in *Kintu*. As a result, all interpretive paths lead back to the same thing, which is the paralyzed situation in which Alinda and her neighbors must await the return of normal life. And whereas Makumbi seeks restoration of the national scale by short-circuiting individual characters' representationality, Nick Mdika Tembo rightly argues that Hoima, the village of *Waiting*, "represents the Ugandan nature in miniature" as it grapples with the suffering wrought by Amin (93). The novel is therefore bound to a historical event (Amin's violent, drawn-out retreat) even as the political dynamics behind it are out of view. Because the mythological references in the book are *not* pursued beyond the level of their "typical" presence in verbal exchange, they serve as indices of the social status quo that has been indefinitely suspended.

As in *Kintu*, the persistence of traditional beliefs is later exemplified by a curse, of sorts. An old woman and healer named Kaaka, who lives near Alinda's family and hides with them in the bush, is shot in the stomach and killed by one of Amin's men. "The day we buried Kaaka," Alinda narrates, "there were three graves. The smallest was for the baby that was said to have been discovered in Kaaka's stomach. It was wrapped in barkcloth, and I could not get a glimpse of it" (59). This observation prompts her to recollect what Nyinabarongo had earlier explained was the source of Kaaka's permanent pregnancy. Referred to as "a child of the spirits," the unborn baby is supposedly the result of the old woman's having uncovered her special powers as a child. After announcing to her mother that she has imbued her *kanga* (fabric wrap) with "permanent medicinal value" by absorbing fluids from a pair of mating snakes, she is told that this is disastrous, as she will now be unfit for marriage. "People like you, who possess such medicine, belong to the community" (60), her mother chides her, to which Kaaka responds that she is already pregnant and in love. This is cause for even greater shame, and her mother takes her to a healer "who will make the pregnancy invisible" (61) until after the marriage has taken place. Ultimately, however, Nyinabarongo tells Alinda that Kaaka never delivered her baby, and so her "stomach remained swollen since that time" (61). It is out of anger at her husband for blaming her therefore that Kaaka ends up living with Alinda's family, and so the story of her cursedness is cast as the catalyst for the book's social configuration (again, diverse routes to a central condition).

In a similar way to the mention of Sun and Moon, Kaaka's unseen "child of the spirits" is significant mainly as a means of presenting a world in which the *social transmission* of supernatural explanations is of paramount importance. Whether or not Alinda believes that Kaaka carried a child in her stomach through old age is not the point; what matters is that Kaaka is fully absorbed through description of her past into the discursive life of Alinda's extended family. This, in turn, matters a great deal because the primacy of family—as well as the family's capacity to represent a larger national reckoning—are the fronts on which *Waiting* both extends and departs from the novel form's well-known investment in individual development. In this I follow an astute reading by Emily J. Hogg in which she argues that the book is "characterised by the sudden truncation of seemingly significant events in the plot, and the deferral into the un-narrated future of those modes of social engagement (school, work) which generally signal maturation" (10). *Waiting* depicts a Uganda in which a traditional form of *bildung* is precluded, replaced with deep bonds of both nuclear and adoptive family as that which withstands social upheaval. Whereas the European *bildungsroman* in its ideal form privileges a main character's departure from the home, Hogg rightly claims that "*Waiting* emphatically asserts the familial and presents it as inescapable: in particular, blood, the body and birth are repeatedly, excessively present across the text" (11).

Kaaka's permanent pregnancy is not affirmed as evidence for the truth of the traditional faith practices that created it (Alinda does not *see* the fetus), but neither is its veracity questioned. Kyomuhendo renders its epistemological status as a given in order to grant it the capacity to facilitate a more immediate kind of social "stickiness" in the world of the text. This emphasis on family sociality in turn stakes claim to a distinctly Ugandan brand of historic representation, anticipating but stopping short of *Kintu*'s deep dive into the belief systems that attend it. *Waiting* is not a novel of ideas, and it is by no means a criticism to acknowledge that it is up to something different and significant in its own right. The comparison nonetheless sheds light on the curious fact that the universalizing ambitions of *Kintu* seem *less* replicable than do the event-bound aims of Kyomuhendo's book. By this I mean that *Waiting*, in its use of a young protagonist to upset a trajectory of individual fulfillment outside the bounds of her extended family setting, might conceivably keep going forever. Historical events whose locus lies beyond the novel's narrative scope are taken into the construction of a cross-generational story-web. Makumbi, in contrast, works from the ground up to give such "stories" a knowledge value of their own, made possible only by lines of pointedly diachronic character development.

On the other end of the spectrum of presenting supernatural causation without interrogating its veracity, assuming not its naturalness but its artifice, is Peter Kimani's 2017 novel *Dance of the Jakaranda*, which adopts a wry, knowing tone in relation to its multiethnic, multigenerational cast of characters. Kimani's book has been hailed as one of the most outstanding African historical novels in decades—one Kenyan writer identified it as the *only* true literary novel to be published there in a five-year period (Baraka)—in part owing to its refusal to pander to ethno-nationalist orthodoxies about identity. The book's plot revolves around the British-led construction of a railroad from 1897 to 1901, though parts also take place just after Kenyan independence in 1963. As Meghan Gorman-DaRif has usefully summarized:

> The novel explores the dynamics of race, identity, and imperial exploitation through the connections between its characters, including Edward McDonald, a settler colonialist who oversees the work of the railroad and stays on . . . after independence; Babu Salim, one of the thirty thousand Indian workers engaged in the construction of the railway; and Nyundo, an African drummer who mobilizes the workers and later joins the resistance against the British. (617)

Dance of the Jakaranda is, in effect, a socially eclectic prehistory of the independence history most often used to justify the nationalist dynamics of recent and present-day Kenya.

In keeping with Gorman-DaRif's take on the novel, it is also true that Kimani's "narrator emerges in the privileged position of knowing the 'truth'" (617), with frequent asides to the reader and liberal doses of obvious tonal judgment. "Master's real name was Ian Edward McDonald," he informs the reader early on, "but there was nothing real about his identity"

(20). Lively descriptions of self-mythologies, self-delusions, and the widespread misunderstandings they yield are punctured with the sharpness of a needle. After describing the "legend" of the grand, "towering" house in Nairobi that McDonald builds for his absent wife, Kimani interjects that "what happened for a fact is that Master turned his castle into a farmhouse and brought in dairy animals" (18). The crux of the book, in this way, is quickly established as a vacillation between the registers of myth and mundane revelation. As the house is transformed from a "monument" (21) to love lost into a post-independence hotel, so too does Kimani suggest the importance of replacing the *language* of civilizational monumentalism with one of shared, fallible humanity. While illicit cross-racial liaisons are depicted as social tragedies in the novel's turn-of-the-century sections, the 1963 parts achieve equality through no-holds-barred humor. Rajan, the Indian railworker's grandson, attributes different details to different ethnic typologies when he tries to determine who kissed him in a dark room. "Some of the African girls he had kissed dabbed their mouths with Bintel Sudan balm," Rajan thinks, whereas "village girls smeared their faces and lips with the milking jelly" and Indian girls favored Vaseline (24). Black, white, and Indian identities are all on the surface here, denoted by trivial grooming habits that are not meant to indicate deeper social divisions.

Kimani's no-nonsense, myth-busting narratorial tone is what buys the novel its candor as regards Kenya's ethnic composition. The book's reference to a curse occurs as an obvious manifestation of social tension when, aboard a ship that gets stuck on the journey from India to Kenya, Babu pokes fun at a Punjabi elder for thinking that prayer is an effective solution. "Even those who did not know the language understood [the older man's] gesture of ripping hair from his depleted pate," Kimani writes. "He was issuing a curse against Babu. 'I think you have water instead of brain in that head. May Allah, the Almighty God, whose faithful servant you have scorned, curse you and your bloodline!' he wailed" (103–4). Later, Babu's wife Fatima believes that the curse is why she temporarily loses the use of her legs following the shipwreck that ultimately befalls them. "She blamed him squarely for the loss of the use of her legs," we read, while Babu as "the proper target of the curse, could barely stand still" (131). Cursedness serves as a cipher here for the growing resentment in Babu and Fatima's marriage, with Kimani's knowing access to Fatima's *real* misgivings—her regret over "having left home to join a man she now considered completely mad" (ibid.).—anchoring the reader's viewpoint. There is no real question of the curse's legitimacy as one of multiple explanations for Fatima's short-lived disability; instead, it is one of multiple expressions of an unequal, underlying social structure. *Dance of the Jakaranda* is a book about the misapprehensions wrought by social inequality, not the epistemological conflicts that attend efforts to *re*-entrench a universal order.

Dance of the Jakaranda is thus best read as an effort to surface Kenya's violent past in order to neutralize it. Race itself *is* a myth, and so racially coded belief systems are a necessary casualty of its demythologization in Kimani's hands. At one point he interjects that "since the English bear the special gift of transforming even the most humiliating spectacle into a historical epoch, it is a safe bet that the truth resides somewhere else other than where it is presumed to be" (201). The novel scripts this truism in a literal way. One of its central plot elements is the mystery surrounding who impregnates a young Maasai woman named Seneiya, an event whose perceived shame is linked with British occupation of Maasai lands in 1896 (174–76). Though he is not the father of the child (he suffers from erectile dysfunction), Babu does at one point try to have sex with Seneiya, and she claims publicly that he is the father, because "all Indians looked the same—though this one had the kindest face" (207). His ensuing imprisonment and escape from prison bring Babu to a new understanding of race relations in Kenya. Uprooted from his immersive work on building its railroad, and observing it now from a mental distance, he sees the country as part of the landscape across which he must furtively travel to find safety. He suddenly realizes that he is but a cog in a racialized labor machine and knows that he has to "do something about the white domination taking root before his very eyes" (233). The crucial point for this chapter, however, is that this is another moment at which reference to traditional forms of knowledge punctuates a recognition of causality that is fundamentally social. "This was the turning point in Babu's life," Kimani writes, "one that, unknown to him, established links with local seers like Me Katilili and Kioni, who foresaw the train as a beast whose belly would require communal feeding for eternity, accurately presaging the years of colonialism that lay ahead" (233).

There is much more to be said about *Dance of the Jakaranda*, but the examples cited here will suffice to mark its differences from both *Waiting* and *Kintu*. All three works are invested in shaping East African histories into truths that are unhindered by Western scripts, and all three are attentive to the tricky balancing act this requires between local epistemologies and universal intelligibility. This might also be usefully imagined here as a balance between certainty and doubt. Kyomuhendo knows just what kinds of social bonds are required to ease Uganda's passage to posttraumatic maturity, which her book indefinitely awaits. Ten years later,

Kimani unearths the racial mythologies of Kenya's colonial past to dispel their chances of gaining a foothold in the future. *Waiting* is certain of what truth is, and *Dance of the Jakaranda* is certain of what truth is not. The first is a historical novel about African development's violent and yet intimate suspension, and the second a historical novel about development's violent material inception. *Kintu*'s achievement in the intervening years is to have laid bare the most fundamental questions about what it means to conceive of truth or history at all. What constitutes "the social" as people perceive the same events through different lenses? And how can individuals make reasonable choices in reaction to layer upon layer of dual possibility? While *Kintu* may not offer one solution that moves readily from place to place, it affirms the importance *of* place in thinking through conflicted but life-determining evidence—even if that means giving over to belief or opting into the mind's limitations.

CHAPTER FOUR

Bodies Impolitic

AFRICAN DEATHS OF PHILOSOPHICAL SUICIDE

THE STORY OF the novel as it approaches global modernity has often been told as the story of representational failure: from Adorno to Achebe, Raymond Williams to Wole Soyinka, long-form narrative is cast as the genre par excellence of civilizational elegy and disruption. It is, quoting Lukács's foundational *The Theory of the Novel*, "the epic of an age in which the extensive totality of life is no longer directly given . . . yet which still thinks in terms of totality" (56). The form imagined this way is a record of striving through loss, climaxing in the convergence of modernist and late-/post-imperial accounts of cultural crisis.[1] In an essay on Adorno's aesthetics and the postcolonial novel, Timothy Bewes goes so far as to suggest that a pining for bygone wholeness is the chief artistic criterion of our age: "What could it mean," he wonders, "to understand the historical moment as one in which failure becomes precisely the 'measure of success' of an artistic work?" (171). While African writing has been seen in the past as a "next frontier" or an antidote of sorts to Western philosophical ennui, the hyperconnectivity of the global or even "postglobal" era, per Tejumola Olaniyan, demands more flexible models. From this view, the recent flurry of international interest in a small cohort of global African writers misses the real possibility of the moment. Instead of marking yet another turn in an inverted historical progression that moves from a shadowy Western center to more enlightening peripheries, we should now be trying to figure out how the African novel, too, meaningfully fails.

A second common story of the novel holds that it is a liberal bourgeois institution that naturalizes individual development over collective structures as a cognate for imperial notions of progress. "Individual

[145]

development," in this narrative, becomes an alibi for sustaining the geopolitical inequalities underlying unevenly enforced norms of universal self-fulfillment. One noted effort to treat "world" African texts, Joseph Slaughter's *Human Rights, Inc.*, upbraids the "image of human personality development" encoded in much human rights law for joining with the novel as "part of the engine and freight of Western colonialism and (neo)imperialism over the past two centuries" (5). By and large, this critique still holds sway over the African literary field: liberal selfhood valorizes self-determination, which in turn assumes conditions sufficiently unconstrained by hardship to make freedom a meaningful idea. Western institutions that champion individual progress too often skip the work of ensuring that its potential is the rule, not the exception. In its quintessential *bildung* form, then, the novel is guilty by association of narrating the self-fulfillment of the few instead of the many. This is nothing new, as important work in adjacent fields over recent decades attests.[2] It follows that much work in African literary criticism looks to the novel's potential to mobilize past and present forms of radical collectivity. Unlike where this book begins, with Casely Hayford's use of the novel to toggle between intellectual solitude and public calls to arms, sharp individuation is now often seen as at odds with more porous constructions of group affiliation and identity.

As I have indicated elsewhere, much of this has been for the good by turning a robust critical eye to African cultural forms that might otherwise be ignored in broader literary histories. In the spirit of restoring some measure of balance between an optic of individual contemplation and one of collective representation, however, this chapter turns to some of the recent African literary "few"—unabashedly intellectual novelists—who *de*-couple a deep focus on individual cultivation from an insidious enforcement of social exclusion. They do this, specifically, by inviting contemplation of what I call "philosophical suicide," a concept with a long literary pedigree that imagines intellection in relation to self-will and death. Far from either announcing a loss of totality, on the one hand, or providing ideological cover for (neo)liberal regimes, on the other, the works I take up in the sections that follow invert *both* of these common framings of the novel at once. They wed pioneering models of dense spatial connection—what we might call "global form"—to a rediscovery of deep private reflection. The searching individual mind presents, however, as cognate with social illegibility, unable to follow through on the notion of a significant death. This chapter thus concerns texts that "fail" to make the thinking subject speak for a shared condition but succeed in representing the recent challenges of sustaining a meaningful relation of part to whole. In the nascent literature of Africa's twenty-first century, the cultivation of individual intellect comes full circle from an insidious ideal to a lonely idea, free of the political valences by which it has long been burdened.

Philosophical Suicide as a Conceptual Tool

The second and third parts of this chapter will be devoted mainly to two contemporary southern African novelists who foreground the relationship between thinking and dying: the Zimbabwean writer Tendai Huchu and the South African writer Imraan Coovadia. Both of their most recent novels, at the time of this book's writing, were published in 2014, and they bear strong resemblances to one another in terms of their diffuse plot structures, coordination of contemporary nationhood across multiple transnational points, and somewhat fatalistic political outlook. Furthermore, Huchu's *The Maestro, the Magistrate, and the Mathematician* and Coovadia's *Tales of the Metric System* were published in the United States by the same small academic press (Ohio University Press), a sign of their similar positions in a highly stratified African literary marketplace. I then offer a brief coda on a third novel from the region, Masande Ntshanga's *The Reactive*; published in the same year, it likewise demands reflection on the relation between self-reflection and self-killing. First, however, I want to establish a thematic locus for these books' engagement with "ideas" clearly marked off as such. To this end, this first section elaborates literary suicide as a key to understanding the deeper shift in these works toward socially impotent rather than representative individualism. All three novels feature alienated, contemplative characters whose intellectual dispositions lead them, in some way, to court death.

Tendai Huchu is the natural place to begin, because *The Maestro, the Magistrate, and the Mathematician* (cited periodically hereafter as *MMM*) makes numerous explicit references to one of the most famous suicides in literary history, that of Alexei Kirillov from Dostoevsky's classic 1872 novel *Demons* (or *Besy*, in Russian). I do not yet want to situate Kirillov specifically within *MMM*—that will be the task of the next part of this chapter. Instead, I'd like briefly to sketch a broad-strokes comparison of two different versions of modern literary suicide that aim to represent a broader condition, the first through self-abnegation, and the second through self-actualization. This is *not* a psychological or sociological claim (at least not in terms of the critical archive on which it draws) but a structural one. I mean "representation" here to refer to different variations of how parts (that is, individual characters) relate to wholes, be they social, spatial, or conceptual. A noted tradition of suicide in modern African literature—exemplified by Wole Soyinka's *Death and the King's Horseman* and Chinua Achebe's *Things Fall Apart*—stresses a civilizational quandary that foregrounds the correspondence of the personal to the social. As Adélékè Adéèkó has suggested, suicide for these writers is by and large a historical act, despite its metaphysical weight in the worlds of the texts. "As entrenched in the narrative and dramaturgic responses to Okonkwo [from *Things Fall Apart*]," he writes, "certainties about how the world runs fail the protagonists and something in the emerging colonial configuration threatens their physical existence" (2011, 72–73). In other words, they die within the widening gap between their cultural worlds' past and present authority.

Per Adéèkó's argument, these two most famous African literary suicides—of Achebe's Okonkwo and Soyinka's horseman Elesin (followed by that of his foreign-educated son, Olunde)—inscribe what is effectively a jurisprudential changing of the guard. In different ways, both Soyinka's Yoruba polity (based on real events) and Achebe's Igbo one (whose details are fictional) are denied their authority to enforce social norms through violence: these are classic texts of African cultural norms' tragic collision with the disenfranchising force of the colonial state. Suicide, then, becomes a literal, individualized leave-taking from a society within and to which the power to uphold value has now been denied. "The self-appointed leader of the native's war of independence in *Things Fall Apart* forcefully removes himself from consideration only when he realizes that he has lost the means of pressing on the rest of the society his views of the justness of the ways he endorses," Adéèkó continues. Similarly, Elesin's suicide in Soyinka's play ends up being not an honorable fulfillment of social duty by following his king to the afterlife (which right he is denied by a colonial administrator), but a shamed, desperate attempt to salvage some measure of individual pride. While the details, Adéèkó grants, vary here from touchstone text to touchstone text, suicide generally "addresses a similar philosophical quandary on the lawful seizure of power and the just enforcement of rules in early colonial circumstances" (73). Considered in these terms, suicide foregrounds, as an African literary trope, a concern not with asserting self-will, but with mourning the loss of self-rule. For Achebe's and Soyinka's suicidal protagonists, a life robbed of continuity between law and belief is not worth living.

A number of scholars have adopted a similar line as regards Okonkwo specifically, arguing that his suicide by hanging is a positive (rather than passive) response to the colonial evacuation of Igbo belief systems. While he "could allow himself to be killed," Alan R. Friesen notes, "thus assuring his reincarnation or his enshrinement along with his ancestors" (7), Okonkwo instead commits the far graver Igbo transgression of suicide. The "tragedy" here, to use a term often applied to both *Things Fall Apart* and *Death and the King's Horseman*, is that Okonkwo betrays a system whose power to punish him has already waned. In a real sense, then, the emergence of "modern African literature" in English is itself marked as tragic. If we take tragedy to signify resignation in the face of inevitable human frailty and compromise, Achebe's choice to write an English novel about cross-cultural contact is a compromise of its own. As Abiola Irele has memorably explored, the tragedy of *Things Fall Apart* is written right into its form, which conveys an intrinsic ambivalence surrounding the balance between individual critical consciousness and cultural identity. "Achebe's novel is not by any means an unequivocal celebration of tribal culture," Irele writes. "We are presented rather with a corner of human endeavor that is marked by the web of contradictions within which individual and collective destinies have everywhere and at all times been enmeshed" (2000, 2). A different way of putting this is that Achebe, with the novel as a tool, can reflect at a distance on the pitfalls of the culture whose denial he nonetheless protests. He is at once a cool intellectual observer and an invested political actor, innovating the novel form even as he regrets its new aptness to express Nigerian truths.

There are, of course, other suicides in modern African literature, but these brief examples, on which much has already been written, should suffice to set the stage for its broad significance.[3] This literary lineage also coincides with African authors' emergence into global visibility and would thus seem to be an obvious point of departure for bringing the discussion back to contemporary African writing about individual choice within contexts of felt historical disenfranchisement. In fact, however, while the postcolonial context is a key background element to the works of Huchu, Coovadia, and Ntshanga, their focus is more on the alienated, philosophical individual as such than on the individual's *representative* role in a particular social or cultural order (with Ntshanga as a partial exception here). Dostoevsky's suicidal figure Kirillov, in this light, is not a surprising choice of literary allusion for Huchu: the Russian character is infamous in studies of the nineteenth-century novel for channeling his triumphant individualism toward a "suicide of ideas." Kirillov kills himself in the name of individual will, or total autonomy; he aims to secure man's triumph over God and his ascent to a godlike status. As part of Dostoevsky's larger

Christian vision, however, he becomes a limit-case that reveals just how fallen humanity is, in need of God even, or especially, in the act of his intellectual repudiation. Kirillov's suicide by a shot to the head is also a key moment for the relation between the novel and philosophy in literary history writ large: he makes manic use of philosophical learning to argue for suicide as a world-transforming act. At one point in *Demons*, responding to Kirillov's vow to kill himself when it will be of maximum use to humanity, the enigmatic leader of their nihilistic-revolutionary intellectual circle mutters, "Old philosophical places, the same since the beginning of the ages" (237). Kirillov is delighted with this reception, because it situates his decision to commit suicide firmly within an *abstract* universal domain rather than a historical one. "The same!" he cries. "The same since the beginning of the ages, and no others, ever!" (ibid.).

As the Russian novel scholar Irina Paperno has pointed out in her exhaustive book on Kirillov's social and historical context, *Suicide as a Cultural Institution in Dostoevsky's Russia*, *Demons* also casts Kirillov as a locus of philosophical compression—that is, the book collapses a long and disparate tradition of philosophical suicide into a key individual character. In turn, he serves as the part that represents the universal whole of humanity through its Christian redemption; Dostoevsky uses intellect as a tool to work back toward faith. "Indeed, in the death of Kirillov," Paperno writes, "Dostoevsky combined diverse philosophical commonplaces into a single, seemingly coherent pattern." In addition to Plato's death of Socrates and the death of Christ (the first representing secular immortality, and the second its religious variant), Paperno then works assiduously through Dostoevsky's engagements with Kant and Hegel. Unlike what Irele sees as Achebe's ambivalence about investing in a form (the realist novel) that tends to foreground the critical individual, Dostoevsky wholeheartedly embraces the displacement of a civilizational whole onto the part of Kirillov. This is, after all, the only point from which he might then hope to work *back* toward all of mankind as something restored from its fallen present state. The catch here is that, for Dostoevsky, what we might alternately describe as a social or cultural totality—"the Yoruba" or "the Igbo," going back to the examples of Soyinka and Achebe—is made subordinate to the religious and philosophical totality of "humanity." I want to be clear that I do not mean to affiliate African writers with "anthropology" and Russian writers with "universality," but merely to point out the different canvasses or scales of political awareness on which these writers worked, at very different historical moments. Universal claims are rightly suspect in a postcolonial context, where local traditions have been disempowered or denied. The flip side of Dostoevsky's ambition, after all, was his civilizational hubris.

And of course, the transformation of humanity from something that is divinely ordained to something that can be rationally "tested" was a familiar facet of nineteenth-century Russia's epistemological revolution as it turned toward positivism and the natural sciences. (The foremost literary relic of this period is Ivan Turgenev's *Fathers and Sons*, in which the main character rejects everything but science before dying, ironically, as a result of a laboratory mishap.) It follows that Kirillov is only able to assume universal significance, for Dostoevsky, because of the limited, national context in which he operates. While nineteenth-century Russia was caught up, like any other place, in all sorts of transnational networks, the important point here is that Dostoevsky had not yet internalized "globality" as an active challenge to the linear part-whole logic that Kirillov embodies and that is the very essence of narrative representation. In this sense, philosophy takes on a particular *metonymic* significance in Kirillov's death. The motivation for his suicide is intellectual, not psychological: inspired by Schopenhauer and prefiguring Nietzsche, Kirillov seeks to realize mankind's supreme authority by mastering his own fear of death.[4] This thinking assumes, however, that there is an actionable relationship between the "part" of Kirillov's life and the whole of everyone else's. His self-sacrifice, in other words, makes sense only given a clear understanding of the public on whose behalf that sacrifice can occur. The national context of *Demons* thus matters a great deal in terms of its philosophical ambitions, as well as for Dostoevsky's conservative Slavophilic politics: the universal import of Kirillov's suicidal intention stems from a tacit conflation of Russia with the world.

This makes Kirillov a provocative point of departure for a self-consciously "global" African diasporic writer like Tendai Huchu. Whereas the examples of literary suicide from Soyinka's and Achebe's oeuvres hinge on their anxieties about cultural denial or disruption by British colonial incursion, Kirillov's suicide in *Demons* relies on Dostoevsky's sense of Russian ascendance to a universal role. To push this contrast still further, Huchu's invocation of Kirillov as a transnational touchstone for literary suicide—rather than a canonical African precursor—invites contemplation of a *desire for*, rather than historical suspicion of, universal representation as an intellectual project. More specifically, this contrast helps us to think through the limitations of a spatial and multicultural, rather than abstract or philosophical, notion of wholeness. This setup then crystallizes some of the most pressing issues facing global literature as a field.

African literature, as I have argued elsewhere, is subject to an ongoing effacement of the novel's mediated status, in favor of a direct conflation of literary form with historically trenchant ideologies (in part, because literary critics then seem to be offering social rather than literary commentary).[5] This means that novels from Africa are usually read through one of two lenses that speak to the eager assimilation of narrative structure to political institutions, à la the example of Slaughter's *Human Rights, Inc.* The first, anti-essentialism, valorizes flux and multiplicity as a means of resisting the transformation of experience into abstract truths that may then become too rigid. The second looks more like a countervailing assertion of collective historical identity, which aggregates individual experience into politically useful social and cultural formations. To be sure, these lenses are not mutually exclusive. Even as activist an intellectual as Frantz Fanon describes the necessary wedge in consciousness between nuance and mobilization during the process of epistemological decolonization. In "Racism and Culture," he writes with some ambivalence about the "precipitous re-valorisation" of tradition that often accompanies African revolutionary movements, noting that it is "not structural, but verbal"—that is, glossy content and not deep form—and must remain so because it "covers paradoxical attitudes" (130).

Embracing the need for literary structures to directly correspond to political ideologies is completely understandable amid the demands of decolonial and immediately postcolonial African literary history. In its residual forms, however, this parallelism between the structuring of fictional characters and that of large-scale historical narratives (for example, "the liberal subject" as a term of suspicion) has resulted in an oddly flat, one-to-one sense of how individuals and historical processes relate. Instead of instrumentalizing individual development (as in the novel's liberal origins), the global literary field now instrumentalizes individual fluidity. The Global South subject thus plays a relativizing role, not a universalizing one, even as the Global South itself—as a network of spaces or social geographies—is explored in greater critical depth. This is because the "totality" in terms of which the novel now thinks is implicitly *already there*: the globe, rather than the nation or mankind, has become the default literary-analytic context. Another way of putting this is that totality is not an imagined projection toward which the novel must build so much as an empirically "real" or spatialized fact against which the novel is read. As Pheng Cheah argues similarly in *What Is a World?*, it may be that "the ascendance of a spatial [as opposed to a temporal-developmental] conception of the world in literary studies is part of a broader attempt to reckon with the implications of globalization for the study of literature" (27). As a result, there is a direct, if complicated, genealogy that links postcolonial criticism to more current global theoretical trends by virtue of a clear line from narrative form to ideological endorsement. The discipline's scope has broadened, however, so that speaking of a nonspatial or empirical whole has become more difficult. By extension of Cheah's efforts to disaggregate "world" from "globe," there is nonetheless an important distinction to be drawn between subjectivity as a tool for distilling spatialized forms of *connectivity* and subjectivity as an end in itself and a point of sustained reflection. In other words, the individual as it evolves from postcolonial to global criticism has remained instrumentalized.

The critical canonization of two broad schools of Anglophone writing clarifies the close relation between global space and global subjectivity. The first, typified by the Anglophone Indian writer Amitav Ghosh in his novels of vast archival and cartographic spread (particularly *Sea of Poppies* from 2008, the start of an epic trilogy about the opium trade), focuses on previously underrepresented transnational constellations to shed light on the historical vicissitudes of multidirectional commerce. Gosh's novels are famously encyclopedic, replete with data like shipping terminology, multilingual period vernacular, and dozens of characters spread across social classes. To quote the Indian Ocean scholar Isabel Hofmeyr in a 2012 essay subtitled "The Indian Ocean as Method," anachronistic categories like "domination and resistance" or "colonizer and colonized" have given way here to a copiously detailed transnational historicism. A creole space like the Indian Ocean "requires us to take a much longer perspective, which necessarily complicates any simple binaries" (589), including the nationalist counterassertions of decolonization. It is fitting, then, that virtually every major scholar of Indian Ocean studies, including Hofmeyr, Gaurav Desai, and Françoise Lionnet, takes Ghosh's novels as a primary source in their South-South literary archive. This historical-archival approach to theorizing global literature derives a nonlinear geography from a focus on how texts actually move around the globe, both facilitating and drawing on transnational networks that break with a clear line from North to South.[6] As part of a varied arsenal of critical tools, it constitutes an important intervention. It tells us little, however, about contemporary writers for whom a *breach* in continuity between subject and society is a primary source of speculation.

The other most visible transnational conjuncture of global-cosmopolitan novels and global-cosmopolitan criticism is perhaps best captured in the essay title "To Hear the Variety of Discourses" (2011), by the acclaimed South African "coloured" writer Zoë Wicomb. This strain of global literature strives to represent social flux on a more limited, subjective scale. In Wicomb's case, this is often a mixed-race female character in the hybridistic, littoral city of Cape Town.[7] This latter kind of globally conscious writing, in sum, valorizes racial and cultural nonfixity by charting its interplay with equally fluid geographies (again, in Wicomb, with special focus on the Indian Ocean region). Spatial mobility as it inflects individual lives is also the hallmark strategy of nearly all the highest-profile recent African novels, from Chimamanda Adichie's *Americanah* (2013), with its many-pronged world aviation network and kaleidoscopic view of diasporic sensibilities; to Taiye Selasi's *Ghana Must Go* (2013) as it charts convergences between Ghana-based and diasporic families and institutions; to Yaa Gyasi's *Homegoing* (2016), which bounces between Ghana and America, and between past and present; and even, looking back, to a book like Binyavanga Wainaina's *One Day I Will Write about This Place* (2011), a literary memoir built of porous, atemporal, and synesthetic moments of intra-African movement and self-formation. Admittedly, this list, to which dozens of books could be added, traverses a wide range of literary sensibilities. But what these titles have in common and what, one suspects, makes them so appealing to literary scholars and critics is that they can be read to equate the self with social and historical trends. The lives they chronicle can be viewed, that is, as portholes to social and cultural "situations," as people become signs of places and times.

There is a third model of African writing that also needs to be mentioned here: the great many novels that are more local than global or even continental in their structural ambition and critical recognition. This is not an evaluative statement, but a descriptive one. (In fact, it describes much of the continent's most prized writing.) As the Tanzanian scholar Michael Andindilile has noted, "Africa" fails to capture the sheer range of difference denoted by this geographical constellation, instead always implying the "two Africas"—that of Western signifier and that of "real life" signified—that constantly seek reconciliation (127, 128). This line of critique is also familiar in the more popular register of those who keep pace with contemporary African writing from debates surrounding the Caine Prize, a high-profile short-story competition based in London and open only to authors of "African descent." These conversations, which tend toward polarization, focus on the limitations imposed by the term "African" as well on as the attendant risks of what is often called "poverty porn."[8] It is not surprising, then, that amid a resurgent insistence on an as yet unfulfilled decolonial imperative in the Africanist intellectual sphere, some writers have also opted to eschew the question of Western influence and involvement altogether. In the realm of literary production, this requires efforts to relocate African literary "prestige"—in the form of publishing and prize-granting institutions—from Europe to the continent.[9]

For a certain kind of novel, this emergent publishing infrastructure can encourage a focus on localizing and refining conventional elements of plot and character, which is also a step toward reconciling the idea of Africa with its manifold realities. It is a project, so to speak, of "telling Africa's stories" outside the imperatives of Western cultural consumption. Because the construction of "Africa" has been so fraught with historical occlusion and foreign projection, one might argue that there are still plenty of localities and identities that demand some sort of truer, deeply embedded representation. Examples of writers who do this particularly well might be Zukiswa Wanner (especially her 2010 novel *Men of the South*); Yewande Omotoso (author of *Bom Boy* and *The Woman Next Door*, published in 2011 and 2016, respectively); and Abubakar Adam Ibrahim (who won the Nigeria Prize for *Season of Crimson Blossoms* from 2015). All of these books narrate "small" lives—that is, the day-to-day realities of people without access to transnational social and cultural elites—in rich detail and with differently bracing styles. At their best, such novels challenge the restrictive identities placed on African writers and turn an empathetic eye to the real trials and tribulations of African subjects. As a possible downside, however, the widespread celebration of such writing (which is usually quite formally straightforward) can confine African literature in a different way, this time to discussions of identity and social roles, rather than meta-level contemplation of either.

For writers and critics with a strong investment in the novel's ambitious capacity to model intellectual challenges rather than only reveal experiential ones (we might think, again, of Kirillov's effort to turn reason itself into a metaphysical domain), this conversation can sometimes seem stagnant. Cheah's argument in *What Is a World?* is again pertinent here, as he worries that postcolonial literature is too often confined to either a derivative status or a negative one, both of them limited. Literature in his formulation can only hope either to model the world system as it already exists or, alternatively, to reject it: the first variant applies to the current crop of "global novels" that try to represent the heavily networked present, and the second might apply to more "local" African writing that refuses to see its realities absorbed into a larger, economically disadvantaging structure. In Cheah's words, "The formative imagination either portrays the complexity of present reality by embedding it in the history of its making, or it negates and points beyond this reality by generating a picture that perpetually contradicts this reality" (82).

Literature, for Cheah, to be blunt risks confinement to being either implicitly "for" or explicitly "against" depicting a globalized world that is already, in some ways, a forgone conclusion. This in turn threatens to squeeze out the novel's layered representation of temporality in order to effect conceptual and ethical renewal. In the more delimited scope of my project here, it is also unclear where the "idea" might now lurk—even literally, on the page—because the possibility of its fulfillment through a representative figure has been lost. One might think here of the main character Ifemelu from Chimamanda Ngozi Adichie's smash hit novel *Americanah*, who ponders things like economic freedom and race in her blog posts in a way that grows directly from her shifting social space (from Nigeria to Pennsylvania to Connecticut and New Jersey, among any number of other locales). She is able to offer a salient critique of US race relations precisely *because* she occupies a peripheral rather than representative position vis-à-vis the American academy. Self and space here are bound in a project of piercing rather than facilitating various truths.

In sum, studies of the African novel tend to prioritize questions of *who* one is, and *where* one is, and to downplay less immediate intellectual projects. Where is the space, then, for the idea? Is it possible to broach an intellectual realm that is not directly instrumental of some other, more urgent priority? And where might we turn, in an African literary scene that can be dizzying in its cultural and geographical multiplicity, to meditate more deeply on the trade-offs between self-exploration and self-sublimation, between movement in the world and stillness with one's thoughts? In the section that follows, I turn to Tendai Huchu's work to begin answering some of these questions. In the *Maestro, the Magistrate, and the Mathematician*, following on his 2010 debut novel *The Hairdresser of Harare*, Huchu experiments with shifting the balance away from an individual's being in social space and back toward his thinking in a private one. I mean this contrast to be as sharp as it sounds—a division between living and learning that recasts philosophical suicide, owing now to a *lack* of will, within a context of transnational migration.

Tendai Huchu's Maestro of Lonely Learning

The Zimbabwean writer Tendai Huchu is provocative here because he does not simply back down from the challenge of global representation in favor of deceptively "local" realities. He does not, in other words, revert to writing competent but structurally unoriginal realist novels when faced with the impossibly dense (and unequal) human archive of globalization. As Adam Kirsch has argued in his short book *The Global Novel: Writing the World in the 21st Century*, "Ambitious novelists [now] will find themselves writing global novels, not out of a cynical desire to elevate their commercial or critical rewards, but because individual lives are now lived and conceived under the sign of the whole globe" (loc. 236). This is true of *The Maestro, the Magistrate, and the Mathematician* on both counts: it follows the lives of three Zimbabwean transplants to present-day Edinburgh, Scotland. Owing, presumably, to its formal experimentalism and many Shona points of reference (including passages of untranslated Shona), it nonetheless has not had anywhere near the commercial success of Afropolitan counterparts like Adichie, Teju Cole, Yaa Gyasi, and the like. Like Coovadia's *Tales of the Metric System* (discussed in the next section), however, this may also be because Huchu "tests" globality as a literary genre by reintroducing an outdated kind of novel of ideas within it as a hostile interlocutor. While the novel of ideas plotline is just one among many modalities within the novel's confines, it nonetheless indicates globality as something that might be otherwise.

This means that while I agree with Kirsch on the basic premise that representing global connectivity is a key challenge for many ambitious contemporary novelists, his statement requires significant filling-in. One might better argue that globality is unavoidable for a particular *sort* of novelist, which is to say one with a bent toward macrocosmic "structure" rather than, say, style on a more local or syntactic level, or even character. In introducing this caveat to Kirsch's case, "globality" also acquires more precision and argumentative heft. While Kirsch claims that it is "impossible to say that all global novels have certain formal qualities in common," because "the global is best thought of as a medium through which all kinds of stories can be told" (loc. 227), I would argue that globality is most useful to the novel as *precisely* a formal designation. To be specifically "global," rather than the closely related "world," "transnational," or "diasporic," is to emphasize far-flung spatial connection as a fundamental component of plot or character composition. It comes closer, in the critical literature, to what Caren Irr has summarized as the trademark "world novel" features of "multi-stranded narration, broad geographical reach, cosmopolitan ethics, multilingual sensitivity, and a renewed commitment to realism" (175). And indeed, both *MMM* and *Tales of the Metric System* connect their national origins—Zimbabwe and South Africa, respectively—to a transnationally disarrayed plot structure. But Huchu's three-part multi-stranded narration crucially forces each of the recurring narrative lines to relativize the other, creating a series of interlinked disruptions instead of orchestrating cohesion.

This puts a more cynical spin on what Rebecca Walkowitz, in *Born Translated*, calls the global novel process of "[collating] multiple voices and [transforming] selections into examples" (128–29). Rather than assist in "gathering and affirming social groups," a social anthologizing function that Walkowitz attributes to the British-Caribbean novelist Caryl Phillips, Huchu's *MMM* ends up revealing what globality *cannot* structurally support: namely, intellection. Philosophy is diffused by the multi-stranded structure of the novel in which it appears, piquing the reader's interest in it as one possible mode of existing, but never quite seeing through any single idea. Huchu uses the novel form to in some sense audition death-by-ideas through *Demons*, reflection on which he eventually nests within only one of his three interwoven, character-driven plots. The Maestro, a Zimbabwean who works at a grocery store in Edinburgh, is soul-deadened and overwhelmed there by "the incredible range of choice on display, so that an elementary defense mechanism [kicks] in, a fuse breaking the circuit, shutting it down" (37). He lives by himself, mostly on greasy takeout food, inside a small, disheveled apartment, with books "piled on the floor, against all four walls of the room, rising up to window level" (41).

Notably, the Maestro is the last of the three central characters to be introduced, so that his narrative through line appears as an exhausted punctuation mark to the less-examined lives of the Magistrate and the Mathematician, with which the reader is already engaged. The Maestro is described just six pages into his first appearance in full thrall to the medieval Roman philosopher Boethius's *The Consolation of Philosophy*, "which he was reading, and had been, slowly, contemplatively for a week" (ibid.). Written during Boethius's year in prison while awaiting execution by the Ostrogoth king Theoderic the Great, the text is structured as a conversation with Lady Philosophy, loosely inspired by the form of Platonic dialogue. And yet the Maestro is decidedly a loner, communing only with his books, to which he returns "time and time again, hoping with each reading to unlearn the last and discover it anew. Each time he read the poetry of the words, he felt a kinship, as though he too was in bondage, searching for a higher meaning to life through reason" (ibid.). His reading doesn't culminate in a renewed understanding of life so much as it perpetuates a self-isolationist cycle of thinking about thinking.

To this point, the Maestro's philosophical contemplation is *always* closely linked to a literary point of reference. "Did this moment exist before he'd read [Jon] McGregor," he asks himself at one point during a Boethius binge, "or had it always been there? And if it had, then why hadn't he noticed it before? Perhaps, he thought, it did not exist and only came to be after I read the book. If that was the case then he had to accept the terrifying notion that fiction had created a real moment in the real world from nothing but word" (42). It is also his anxiety about the power of language over life that prompts the novel's first musings on suicide, as a means of "testing God," boldly echoing Kirillov's literary-epistemological significance but not yet venturing to invoke him directly. "In that moment," as the Maestro hangs out reading on his windowsill and his thoughts veer to the exuberance of mortality, "he pondered if he were to let go, to cast himself down from this ledge . . . if he let go, would He send one of His angels so that not a hair on his body would be harmed" (ibid.). In fact, however, the Maestro is just waxing poetic with the notion of divine salvation. His outlook on life is dire, and worth quoting at length:

> The Maestro always came to the same conclusion, he would hurtle into the void, accelerating at nine point eight metres per second squared, simple physics, the predictable effects of gravity on an eleven stone, twenty-seven year old male body falling through the atmosphere, leaving only the hope that through the panicking, firing neurons there would be a moment of clarity in which everything is illuminated, a split second in which life itself was explained, the meaning of it all, past, present and future laid out, all making sense so that when, when he hit the ground, then at least it would have been worth something more than the aching emptiness he felt every day with each sunrise and sunset. The image of the falling man from 9/11 flashed into his mind. What had the man thought on the way down, was he just thinking, oh fuck, oh fuck, or was there some fundamental insight on the journey, plummeting to earth, the concrete-scarred ground rising to meet him? (42–43)

This, then, is the immediate context in which reference to Dostoevsky first appears: he is immediately listed on this page alongside Kafka, Sartre, and Nietzsche as one of the Maestro's hopes for understanding. His free-indirect narrative style grows increasingly febrile as he moves deeper into intellectual solitude, and the Maestro's first section is then jarred into coming full circle to where it started; that is, with the disillusionment of infinite choice. The phone rings; he speaks briefly with his one point of social contact, a Polish woman named Tatyana, and then reverts to aloneness in his hovel. "He switched the TV on," Huchu writes, "flicking through many channels, and failing to find anything worth watching" (44).

The Maestro's habits of mind can be summarized as follows: philosophy gives way to literature; literature gives way to a sense of meaninglessness and mediation; and yet following through on this sense of meaninglessness gives way to technological disruption. (Or, in order of topic, Huchu moves from Boethius to Jon McGregor to suicidal ideation to distraction with a transnational cable television package.) Suicide comes into view here as an "idea" in its own right rather than as an action meant to fulfill an intellectual proposition. The hazy line between lived and secondhand experience also seems to deflate the importance of "experience" altogether as the bedrock of self-formation. Indeed, the blur the Maestro experiences of acute, imagined sensation (the feeling of concrete) with a received virtual image (the falling man on 9/11) is part of his profound self-disorientation. As Simon During suggests as part of a broader argument in *Against Democracy*, in devaluing "experience" as the Maestro's main currency—his life is the thing that *disrupts* his thoughts, not that which sees them through, or makes them meaningful—Huchu in some ways departs from the conceptual basis of liberal democracy. "The category [of experience] is so valuable to democrats because experiences seem to precede traditions, learning, hierarchies, and morality," During writes.

> Furthermore, experiences . . . are like democratic citizens who enter into their privilege simply by being born . . . in a particular place at a particular time, and who need share little. From within this logic democracy [offers] experience itself as a basic criterion of value, as if societies are good just to the degree that they deliver rich and full experiences rather than to the degree that, say, they encourage virtuous living or offer social order or unity or purpose. (6)

The Maestro does not think and therefore exist; he exists in the contemporary world and is therefore unable to think. He is certainly disillusioned with the populist leveling that technological connectivity as a form of shared experience has brought (or at least, that it has accompanied), but there is no clear political or economic association with his elitism here.

The Maestro's inability to avoid distraction continues apace with his self-isolation as his plot progresses, always with at least one other plot intervening between each of his appearances. Interestingly, references to a global literary marketplace increase as his determination to sequester himself from it grows, creating a gap between the Maestro's will and his context. Prompted by a return to the Doris Lessing novel *The Grass Is Singing*, he contemplates his involvement in a particular liberal-multiculturalist niche of global publishing by acknowledging that "most of his choices were made for him by the Guardian, or a short reference in the introduction of some seminal text" (131).[10] While he judges films freely, owing to a lack of real knowledge, with novels he "was more likely to fear that he didn't get it, rather than to say that a book was bad. He envied the brave souls on Amazon, the dissenters hiding behind anonymous avatars, who gave War and Peace one star and told Tolstoy to go stuff it—too long, too slow, too many characters, what's with all the digressions, just get on with the story, Nikolayevich" (ibid.). This creates an oddly tense context for the moment when the Maestro comes around to openly likening himself to Kirillov. After a particularly frenetic passage in which he throws away his phone, internet router, and computer in the name of claiming reading as "a religious vocation, a retreat," from which he "had to push the world out so he could focus" (137), he announces that he "felt like Kirillov, an idea incarnate" (138). At this point the reader might well ask, wait, *what* idea? Kirillov's incarnation of philosophy is specific: he wants to kill himself to stretch free will to its limit, thereby liberating the world from the need for a higher authority. The Maestro here claims only the idea *of* ideas, an escape from the public rather than an assertion of his individual power to represent and redeem it.

On some level, then, literature here serves as a buffer between ideas and their acquisition of any real social force. In the section after the one in which Kirillov appears as a sign of ideas made incarnate, the Maestro has already returned to reading material with a global spatial orientation. Specifically, he is reading David Mitchell's 1999 novel *Ghostwritten*, which is in some ways a structural precursor to Huchu's *MMM*. As Rita Barnard has suggested in an essay on "Fictions of the Global," *Ghostwritten* is a quintessentially "global" novel, leaping from continent to continent and voice to voice in a way that approximates hyperlinked online reading. Reading it, even admiringly, sends the Maestro into another fit of doubt as he turns again to Dostoevsky (this time, the Grand Inquisitor from *The Brothers Karamazov*) to wonder whether he shouldn't turn instead to a "single book" in order to "find someone quickly to whom he can hand over that great gift of freedom with which the ill-fated creature is born" (172). The books he has in mind are religious texts, and the relation of free will to divine power is a recurring concern for the Maestro as he languishes in freedom as an overabundant commodity. As he delves further into trying to limit that freedom by his own means, he grows accordingly hungrier for some intervening authority or purpose. His apartment is squalid, he hardly eats, and he burns his books in an act of desperation to release himself from the "slew of minds linked through time and space [that] had resided in the flat with him, challenging one another, contesting, arguing, seeking a higher truth" (211). Desire for a single book could be glossed here as desire for a *singular* book, one that allows for decision and direction instead of modeling a diffuse network of back-and-forths.

In some ways, such pressure on freedom might seem to recall what has become a very well-worn kind of modified secularization narrative, which explores religious authority's widespread evolution, in Latin modernity, from social requirement to private choice. This line of theorization is typified by the Canadian philosopher Charles Taylor's concept of "buffered identity" from *A Secular Age*, in which he explores "the fragility of any particular formula or solution, whether believing or unbelieving" (303). The proliferation of choice here is liberal pluralism's strength and weakness. At its best, it results in what Taylor calls "the positive features of the present spirituality of search" among today's highly "disciplined, conscious, committed individual believer," or a "pilgrim seeker [who is] attempting to discern his/her own path" (532). To be sure, some part of this story may ring true for the Maestro in *MMM*. (Dostoevsky, after all, believed in a Christian God, while for Huchu God is more or less immaterial.) The timelier problem that the novel takes up, however, is that the contemporary literary imaginary (and market) privileges *space* over mind as the font of subjectivity: people are determined from the outside in, not the inside out. In Huchu's case specifically, the frustration of the Maestro's uncontrollable swings between old philosophy and new fiction—between Boethius and *Ghostwritten*—stems from the fact that *Ghostwritten* has already won out. There is in fact no socially viable choice between the two, even though the Maestro attempts to structure his private life as if there were. He *already* inhabits a hyperpluralistic "global" structure: multi-stranded, multi-voiced, and broadly cartographic in its points of reference. A model of modernity like Taylor's sees pluralism as the public commons in which all sorts of faiths and belief systems come together. On an individual level, for him, people and communities can still pursue a coherent line of thinking; the challenge comes in mass coordination. A novel like Huchu's sees "systematicity" itself—that is, an emphasis on networks, connection, and multidirectional movement—as prohibitive of even privately following ideas through. In his insistence on claiming a space to think deeply and hard, he forfeits his social legibility.

Before dwindling down to the Maestro's "inadvertent" suicide at the end of his portion of the novel, it is worth noting here that his heady musing stands in stark contrast to the book's two other plotlines. In story arcs that follow two fellow members of Edinburgh's Zimbabwean diaspora, each of these main characters moves steadily *away* from their intellectual modalities and toward some form of social integration. To be clear, no one benefits from this: by the end of *MMM*, all three lives are either over or mired in deception. Unlike the Maestro, however, the Magistrate and the Mathematician at least make some kind of peace with themselves amid their respective national and class mobilities. The Magistrate, the ex-judge with whom the book begins, does so by abandoning a staunchly patriarchal vision of legal and historical cultivation in order to live with the downward mobility his emigration entails. This normalization correlates strongly to the textual medium by which he imagines his relation to the world. He is first revealed when described as not "one for fiction anyway. A serious man concerned himself with facts, newspapers, journals, textbooks and the occasional biography, especially if the subject was an influential figure in law or politics" (4). By the end of the book, however, the Magistrate has learned to accept all manner of contemporary disorderliness: his teenage daughter Chenai breaks with Shona conservatism when she becomes pregnant with a white boyfriend's child; the Magistrate takes a job in a nursing home in order to help pay bills at home and save his flailing marriage; and his media diet is the music on his Walkman (71). By then, there is no further mention, let alone valorization, of the written word.

The Mathematician, an economics doctoral student named Farai, is likewise ushered into social integration in Edinburgh. He starts off living mainly through his penchant for abstraction of a "real" rather than philosophical sort: an avid number cruncher and stock market buff, he frequently calls his father in Zimbabwe to check on their gains and losses. Here too, the Mathematician's mode of thinking is symbiotic with his media consumption. The second line of his introductory section describes his LCD radio clock, even integrating a digital font into the text. Huchu proceeds to use literal symbols continuously through the rest of the section, with arrows marking the direction of various stock prices and the digital font reappearing as Farai watches CNN. In a deliberate echoing of the Magistrate's introduction, he also insists to a coffee shop acquaintance that he's a "serious man." "I don't read novels," Farai continues. "They're a waste of time. The last one I tried was Don Quixote, which was forced on me in my lit class in high school. I didn't even bother; I just bought the video and even that was boring. I thought, *sod this for a game of marbles*. In the end, I dropped the subject. Give me numbers, $, £, symbols" (24). Farai is also the novel's cipher for discussion of the rapid, shallow pace of contemporary media consumption: he "scans the familiar diet of war stories, crime and scandals" (ibid.), laughs cynically at Fox News (151), and scrolls through his email. He is largely inured to an earlier generation's indignities of race and politics, laughing off a racial insult and thinking callously that his former Zimbabwean house guard, having been beaten by ZANU-PF officials, "looks like 1 of those slaves from *Roots*" (154). All the while, Huchu shows Farai communicating in fits and starts via text message, especially with a working-class Scottish girlfriend, whom he eventually finds in bed with his contentious roommate, Scott. By the end of his plotline, however, the SMS medium channels more meaningful romantic prospects: he connects at a club with a woman named Supriti, by whom he is "pussy whipped," he ends up gladly admitting, while texting her things like "I dreamt of u last night xx" (247, 248).

But at this point Farai suddenly dies, bringing to fruition what has thus far seemed like a background plot of local ZANU-PF machinations. In the meantime of his social trials and tribulations, he had stumbled on a Portuguese research archive with incriminating details about Zimbabwean involvement with Mozambique. It is for this reason that he ends up stabbed by a political operative, who frames his wayward roommate for the crime. In one light, this twist may seem like a timely (even trendy) instance of genre fiction intruding on a more literary-experimental novel, as Tsitsi Jaji and Lily Saint suggest in their recent introduction to a special issue of the *Cambridge Journal of Postcolonial Literary Inquiry* (156). Crucially, however, Farai's thoughts at death drift from words into video game icons, with small, black Pacman faces punctuating and then disrupting his last inner monologue about his new love. While the Magistrate can to some degree be read as representing an older African literary model of the migrant, a figure who moves from a "peripheral" nation and is forced to make his or her way within a former imperial center, Farai serves as Huchu's exemplar of a younger, tech-savvy Afropolitan. His death quite literally seems to embody Paul Virilio's seminal concept of the "dromosphere," defined as the violent conversion of speed itself into modernity's primary medium as it races toward what he calls the "hidden figure of catastrophe and of catalytic accident" (156). As if purposefully describing the hyperconnected Farai's swift replacement, on the page, with a tiny digital icon, Virilio links speed through technological advancement to a "crisis of dimensions," a process of "miniaturization," and "the will to clear away obstacles" that accompanies "an accelerated depression of forms and volumes" (ibid.). Were we only dealing with the Magistrate and the Mathematician, an interesting if fairly straightforward reading of *MMM* would thus present itself: the intrusion of genre fiction in the form of a political thriller stages the collision of postcolonial and global modernity through Shona culture and politics. Huchu's work, were one to follow this thread, would be innovative because it pairs the highly convention-driven (and thus "universal") appeal of urban crime fare with more distinctive traits of the Shona diaspora.[11]

Indeed, in the background plot of what turns out, under Robert Mugabe's regime, to be maliciously engineered diasporic opposition politics, Shona is a crucial ingredient in the reader's understanding of Huchu's humor and, later, of plot foreshadowing. The language thus seems to work as a specific medium for what could find broader relevance as an example of African languages' subversive "multiple modernity."[12] Shona is both the platform *from* which the Magistrate globalizes in his acceptance of his young daughter's mixed-race, English-speaking, MTV-obsessed life and the platform *to* which Farai and his friends revert in their most generationally quintessential moments. "Loud music pours from the [party] building," we read at one point. And then, without translation, the atmosphere is set with "Ndizvo chete, zvandinoda, kukutaurira asi ndashaya mazwi" (All I want is to tell you, but I can't find the words) (187), which a Shona-conversant reader will recognize as a popular Zimbabwean "urban grooves" song from the pivotal year 2000. Elsewhere, at a hilarious anti-Mugabe rally, people shout "Pamberi nemusangano" (Onward with the meeting), "Pamberi naPresident Tsvangirai"(Onward with President Tsvangirai), and "Pasi nemadzukatsaku" (Down with insurgents) (104). Most notable, however, is Huchu's switch to Shona in a conversation about the difficulty and expense of shipping an unknown local Zimbabwean man's body home. (Either Farai or his friend Brian is speaking; it's not quite clear.) "I heard of a dead singer who was stuck here for a year because his family couldn't afford to ship his body home," one of the young men says. "*Inobva kupi 5* grand *yekubhururutsa chitunha nendege?*" (It starts at $5,000 to get a body flown home) (249). Farai, the would-be high-flying financier, might as well be discussing his own impending death.

In fact, they are speaking of the Maestro's death, in a scene that perfectly captures the larger dynamic around which I have structured this chapter. Two men, standing in for two different means by which the African novel comes to its global contemporary expression, converge in a discussion of a third man, who has died in an act of prolonged resistance to this same historical inertia. For in his own final pages, the Maestro is revealed to have succeeded in locking himself within the impenetrable confines of his own mind. Though he decides at the last minute that he wants to find love with his Polish friend instead of starving to death, it is too late: he lies down to rest in the snow outside her house and freezes to death, reminiscing for the first time about Zimbabwe, before he breaks off midsentence and lapses into death (221). As the book's sole inheritor of the "literary-philosophical" strain of intellectual life, he is also the most socially isolated of its characters, both in life and in death. Huchu posthumously reveals that the Maestro's real name was David Mercer; he also reveals that Mercer was white, and thereby removed from even the Shona medium by which the political shadow-novel has been progressing all the while. Mercer's removedness, then, which results in his long, drawn-out suicide by seclusion, also applies to both the genre (the novel of ideas) and the epistemology (literature) through which Huchu renders him. While the Magistrate and the Mathematician are recognizable male Zimbabwean "types," the Maestro lives in and dies by his mind. He is therefore marked as an oddity within a novel that is also, for the most part, an exception to the place-oriented norms of internationally conscious African literary fiction. In two senses, then—one on the page and the other in a novelistic self-conception that is at odds with the global market referenced by the book—Huchu's "philosophical novel" is doomed. In this, however, he also offers the possibility of its global persistence. *The Maestro, the Magistrate, and the Mathematician* stages a timely mix of media savvy, political commentary, multilingual sensibility, and structural experimentation, tempered finally with a rare taste for an almost obsolete register of searching for a sense of why it all matters at all.

Imraan Coovadia's Measured Thinking

Ideas, in *Demons*, precede their fulfillment as death, in both Kirillov's suicide and his nihilist associates' murder of the character Shatov (a plot turn based on the Russian revolutionary thinker Sergei Nechayev's real-life murder of a man named Ivanov, who dissented from group opinion). This is precisely the problem: ideas are *so* damn powerful that they have the capacity to dehumanize those whom they captivate. In *The Maestro, the Magistrate, and the Mathematician*, Tendai Huchu invokes Kirillov in a context of global migration to reverse this formula. Ideas still fuel the Maestro's self-starvation as he fights to claim a space of deep private thought, but his death illustrates philosophy's structural powerlessness instead of its agency. In his crowning achievement, *Tales of the Metric System*, journeyman South African novelist Imraan Coovadia inverts this equation: the novel positions philosophy, not as an agent of violence, but as its by-product. Coovadia's book, like Huchu's, affects a "global" form by moving erratically among multiple plots, at different locales, carried by different characters whose lives intersect just briefly (and often at random). As he describes his process of writing the book in a recent issue of *Current Writing*, "I kept wanting to figure out how do you include lots of different spaces without it seeming artificial or too much like an obvious contrast. I think that's why in *Metric System* I wanted to have like ten different spaces, not one of which was more important than another, but all kind of equally distributed rather than one major contrast or opposition" (96). The ten different plots to which he refers are divided into sections headed by references variously to their period or setting ("School Time," "Soviet Embassy"), to a significant object ("The Pass," "Vuvuzela"), or to a central event ("Truth and Reconciliation"). These sections, each of which appears only once, are arranged in nonchronological order and cover time frames from 1970, when the metric system was introduced in South Africa; to 1999, which saw the close of the post-apartheid Truth and Reconciliation Commission; to 2010, the year of the FIFA World Cup.

This many-faceted structure builds on but also departs from the noted cosmopolitanism of Coovadia's previous four novels, produced between 2001 and 2012.[13] "With the rise of transnational relations and its accompanying theories gaining ground in cultural analysis," notes Ronit Frenkel in *Current Writing*, "and the concomitant shift towards understanding South Africa in terms of its blendings and ambiguities, Coovadia's narratives seem to be one of the forces informing South African cultural and literary studies of the present" (1). And yet *Tales of the Metric System*'s sheer profusion of plotlines, put forth in elaborate coordination, marks Coovadia's first foray into what I have described as a more precise definition of global form. Also owing to this jumpy design, a number of critics have made stock comparisons between Coovadia and David Mitchell (whose *Ghostwritten* appears in *The Maestro, the Magistrate, and the Mathematician* as a foil to Dostoevsky and Boethius) and Adichie's *Americanah*. Huchu's *The Maestro, the Magistrate, and the Mathematician* is in fact a much more apt literary pairing, since it embeds a global structure—that is, a design that favors multidirectional movement across space rather than development over time—within a national set of issues and events. Coovadia, like Huchu as well as Makumbi in the preceding chapter, thereby cedes (probably knowingly) his claim to "global writing" of a more obvious, commercially viable sort. *Tales of the Metric System* is in this sense more of an antagonist to *Ghostwritten* or *Americanah*, which both take for granted that globality is best represented by a *maximally* transnational, and thus perhaps overly literal, jet-setting structure.

Like Huchu, Coovadia also demands significant interpretive work from the reader to make sense of how his plots' rare intersection might matter, as he distracts from the gravity of their contents through visual experiments on the page. Along with the varying section headers, there are small black-and-white illustrations of sections' namesake objects (like a vuvuzela, the infamous little horn from the 2010 World Cup held in South Africa) and other objects that serve as quaint and inviting lead-ins to what are often their socially fraught contents. A section called "Sparks," for example, is headed with a gun, in reference to the career of its main character, Sparks, as an aide and protector to African National Congress leadership in the struggle against apartheid (and also to the real-life figure Sparks is based on, former South African president Thabo Mbeki's spokesperson Parks Mankahlana). "Where there was Sparks there was fire," the chapter opens, a pun on Sparks's role as a "last line of defense" in the tumultuous 1980s: he was known for packing heat in his vinyl briefcase (286–87). Coovadia then abruptly channels his wry style toward a deeply felt focus on Sparks's life ending in a death that results from Mbeki's notorious HIV/AIDS denialism. The labor that sorting through such tonal discrepancies demands is best described by a line from the book itself: a minor character praises novels over life because "in a play or a novel we keep sight of each person and we demand to know what happens to him and to him and to him. In real life, we lose track of people all the time. They simply disappear and reappear without compunction" (279). The narrative nodes of *Tales of the Metric System* converge only rarely, and it is the reader's business to determine when and whether such points are moments of consequence.

It is this attribute of a global reading practice that Derek Attridge, in his review of the novel for *Public Books*, seems to miss when he bemoans that "the attempt to create imaginative fiction that is at the same time an engagement with history results in a confusing mishmash of the two kinds of writing." Whereas Attridge in his use of descriptors such as "uncomfortable," "uneasy," and "discomfiting" seems to suppose that Coovadia's novel of nation would be improved by cohesion of voice (or even genre), in fact *Tales of the Metric System* formally internalizes something more like the final turn in Edward Said's thinking about contrapuntalism. In *Humanism and Democratic Criticism*, Said describes this concept as "a form . . . expressing motion, playfulness, discovery, and, in a rhetorical sense, invention" (25). Whereas *Ethiopia Unbound*, as discussed in this book's first chapter, achieves this inventive effect through wide formal synthesis, Coovadia attains it by putting different genres of the novel—roman à clef, national epic, spy fiction, and philosophical fiction, to name but a few—in erratic collision with one another. The intended effect, however, is the same, in that it models the process of groping toward broad historical connection, which "will always remain open to changing combinations of sense and signification" and "whose usefulness is that it shows us history as an agonistic process still being made" (Said, ibid.). Notably, Said means contrapuntalism here as a tool for critiquing Western-centered humanist methods and institutions in the name of a more enduring humanism. (He takes memorable aim at the Yale critic Harold Bloom.) This goal is especially relevant to *Tales of the Metric System*, as it surveys a wide range of literary and philosophical canons, from Russian anarchism (Bukharin, Kropotkin) to French existentialism (Sartre) to historical materialism (Marx, Mao) to Black Consciousness (Biko). The book suggests that humanism, like history, is a moving target, but one at which it is nonetheless worth taking aim.

One way in which Coovadia stakes claim to working through the deepest meaning of life also specifically coincides with Huchu's novel and its use of Dostoevsky. And yet in Coovadia's intellectual rhapsody about the idea of "testing God" (also one of the Maestro's favorite topics, borrowed, of course, from Kirillov), sacrificial death is what *prompts* a turn to philosophizing rather than the result of a self-consuming philosophic temperament. This occurs in a pivotal section called "The Necklace," set in Durban, South Africa, in 1990 (the title is a reference to a cruel death by burning tire that became a symbol of township violence during apartheid), and the Dostoevskian resonances are unmarked but unmistakable. (I have confirmed the Russian influences on the novel in personal correspondence with the author.) "God doesn't love a young thief," the chapter begins, before the reader is introduced to a desperate boy named Shabelo who is "shouting for his life" as he bangs on a man's window "begging the occupant to allow him to enter" (165). The man here is Mr. Shabangu, a character readers recognize from a previous section of the novel as a local building caretaker and locksmith who also trades in apartheid passbooks (the infamous *dompas*, in colloquial Afrikaans) and steals things to hoard in his room.

Mr. Shabangu's community has no idea that he is a thief, and he calmly stands by as Shabelo is surrounded by an angry mob for the same crime. He does not think very hard about the boy's impending death: "He didn't like the commotion, at his age, so early in the day, nor the fact that the boy had drawn attention to his house. Why today of all days? And what did the boy have to gain? He didn't stand a chance of escaping from his punishment" (ibid.) Mr. Shabangu provides the reader with a historical perspective on punishment, not a philosophical one, as he matter-of-factly describes police passivity in the wake of Nelson Mandela's release from prison on Robben Island (166). The pages leading up to Shabelo's death also offer an almost lyrically detailed and comprehensive description of the South African township as Shabangu observes its tin shacks, its burned-out vehicles, and its recurring characters (167). It is what might recently be called an example of "surface reading," concerned mainly with texture and empathetic facticity. The absence of a clear destination for Mr. Shabangu's guided tour is captured in a telling, free-indirect bit of access to his mind: "He had forgotten how to measure his own life" (168).

As the young Shabelo's inevitable death draws nearer, however, Shabangu is less and less able to maintain his descriptive distance. This also begins a crucial process of separating Shabangu's intellectual consciousness from the township community in which he is physically immersed; his mind comes narratologically unhinged from his body. Musing about what he would say to his neighbors were they to discover that he himself is an inveterate thief, Shabangu departs from rational explanations for his behavior and enters the realm of metaphysical speculation. "He would admit that he was worse than they were," he begins, to himself. And then soon after, "That he neither hated nor loved himself as he appeared to the eye of God. That he was simply the thing that he was. That no man was better than him" (169). Meanwhile, a familiar man, taking charge of Shabelo's fate, coolly "leaned on a length of pipe, listing the allegations. Shabelo had been a long-time nuisance" (170). Shabangu is at one point consulted as to the community's best course of action, and he responds only that they "must do what [they] believe is correct" (171). The chasm between Shabangu's silent intellectualizing and his public pronouncements all the while grows still wider. "How did you measure the right punishment? What were the right units to balance the crime and the penalty?" (172), he wonders internally, locked by choice outside social agency. Even though Shabangu thinks that "Shabelo [is] too young to be murdered in the open" (173), he joins with the crowd in passing a matchbox around to light the neck-tire aflame. This split self—a presentational mind-body dualism—breaks provocatively with, for example, René Girard's classic expositions of collective cohesion through human sacrifice. "Scapegoat indicates both the innocence of the victims, the collective polarization in opposition to them, and the collective end result of that polarization," he writes in *The Scapegoat* (39). What he calls a "full system of representation" entails the individual's inability to recognize scapegoating when he or she is part of a social body that coheres through division (40). In "The

Necklace," however, the crowd is *not* polarized; dissent occurs only within a lone individual mind. If Girard urged humanistic texts closer to understandings of group behavior derived from social science, then Coovadia urges social science back toward a quintessentially humanistic mode of representation. Dynamism here is a private affair that results in nothing at all, not a shared phenomenon of group identity.

The wedge between intellection and community acceptance is fully realized as the section evolves from internal monologue to dialogue. As Shabelo burns to death, Shabangu thinks he also hears the boy philosophically weighing his suffering. Shabangu remarks:

> You could hear Shabelo talking softly but determinedly to his assailants. You heard him explain his plans, reminding them that he had never stolen anything more than a bag of white sugar to make caramel. You heard him distinguish between the man who stole as a luxury, as a way of testing his relationship to God, and the boy who was hungry enough to sell false information and who might have done nothing more than call up the talking clock to find out the time. He muttered that accusation wasn't the same thing as proof. (175)

It's entirely unclear whether this is meant to be an accurate depiction of what's happening—whether Shabangu, that is, has reverted to his descriptive role—or whether Shabangu is superimposing his own intellection onto the victim. On some level it doesn't matter: Shabelo dies either way. My point here is that "testing God," and the turn it signals toward Kirillovesque philosophical stakes, happens *because* of death, not *as* death. The thinking and the dying are two discrete parts of a scene: ideas are not integrated into a socially significant character. Shabelo's death turns Shabangu into a lay philosopher, but at no point does philosophy therefore become a social act. Shabelo's deathly "embodiment" as the ultimate expression of the social will gives way to the utter solitude of deep reflection, possibly even in an act of narrative transference from the burning Shabelo's words to the observing Shabangu's thoughts.

In response to numerous inquiries as to whether something is wrong after Shabelo's body has burned, Shabangu only grows *more* silent, musing on redemption, and Christ, and the moral metrics appropriate to a godless world. (It is interesting, too, that he veers at one point into thinking about fire "in the mining shafts, fire in the workers' hostels and train stations, infinite tides of fire to make the world honest" [178], as a house burning down is also a signal event in Dostoevsky's *Demons*.) At one point, a local friend named Alfred inquires, "Do you have something on your conscience?" to which Shabangu answers, tersely and out loud, only that everyone does. The reader, however, is jarred back into thoughts that could have been lifted straight from Kirillov as he formulates his motivation to kill himself—or, for that matter, straight from the Maestro's sections of *The Maestro, the Magistrate, and the Mathematician*. "There was. There wasn't," Shabangu thinks to himself. "There was no method to answer the greater part of the questions which could be put to a man. There was no such thing as a conscience independent of God" (183). When he then ventures that "he might steal something from God" (186) in exacting his own retribution on himself by reflecting on the necklacing so it "[burns] through his joy until there was nothing but ash in his heart" (ibid.), it is clear that Shabangu's socially alienated mind has taken the place of either God or mankind as the novel's culminating subject of investigation. "What if there was nobody better than a thief to hold the world together?" he finally ponders, in reference to the two men crucified side by side with Jesus. By this point it is quite clear that there isn't: evacuated of ideas for which to seek actions, Coovadia's township public coheres around petty persecutions from which ideas only sporadically emerge as an individually alienating force.

Tales of the Metric System also broaches the domain of professional philosophy in a way that maps readily onto this chapter's multi-stranded discussion of intellection as a close cousin to death. In this case, ideas are again the self-willed cause of a life's ending. The structure of Coovadia's account, however, subverts the notion of literary "suicide" as either a culmination or climax of the will, or as an individual act of historical representation (drawing on the early examples from Soyinka and Achebe). His character Neil Hunter is based on the radical white philosopher of the Black Consciousness era, Rick Turner, whose only book before he died was *The Eye of the Needle—Towards Participatory Democracy in South Africa* (1972). Turner is best known for expounding a radically nonracial vision of South Africa's future in which white and black South Africans would be jointly liberated. As the South African *Daily Maverick* columnist Marianne Thamm polemically reminded readers in 2014, Turner's work also emphasized the power of individual choice in forging new social collectivities. He understood, quoting Thamm, that "people first needed to turn inwards and perform a sort of deep, psychic root canal on themselves to be truly liberated."

In this sense, as Coovadia's imagining of Turner's life suggests through his fictional wife Ann, there was a remarkable consistency between his notion of the individual and that of the body politic. "The contradiction was Neil's all-purpose explanation," Ann thinks. "This country was in a state of contradiction, starting with an economy which made many rich and far too many poor. The individual was also in contradiction between his heart and his mind, the angel and his demon. Anywhere there was life, there was contradiction" (35). Almost certainly assassinated by apartheid state security forces through his window in 1978 (just months after Steve Biko was beaten to death in 1977), the Turner of the novel runs a free university in his home for like-minded activist-intellectuals. He offers a bridge in multiple senses: he moves between the insurgent and mostly young black South African intellectual world, as well as among aging European philosopher counterparts, including Jean-Paul Sartre (ibid.). He is also one of the most frequently recurring figures in the book, stitching together multiple temporalities and character constellations.

Hunter is introduced within the novel through other people whom he has affected, first his wife Ann, who recalls that he "had the strength of his convictions. It made him inhuman in certain respects" (36)—for example, when he did not intervene when Sartre once made a sexual advance toward her. We do not, that is, encounter Hunter first as a living, breathing man, but as an abstracted analysis of manhood. This is also the mechanism by which Coovadia acquaints the reader with Hunter's ideas, as Ann is left to tend to a student discussion group on Fanon when he shows up late. Later a character named Polk, based on the South African playwright Athol Fugard, provides a similarly once-removed account of Neil's intellectual disposition, noting that "Neil doesn't really like plays and novels," as he "prefers abstract concepts instead of life itself. Neil sees the world in a straight line" (69). More consequential, however, is the ensuing introduction of Hunter's death. In a section called "Boxing Day," which takes place among mostly working-class Durban Indians in 1979, a young man named Yash introduces his cousin Logan as a heavy-thinking activist just released from detention by apartheid officials "only because of the publicity around Neil Hunter's murder and Logan's connection to the case" (114).

If this chronology begins to sound muddled, that's because it is: to summarize, we first meet Hunter as a living but peripheral character, and we then encounter him as a posthumous "idea" in his own right. Logan's friend Satya, also Indian, then toes a distinctly cosmopolitan line in his rendition of Black Consciousness philosophy. "Biko teaches us that the real revolution comes in consciousness," he opines. "First, we free our minds. For that we can use the best of thinking from around the world" (118). Like Hunter, he also links Black Consciousness to a strong sense of contiguity between individual and collective. Unlike Hunter, however, he rejects the notion of objective truth. "I would tell him that it matters out of whose mouth the sentence is coming," Satya continues. "That if a true sentence comes out of the wrong mouth, it cannot help but be false" (119). All of this heady discussion of the relation among state, truth, and individual takes place with no actual representation of its focal point in any depth by Coovadia.

Hunter does finally appear as a full-blooded character with a mind, rather than just thoughts rehearsed by others, in the last section of the book, called "The Pool." The reader will note here that the chronology looks backwards from the year of his assassination, which has already been revealed and discussed as a key link between other characters and sections. Hunter, at novel's end, is under house arrest with his new wife (not Ann) and has been granted permission only to swim to maintain his health. "In the pool Neil didn't worry about Logan," Coovadia writes, "the young teacher who had disappeared" (368). Though Hunter is not worried, he is nonetheless deeply engaged in his intellectual project: he thinks through a brief description of his ideal society; meditates on the nature of freedom; and considers French philosophy in light of its climatological situation (368–69). The last point is especially significant, as it situates Hunter's work (and Turner's) very clearly in the locality of Durban. "The hot form of life, the existence in the body," he thinks, "precluded the other form" (369). It is the socially *immediate* philosophy of the humid South African coast that therefore counteracts the "unnecessary death and destruction" of European civilization over the past two centuries (371). The remainder of the section unfolds as a beautiful synthesis of well-known philosophical forms and tropes, namely a dialogue between Hunter and one of his students, and Hunter's reflection on the murder of Socrates "on account of his strangeness" (372). Rick Turner, in this way, is narrativized along with South Africa in its darkest days as the rightful inheritor of a global philosophical tradition, the fruition of thought in the form of a committed individual. Except that the narrative then veers off this course and back onto that of its disaggregated historical plot. We already know that Hunter is dead: he has offered himself as a political target in order for his thinking to persist.

In effect, Coovadia positions Hunter in three different sorts of literary relation to philosophy. In the first, his ideas serve the project of "character" (that is, his role as husband to the narrator of the section we are reading), and in the second his personhood is effaced to allow his ideas to rise to the "abstraction" of intellectual conversation that reveals their social impact (in the reflections of the young Indian activists after his death). Only in the third do we see the man and the ideas in concert. This final unity on the level of character/intellect, however, is the *least* narratively effective instance of Hunter's appearance in terms of the novel's overarching cohesion or what we might call its globally modeled plot (albeit mostly superimposed on a national situation). The chronological flashback that delivers Hunter's assassination—"The window had already splintered into the stars when you heard a gunshot and became aware of the overwhelming scent of gunpowder in your nose" (389)—means that the novel concludes with an anticlimax: the man is dead before he dies.

Hunter's connection to his fellow South Africans beyond a limited circle of like-minded thinkers is purely formal, as we see when Coovadia deploys a narratological technique that he has used a number of times throughout *Tales of the Metric System* to mark death (including the section in which Thabo Mbeki's aide dies of AIDS). It is a subtle switch from a third-person to a second-person singular pronoun, from a "he" to a "you," that seems to connote some sort of intimacy between narrator and character but cannot quite rise to the level of sustaining structural momentum. "You remembered the scenes in classical poems," Hunter thinks just after this perspectival switch, "where someone went down to the underworld, conversed with the people condemned there, and then returned to the surface" (386). In his death on the book's final page, Hunter himself returns to the surface of South Africa, as the moment briefly rewinds to allow him a glimpse of his own assassination. Hunter's ideas have not structurally led anywhere after all; he is not Kirillov, or even a Maestro. Instead, his ideas have been put forth and reshuffled, in life and death, and constitute only one among many broken vectors along which South African history jerks and bumbles from a national to a global set of structural conventions.[14]

Coda: Masande Ntshanga's The Reactive *and the Rewards of Self-Affliction*

Hunter, like the Maestro, has committed a suicide of nonresistance: he has not picked up a gun to end his life, but he has knowingly brought on his death. Although Hunter is killed for his ideas, his death is immaterial to their meaning within *Tales of the Metric System*'s globally disarrayed design (which is not the same thing as saying that they are irrelevant to the novel's depiction of Rick Turner's significance as a thinker). Ideas, in other words, are acted upon from without rather than from within; they circulate through a loosely coherent structure rather than coming to fruition as a representative individual choice.

To end this chapter I would like to turn briefly to a final South African novel from 2014, Masande Ntshanga's debut book, *The Reactive*, to sketch a slightly different version of the interrelation of suicide, intellection, and globality. It is worth noting, too, that *The Reactive* is connected to *The Maestro, the Magistrate, and the Mathematician* and to *Tales of the Metric System* in both the general and specific conditions of its production and international circulation. Ntshanga worked under Coovadia's mentorship at the University of Cape Town's MA program in creative writing, and like the previous two works, *The Reactive* found US publication with a small, independent literary press (in this case, Two Dollar Radio, a forward-thinking family outlet run from Columbus, Ohio). Thus, while Ntshanga's book has met with considerable acclaim, it occupies a markedly different niche of global African cultural production from what has been called the "million-dollar club" of young African novelists currently dominating most discussion abroad.[15]

Part of the difficulty in placing *The Reactive* stems from its self-conscious intellectualism, which is to say both its fluency in a "high" literary and philosophical idiom and its penchant for inward rather than explicitly social projection. As Coovadia put it wryly at the novel's Cape Town book launch, Ntshanga's debut "represents a thirty-year long introspection on being in the world."[16] Its main character, Lindanathi, is a University of Cape Town dropout who lives with two close friends huffing glue, waxing philosophical, and reading books like Camus's existentialist debut *A Happy Death* (24). To do this, they congregate mostly in a bohemian-styled living room adorned with their homemade copy of Rothko's *No 4* painting (13) and very occasionally attend outside parties where they listen to people "talk shit about Nietzsche" (89). The multiracial band of three—Nathi, Cissie, and Ruan—are quickly introduced as outsiders to the norms of apartheid-era South African writing. "The three of us aren't slaves," Nathi observes. "[We] wrote matric in the country's first batch of Model cs [formerly white-only, partly fee-based public high schools]. In common, our childhoods had the boomerangs we used to throw with the neighborhood kids, the rollerblades and the green buckets of space goo." In a single word, then, they shared what Nathi calls "ease" (25). The near-constant drug use effectively becomes the novel's medium, steering its somewhat distant but precise first-person style as it moves fluidly between dialogue (without quotation marks), Nathi's immediate thoughts, and his broader recollections of their friendship and his personal past.

Per Ntshanga's own description in an interview for the website Brittle Paper conducted by my students at Johns Hopkins University (Jackson et al., 2017), the drugs permit a "preoccupation with consciousness; this idea of a fluid mental self and how that self shifts and evolves in relation to various stimuli and its environment." It also speaks to the in-between historical position of the characters: they must search for some sort of self-actualization absent the immediate political pressures of apartheid and without a clear economic future as South Africa's educated "born-free" or "millennial" generation contending with the precarities of finding employment in a globalized marketplace. Lindanathi has HIV, and he and his flatmates play a game called "Last Life" whose only aim is free-roaming speculation on what he should do with the time he has left. Free-roaming speculation, in fact, is the only real occupation Ntshanga offers to his motley cast of characters, aside from cooking glue. "What if babies cry because birth is the first form of human incarceration?" Cissie asks once out of nowhere. "What if it's a lasting shock to the consciousness to be imprisoned inside the human body? If the flesh is something that's meant to go off from the beginning, doesn't that make it an ill fit, since the consciousness, naturally amorphous, is antithetical to disintegration?" (26). At best they are a lost generation, and at worst a self-indulgent group of privileged twenty-somethings.

On this point, however, two key factors intervene to make Nathi a less than ideal representative figure for the "global" South African novel. First, Lindanathi's HIV was self-inflicted while he worked at a research laboratory. He is atoning for his immense guilt surrounding the death, eight years prior, of his less economically well-off younger half-brother, Luthando, whose traditional Xhosa coming-of-age circumcision (an infection resulting from which is the cause of his death) Nathi fails at the last minute to attend. To make matters worse, Lindanathi and his friends financially sustain themselves by selling his antiretroviral medication, so that they literally profit from most South Africans' lack of access to treatment. Second, *The Reactive*'s efforts to depict globality are not structural but stylistic. By this I mean that whereas Huchu and Coovadia subjugate character consciousness to their multi-stranded, transnational plot structures, Ntshanga's depiction of global conditions is entirely through Nathi's mind. And yet these two factors—Nathi's self-infection (and profiteering) and the book's preoccupation with his inwardness—together offer some measure of optimism about the possibility of attaining individual wholeness through reflection. At the novel's end, Nathi has arrived at the capacity to make a decision that advances his life rather than anticipates its ending: he falls in love and opts to return to his hometown in South Africa's Eastern Cape to undergo his own circumcision and thus be inducted into a

Xhosa lineage. As Ntshanga puts it again in the Brittle Paper interview, "I found the idea of [the characters] attempting to 'become,' yet lacking the imaginative vocabulary to do so, given their alienation from the national narrative and its heritage, not only bold, but also hopeful." Building on Andrew Van der Vlies's reading of *The Reactive* in his recent monograph *Present Imperfect: Contemporary South African Writing*, we might say that Lindanathi has deliberately embraced the stasis of his generation in order to think his way toward agency.

It is on this point, however, that some of *The Reactive*'s investments get lost in its reception thus far, which makes little of Nathi's penchant for either self-harm or an ensuing life of largely useless philosophical introspection. Perhaps unsurprisingly, the novel's focus on Nathi's individual sabotage as a catalyst for his later development has gone missing from most of *The Reactive*'s international reception. For example, American reviews of the book for the most part fail to note the fact that Nathi gives himself HIV, creating the impression that he is simply one of millions of poor South Africans infected with and unable to treat the virus during the era of Thabo Mbeki's disastrous AIDS denialism spanning the years 2000 to 2005.[17] The limited academic criticism the book has received is more provocatively divergent from my own reading of *The Reactive*. Van der Vlies writes that the novel may at first seem to operate within a structurally un-incisive market trend of South Africa's young black writers: "speaking in the present tense, about feelings of personal injury and impasse" (156). Ultimately, however, Nathi embraces the lackadaisical "waithood" (to use Van der Vlies's term) of the post-post-apartheid period in an "affirmative" way, in order to recapture a kind of self-examining, self-justifying liberal selfhood as against a fully marketized neoliberal one, epitomized by his selling off his medication (167). Van der Vlies thus worries that the book's final turn back to tradition may be reactionary, which is to say a misplaced valorization of authenticity as an alternative to socially generative doubt. Drawing on the affect theorist Eugenie Brinkema and, in particular, her analysis of anxiety in existential philosophy, he suggests that psychoanalysis, not philosophy, provides the book's most useful analytic tool kit. Freud, Van der Vlies explains, arrives ultimately at the view that anxiety arises from a *failure* to intervene in repressive systems, rather than from a profound awareness of the future's contingency, multiplicity, and possible meaninglessness.

I do not wish to get lost in the deep rabbit holes of either affect theory or psychoanalysis, or to question Van der Vlies's reading of Brinkema and Freud on its own terms. What I do want to highlight is the need his reading expresses to somehow displace the philosophical inclinations of both Nathi and *The Reactive* onto something that better resembles social or political utility (or even its foreclosure). In this way, it has something in common with readings of the novel that eclipse the complicating factor of Nathi's self-harm in order to make more of his social representativeness. One way to think about the difference between my reading of *The Reactive* and Van der Vlies's might be that whereas I see Nathi as mainly a figure through which Ntshanga explores the deliberate loss of and coming back into selfhood amid pervasively hostile global conditions, Van der Vlies urges the text toward the related but not quite synonymous category of social subjectivity. The difference here is perhaps a matter of an "ultimate" morality versus a latent politics, or of self-exploration as a project that is adjacent to but distinct from its social situation. Clearly self-exploration and one's social situation are conjoined, and it is difficult to imagine any target audience for *The Reactive* that is at risk of social unawareness. In *Sources of the Self*, however, Charles Taylor argues that selfhood is "essentially linked to our sense of the good" (51), in distinction, perhaps, to our sense of the "right." For *The Reactive*, this fundamentally philosophical level of self-formation precedes Nathi's discovery of its point of social relevance or intervention. Indeed, the end of the novel points to nothing much more than Nathi's growing capacity for pleasure and mental calm. After a rousing sex scene with his girlfriend on the final page, he remarks, "I close my eyes; but this time, unlike so many others in my life, I don't clench them" (197).

There is no doubt, finally, that *The Reactive* is a book of penetrating engagement with the social and political inequalities of contemporary South Africa, and that Ntshanga is acutely aware of the many pressing challenges of moving the country forward (wherever that may be). But need this mean, qua Van der Vlies, that the reflective arc he traces in Nathi must "lead towards action" that might save the world (172)? The most unusual accomplishment of the novel is its posing of a still *more* difficult challenge than figuring out the manifold ways in which the personal is always political, a message its readers have all heard a thousand times before. Ntshanga, in his own words, seeks to discover "how one actualizes as an individual on their own terms—in a society where their advantage always correlates with—or even depends on—the disadvantage of another" (Jackson et al., 2017). *The Reactive* is an experiment with trying to separate the cart from the horse, mind from matter, or the difficult work of thinking from the inevitable necessity of doing. In the age of incessant disruption and utility, his aims could be much worse.

Conclusion

The denser the archive of human experience, the less clear are the lines of the novel's development. This is true at the level of character (the "global novel" by any precise definition cannot work as a *bildung*), and it is true at the level of plot. (Gone too is the neat first-wave postcolonial fiction of one-way movement from colony to metropole.) More important for reckoning with the novel's most innovative futures, this is also true of the narrative logics by which ideas are fulfilled—or in this case, the logics by which ideas and their human vessels are left stranded. The notion of "free will" finds maximal expression for Dostoevsky in Kirillov's suicide, as philosophical history collapses into an iconic literary moment and then unfurls again into the real-life philosophical responses it inspires. An idea destroys a man speaking to and for his national public; that public, in turn, acquires the capacity to redeem all of humanity by returning to God.

For Tendai Huchu's Maestro, for Imraan Coovadia's Mr. Shabangu and Neil Hunter, and for Masande Ntshanga's Lindanathi, it is now the idea *of* ideas that provides some relief from a grotesquely disjointed and disorienting web of global systems. Intellection becomes not the source of but the solitary response *to* violence of varying sorts and degrees, as philosophical references flicker in and out of focus. In this way, Huchu and Coovadia suggest philosophy as just one among many modalities, but stop short of parsing the highest stakes their novels nonetheless haltingly audition. Ntshanga, for his part, avoids the trap of structural dissolution by chronicling a single consciousness. I am uncertain whether any of this is cause for celebration or solemnity, and I suspect that the writers featured in this chapter are of equally many minds about the novel's future. But together they indicate where we should be looking to keep the form's protean spirit alive: to universalism's former "peripheries," now its doubtful, scattered core.

Epilogue

SPECULATIONS ON THE FUTURE OF
AFRICAN LITERARY STUDIES

ONE OF THE DISCIPLINARY questions this book raises is that of how to navigate literary nonrepresentationality. By this I refer not to an abstract or anti-mimetic aesthetics, but rather ask how to advance a literary field when an implicit or explicit claim to "speak for" a large population grows untenable. For a long time, African literature occupied a marginal place in the Western academies and publishing circuits that drive most global literary commerce. In part as a result, it was seen to *represent marginality*. But in a context in which African writers not infrequently garner million-dollar advances, and in which most critics and scholars at least know enough to feel bad about having sparse knowledge of African traditions, "marginality" has run its course as an undergirding tenet of African literary production and pedagogy. While there is still much work to be done to increase Africa's presence in the humanities beyond African studies, the *reason* for doing so is not because Africa is marginal, but because it isn't. I do not suppose that a million-dollar contract means much to Africans writ large, nor do I think that Africa as an economic construct has risen above hardship introduced from without and upheld from within. But this too is part of the challenge: literary fiction in its own right these days represents little aside from the state of literary fiction, even where it grapples with profound social questions.

If one would be hard pressed to say that the state of a nation is measured in any real way by the vibrancy of its literary production (the United States seems like a strong case in point), then it is well near impossible to use literature to measure the state of an entire continent. The more robust a publishing landscape grows, for that matter, the less representative are any of its individual participants. Bibi Bakare-Yusuf, cofounder of Nigeria's thriving Cassava Press, makes this plain to the *Los Angeles Review* when she describes her mission in terms that diminish the capacity of any one writer to "speak for" a country, region, or identity:

> Nigeria will boast of a rich literary history when the variegated, insane, and complex expanse of Nigeria's human experience and imaginative world are published, known, read and legitimized both in Nigeria and overseas. We will have a rich literary history when the names of writers who are female, queer, and from diverse ethnic, class, or religious backgrounds can roll off our tongues as easily as other male and female writers from a particular ethnic, social, class, or linguistic configurations. The day we can speak of more than ten Nnedi Okorafors (speculative/fantasy fiction), ten Zaynab Alkalis (oft-cited female writer from the north), ten Olumide Popoolas (writing queer humanity), ten Yemisi Aribisalas (food writer and polemical non-fiction), ten Noo Saro-Wiwas (travel writing), and ten Zulu Sofolas (playwright) is the day we can begin to talk about Nigeria's rich literary history. (Mang, 2014)

As African literature gains stature in our institutions of formal teaching and learning, it is similarly fair to say that "African literature" as a term signifies less and less. By and large, this is a good thing. And while it is hard to generalize from any one scholar's experience, my own suggests that African literature is slowly becoming a bit more like my colleagues' better-entrenched fields, in which diversity and dissensus are taken as givens. African literature classes where I teach are routinely oversubscribed, especially at the introductory level. And students' preconceptions about the continent have grown less essentialist: they hail from a range of backgrounds, including African and Afro-diasporic, and for the most part arrive eager to push beyond stereotypes of a mythic "African perspective."

Perhaps I have simply been lucky, but I don't think so: the "African literary renaissance" has been widely remarked on by academics and critics alike. Like any movement that straddles continents and intellectual registers, it is prone to valorizing certain kinds of texts above others (witness, for example, the debate surrounding Chimamanda Adichie's adoring Western reception).[1] Despite this, and despite occasional bursts of resurgent dogmatism from some quarters, Tejumola Olaniyan is right when he writes that the "post-global" era is "tearing to shreds these our long-established canons of the self-understanding of our field. This is the reason for the extreme corporeal, locational, linguistic, formal, and thematic dispersion of contemporary African literature and literary theorizing" (395). He counts this dispersion as a salutary upending of earlier identity "tests" of language and geography and shows how broad humanistic principles might take the place of these tests while maintaining a stake in their goals. In reference to the legendary first African Writers Conference at Uganda's Makerere University in 1962, at which commitment to indigenous African languages was a major point of discussion, Olaniyan looks beyond what he sees as an outdated nativism. "The goal's logical end is still the ideal in any multi-language context: mutual translation," he suggests. "All languages ought to be thriving, not just as mother tongues but, also, and more critically, as tools of social mobility" (393). The overriding message of his intervention is in line with that of *The African Novel of Ideas*. One need not choose between Africa and universality or, for that matter, between Africa and anything else. It's *all* there, to anyone committed to looking.

At the same time, it is easy to feel that if African literature is everything, then it is nothing at all. Paradigms of dispersion, diffusion, or plurality can seem so definitionally weak as to call the very notion of a geographically identified literature into question. A broadened understanding of the field also comes with professional frustrations: I would venture that most "area" scholars now reading this know well the feeling of bristling when a colleague trained in the Victorian novel, or British Modernism, glibly declares that they will now include "an Africa/South Asia/other regional chapter" in their new book. If the pendulum swings too far in the other direction from Olaniyan's "tests," then the notion of expertise also begins to seem moot. There is a lot to be said for prizing knowledge as well as interest, for painstaking research and language training as well as high-flying arguments—in sum, for the granular sense of place and history that fields identified by geography tend to demand and by which their ideas must rise or fall. In other words, while the field of African literature is indeed a big tent, none of whose parts bears more intrinsic claim to "Africanness" than any other, it is still useful to think about what distinctive traits African literary studies and the African writing that it studies might contribute to the discipline at large.

I will start with the field and then pivot to the future of the novel of ideas within it. To my mind, two methodological tendencies born of resistance to Western epistemological hubris now offer strong credentials for discipline-wide leadership. First, the African literary humanities are premised on an inbuilt suspicion of unspoken and unearned generalization. Whereas scholars of European textuality have often simply taken it for granted that they are writing about "literature" or "language" as such, scholars of African traditions have constantly faced pressure to justify their claim to translocal significance. Olúfẹ́mi Táíwò captures this defensive position eloquently in his 1998 essay "Exorcising Hegel's Ghost: Africa's Challenge to Philosophy":

> It is only insofar as we confront, or have to deal with, or inhabit a world constructed by Western Philosophy that we are forced to think of an absence and of how to make sense of it. And we must confront our absence from the history of this tradition because, no thanks to colonialism and Christianization, we are inheritors and perpetrators of this heritage. Additionally, given that the "West" presents itself as the embodiment and inventor of the "universal," we must protest even more loudly that its universal is so peculiar and that its global is so local. (4)

While Táíwò's (attribution of Africa's being locked out of universality to Hegel above others might be arguable, his larger point about Hegel's undersourced and "bastard Universality" (10) still stands.

Táíwò's essay has also proved prescient as regards the conditions of scholarly activity required to begin moving toward a legitimate universalism, which is to say a universalism that is always on guard about the contingency of its identification as such. "Had [Hegel] availed himself of the material available in Europe at the time he was writing respecting African achievements," Táíwò notes, "he would have been forced to a radically different conclusion" (8). While Táíwò fully acknowledges that no amount of reading would have disabused Hegel of his racist views on Africa, he implicitly suggests that a generalized expectation of archival expansiveness might at least stymie unreflexive expressions of the part as the whole. *If* one does the reading, this line goes, ambition to grand claims will be both individually tempered and collectively affirmed: a geographically de-hierarchized academy is truly a group effort. Movements like Global Modernism, Global Romanticism, and V21, among many other initiatives, would seem to suggest that the default standards of argument in the discipline *are* changing. While not everyone will or should work on non-Western traditions, or even on questions of globality per se, it seems fair to say that there is increasingly little tolerance for work that does not acknowledge the challenges that a more pluralistic archive brings to the fore. Rather than see Africanist scholars as evolving toward the tacit assumption of universal status that has formatively characterized the "mainline" of literary studies in the West, I suggest that everyone else should evolve toward the foundational self-reflexivity of "marginalized" fields.

Related to this confluence of self-relativization and more defensible universal claim-making is locatedness, which I see as the second point on which African literary studies is ahead of the disciplinary curve. For better or worse, African writing is virtually *always* identified by location. In recent years, fiction writers in particular have chafed at the limitations this is seen to impose, as, for example, in a 2015 piece by the Scottish–Sierra Leonean writer Aminatta Forna in *The Guardian*. Riffing on a suggestion by Ngũgĩ wa Thiong'o years before that there should simply be one, inclusive Department of Literature, Forna describes her dismay at giving a talk at Oxford University and finding only Africanists in attendance. "All this classifying, it seems to me, is the very antithesis of literature," she proclaims. "The way of literature is to seek universality. Writers try to reach beyond those things that divide us: culture, class, gender, race. Given the chance, we would resist classification. I have never met a writer who wishes to be described as a female writer, gay writer, black writer, Asian writer or African writer." From a market standpoint as well as a moral one, Forna's position is understandable: a writer's points of origin are often multiple, and so even as a practical matter their attachment to a locale becomes difficult to manage. At the same time, her perspective works against the grain of some of the most rigorous African philosophical thinking included in this book (for example, by Appiah, Wiredu, Ramose, and Eze, not to mention Jennifer Makumbi), which seeks rather to model the *process* of getting from an African locality to its universal resonance.

We might thus keep Forna's widely shared frustration in mind while turning it on its head: instead of only non-Western literatures being identified by a point of origin, what if all literary scholars felt equally compelled to take account of their field's relationship to place? Once again, African philosophy has given serious thought to this question. "African philosophy," argues Bruce Janz, "has led the way in taking seriously the places and spaces in which philosophy happens and the constituencies and communities in which it matters. Philosophy in Africa analyzes (its) place as an object of inquiry, and also exists in that place in a wide variety of ways" (2017, 155–56). Janz, like Táíwò, sees this priority as having emerged from Africa's dis-privileged position in self-conceived "generalist" disciplinary conversations, so that it has been, from the get-go of its institutionalization, forced both to argue against Africa's "imposed identity in world history" (157) and to instantiate its far-reaching diversity of thought in reference to it. If, Janz continues, "epistemology has been constructed in the West as if there is no geography," or at least as if "any claims about responsibility to geography [are] less than philosophical" (159), then African philosophy has developed via acute attention to geographical and social-geographical barriers. It is crucial to note, too, that he is careful to differentiate place from space, in the sense that "space" can quickly become an abstraction devoid of the accountability to particularity that place demands. "Place" also allows for the critical bypassing of identity essentialisms, as it attends to ideas' interaction with geographical conditions rather than to categorization of their human arbiters in geographical terms.

I do not by any means intend for these traits to be a comprehensive list of what African literary studies has historically done well, or to imply that there are not other fields that have developed with similar emphases. What I *am* arguing is that moving our field forward requires helping it to generalize some of its main tenets: as Africanists look toward questions of broad relevance, so too should other fields internalize some of the pressures that Africanists have long faced. For this reason, one way to imagine strong work in African literature going forward is as a project of explicitly coupling a place-designated archive with a theme-, form-, or method-driven field. Instead of producing more work that offers readings of themes *in* literature, or that looks only at a given African archive's local or national implications, we might ask how African literature's meta-analytic investments can sharpen those of a field that is less geographically bound, and vice versa. Though this list is very far from exhaustive, some of the most provocative recent work in African literary and cultural studies has moved in this direction. Ato Quayson's *Oxford Street, Accra* (2014), a multicentury cultural history of a small but important piece of Ghana's capital, attracted attention from African and postcolonial humanists as well as urban historians, even winning a prize from the completely nonliterary Urban History Association in 2015. Cajetan Iheka's book *Naturalizing Africa* (2017) situates itself equally within African literary studies and the environmental humanities, making a persuasive case that Africa is at the vanguard of the latter field. Going back a bit further, Tsitsi Jaji's *Africa in Stereo* (2013) drew on Anglophone and Francophone African literary traditions, coupled with a deep formal understanding of music theory, to converse with the fields of musicology and sonic studies. I could go on.

Instead, I turn now to some further closing remarks on the African novel of ideas more specifically: I have structured this book around where it has been, and that raises the question, in turn, of where it might yet go. The first part of this epilogue maintains that African literary studies have an important stake in shaping the literary-critical field at large as it labors toward geographical de-hierarchization. It follows, then, that attending to particular African forms and genres can also crystallize broader challenges and (foreclosed) possibilities for the novel as such. The representational brand of philosophical individualism whose fate I have traced to this point is, I admit, untimely. This does not mean that it is outdated: it will continue to exist as a meaningful, if minoritarian, concern. At the same time, philosophical individualism is not what typifies the novel's response to current economic, political, and ecological crisis conditions, felt all the more acutely on the African continent. All of the novelists featured in *The African Novel of Ideas* share an investment in a capacity for reflective individualism that exists formally apart from the polity in which it is enmeshed, *even* in those cases where the two work in salutary relation to one another. Insofar as this is a realist preoccupation, however, the novels I discuss in this book's final chapter seem to have reached the end point of what new work this kind of philosophical figure can perform.

It is notable, then, that all three of the writers treated in this book's final chapter have turned to some variant of speculative fiction in recent years. Tendai Huchu has seen growing success in this arena with short stories published under the name T. L. Huchu, and in 2019 he signed a two-book deal with the prominent science fiction and fantasy outlet Tor Books. The first of the new titles will interweave Scottish Enlightenment philosophy with a plotline about magic. In 2018, Imraan Coovadia published a novel called *A Spy in Time*, about a post-apocalyptic philosopher–cum–secret agent–cum–time traveler. And in 2019, Masande Ntshanga followed up *The Reactive* with *Triangulum*, which chronicles South African history from the vantage of its ecological devastation in 2040. Even Ntshanga's publisher's copy foregrounds its wedding of philosophical ambition to generic hybridization.[2] The overarching effect of these careers, viewed alongside those of other spec-fic stars like Nnedi Okorafor, is thus to suggest that the forceful presence of ideas in fiction is retained by exceeding African locales as they "really" exist. This is *not* to indicate that Africa is somehow less philosophical than anywhere else; *The African Novel of Ideas*, I hope, has led its readers to the opposite conclusion. On the contrary, I mean to position African writers at what is perhaps an alarming vanguard: a philosophical selfhood with worldly and narrative force would now appear to be a globally fantastic premise.

Realism, meanwhile, has moved on—or more accurately, circled back to keep on doing what it has always done well. There is no shortage of lives and situations demanding scrupulous attention, no dearth of social worlds ripe for nuanced and perhaps sympathetically mobilizing characterization. At its best, this is what the bulk of critically acclaimed Anglophone African fiction offers: the African novel need not be conceptually innovative, just formally *good*. The measure of realist success, in this view, is in the richness and to some degree the accuracy of the content. While it may not make for duly thrilling academic explication (though it *does* often make for rewarding teaching), it is worth remembering that it is no easy feat to put the present on the page, or to give the past a vivid new life. This is doubly true when writers are able to make multilingual experience legible to readers who lack the same translational skills, as in some of the best recent African historical fiction. The high-profile valorization of African realism becomes more troubling, however, when the content in question is neither deeply knowledgeable of place nor committed to boundary-pushing thought and yet lays superficial claim to both. Ashleigh Harris, in *Afropolitanism and the Novel*, associates the narrativized divorce of what we might call Africa-as-brand from the bulk of African realities with the term "de-realization," which she argues "is a condition that the novel form cannot ultimately surpass" but can only replay again and again (loc. 481). In illustrating her point through discussion in part of prominent so-called Afropolitan novelists like Taiye Selasi and Chimamanda Adichie, she articulates what has become a common critique of Western-facing African cultural production. In this reading, the future of the novel form in Africa is found on the streets, in Harris's case quite literally as she works to compile a searchable database of informally circulated African genre fiction.

This kind of democratizing work will no doubt play an increasingly and justly prominent role in the field moving forward, but it is a very different kind of project than that undertaken by *The African Novel of Ideas*. To put it bluntly, the juxtaposition between outward-facing (that is, seen by the West as representative but in fact not) and locally popular (actually representative but internationally unseen) African fiction misses the challenging, persistent subset of what we might call the philosophical fringe. And the self-conscious "fringey-ness" of that fringe, which I have briefly linked here to speculative fiction, marks *it* as the more salient oppositional construct to the world of million-dollar Afropolitanism. It is a brand of literary expression committed to preserving a space of intellectualism for its own sake, not as a turn away from the political exigencies of the continent, but in the desperate, dogged hope that a space *might* remain there for seeing the world in a way that we have not yet. How different this is from the prepackaged insights of the hit *Americanah*, in which the monologic, set-off form of the blog creates the palatable illusion of an open mind. In fact, only the social repackaging of key terms is on offer there, with the "right" conclusions waiting at the interpretive finish line. "Obama Can Win Only if He Remains the Magic Negro" (321), a typical blog title reads, mistaking common critique for novel insight. How different it is, even, from the more earnest thoughtfulness of Yaa Gyasi's magisterial *Homegoing*, where transatlantic racial history can sometimes look like a backdrop for self-knowledge served up as adage. "Strength is knowing that everyone belongs to themselves" (38), one of its characters offers, typifying the liberalism that so often obscures the more laborious, historicized, and yet self-transcendent individualism of this book.

Let me conclude this epilogue with a plea that unites the work done by the African literary field and that done by the African philosophical novel. Where there is ample cause for both cynicism and for an overcorrective "championing" of African writing, the African novel of ideas should stand as an invitation to undertake the rigorously untenable: to maintain faith in modes of questioning that are not reflective of the certainties and fast feelings demanded elsewhere, and that may no longer even make sense outside their narrative exposition. If African literary studies have evolved around suspicion of false universalisms, then at least a searching minority of African writers and philosophers have been just as attached to the promise of one that is true. Novels will not save the world. But somewhere, in the push and pull of individualized thought and institutional pressures, is the quality of mind that makes it feel worth saving.

NOTES

Introduction: Disaggregating Liberalism

1. It is difficult to imagine a special issue of a major journal on novel theory addressing "the liberal self" these days in any terms other than requiem. A recent issue of *Novel: A Forum on Fiction* on the theme of "International Fiction: Frontiers, Systems, Connections" (2018) is more representative of where the broader field is headed, which is to say toward prioritizing the form's capacity to model interconnection between humans and the material world. African and Global South literary studies are likewise, and with good reason, moving toward an ecological approach, both literally on the level of theme and in terms of its interdisciplinary methodological emphasis. Cajetan Iheka's *Naturalizing Africa* (2017) is a strong example of this shift on the Africanist front, as is Jennifer Wenzel's *The Disposition of Nature* (2019) on a slightly broader scale.

2. See Chibber's much-discussed *Postcolonial Theory and the Specter of Capital* (2013). For a thorough and provocative overview of its institutional context, see also Chris Taylor's review essay, "Postcolonial Studies and the Specter of Misplaced Polemics against Postcolonial Theory: A Review of the Chibber Debate," in the *Cambridge Journal of Postcolonial Inquiry* (2018). Also relevant here is Bruce Robbins's recent *American Literary History* review essay, "Everything Is Not Neoliberalism," which argues for the possibility of cultural expression that exists outside various controversial definitions of all-encompassing capitalism.

3. As Omedi Ochieng summarizes in his book *The Intellectual Imagination: Knowledge and Aesthetics in North Atlantic and African Philosophy*, "The flaws of the Cartesian project . . . remain as glaring as ever. The mind, according to the Cartesian formulation, is posited as the executive 'cause' of bodily behavior or actions" (loc. 306). Ochieng rightly sees this assumption as indicative, among many other sources, of the limitations of canonical Western epistemology for constructing a socially and somatically attuned model of rationality. At the same time, a division between mind and matter may well remain a compelling facet of African and other narrative and/or historical imaginaries.

4. For a comprehensive overview of this debate, which spanned years and a wide range of texts (some of which are cited later in this book), see the political philosopher Ajume Wingo's entry for "Akan Philosophy of the Person" in the *Stanford Encyclopedia of Philosophy* (December 27, 2006).

5. Avram Alpert's book *Global Origins of the Modern Self: From Montaigne to Suzuki* (2019) is worthy of mention here, as it takes a different but complementary approach to expanding the geographical range attributed to what has become known as "the liberal self." Drawing on some canonical figures (Rousseau, Hegel, Emerson) but also more surprising ones (Du Bois, Fanon, and Suzuki), Alpert argues that "the question of global self-making is at the heart of even the most Eurocentric thinking,"

and so he means to shed light on their "single, shared, wildly uneven, and violent history of global self-making" (4). His founding contention is that "the Cartesian moment of turning in is not the founding moment of modernity, but the evasion of its global demands" (2–3), suggesting that globality is, so to speak, the elephant in the room of interiority. Whereas Alpert is concerned with recovering the pluralistic origins of what has been passed down as a Western tradition of selfhood, my book is addressed to discrete narrativizations of African philosophical individualism that emerge of their own accord.

6. Siedentop's *Inventing the Individual* (2017) interestingly locates the development of an association between the individual and inwardness in Europe in the sixteenth century. He writes that "The emphasis on innerness, on something felt, contributed to a new kind of humility and a revaluation of the role of the mind" (341).

Chapter 1. Ethiopia Unbound *as Afro-Comparatist Novel: The Case for Liberated Solitude*

1. On the history of the field's Eurocentrism, see the chapter "Grounds for Comparison" in Natalie Melas's *All the Difference in the World* (2006), as well as Harry Levin's essay "Comparing the Literature" as anthologized in *Grounds for Comparison* (2013), based on his 1968 inaugural address to the American Comparative Literature Association.

2. Nathan Suhr-Sytsma and I have written of a similar impasse within efforts to decolonize American literature in a 2017 special issue of *Research in African Literatures*. "If the goal of the most innovative new work on secularity is to move toward the global," we suggest there, "then African studies has already been there long and constitutively enough to see the global as an equally fragile frame" (xi).

3. In *The Postcolonial Unconscious* (2011), Lazarus goes so far as to accuse the academic discourse of postcolonial studies of having consolidated itself around an outright "refusal of an antagonistic or struggle-based model of politics" (21).

4. Melas describes comparative literature's positivism, in fact, in similar terms to common critiques of white European Africanists. Biodun Jeyifo, for example, has characterized Albert Gerard and Bernth Lindfors as pursuing "the claim of historical depth and the demand for a rigorous, conscientious scientificity" (1990/2007, 438).

5. Casely Hayford's most prominent long-form intellectual work aside from *Ethiopia Unbound* is *Gold Coast Native Institutions* (1903), in which he argues for the integration of Fante and Asante systems of governance with British ones. In the journalistic realm, he is best known for his work as both writer and editor at the *Gold Coast Chronicle* and the *Gold Coast Leader*.

6. For a broad overview of the intellectual life of this period, see Robert July, *The Origins of Modern African Thought* (1968).

7. This image is not helped by the Bond of 1844 (originally called the Fantee Chiefs Declaration, 1844), in which an alliance of Fante chiefs signed over to the British criminal jurisdiction over their coastal territories. A common interpretation of the treaty is that it paved the way for increasing British control of the Gold Coast, partly in the form of property taxation, to which Fante chiefs did not consent. The Fante

motivation for signing the Bond was to gain protection from incursion and trade disruption by neighboring Asantes (with whom the British were often at war).

8. From 1916 until his death in 1930, Casely Hayford was also at the helm of the National Congress of British West Africa, which sought a specifically regional scope for its legislative activism. Whereas the Aborigines' Rights Protection Society sought the preservation of traditional institutions, the National Congress of British West Africa had the more ambitious goal of developing new institutions.

9. Given the significance of philosophy "in the air" during and after the Fante Confederacy intellectual era, it should not be quickly overlooked that Casely Hayford grants narrative authority to *Ethiopia Unbound*'s narrative by frequent and explicit reference to his main character's status as a philosopher who "[drinks] freely from the vital springs of knowledge" (29). In the context of this larger book project, it is worth a short detour here to note that philosophy was perhaps the chief intellectual currency of the proto-nationalist Fante intellectual world with which Casely Hayford was associated. While he was formally trained in Methodist theology and law, he had a strong penchant for corrective appeals to reason in his anti-colonial work as a journalist— most prominently for the *Gold Coast Echo* and the *Gold Coast Chronicle*—and as a political leader. He helped found the prestigious Mfantsipim School and succeeded Mensah Sarbah as president of the Aborigines' Rights Protection Society, in addition to his appointment in 1916 to the Legislative Council of the Gold Coast and in 1920 as a representative of the National Congress of British West Africa in London. Kobina Sekyi, for example, author of the 1915 satirical and bilingual drama *The Blinkards*, similarly illustrates philosophy's indigenizing cachet in the post-Fante Confederacy milieu. While his fictional work is very different from Casely Hayford's in genre and tone, Sekyi is likewise engaged in what we might truly call "decolonizing" rather than, say, deconstructing rationality. Sekyi graduated in 1910 from University College, London, with honors in philosophy, before graduating with a philosophy MA from King's College in 1918. (He also took degrees in sociology and law.) Sekyi's philosophical work mainly involves refuting Darwinian evolutionary theory as it is used by other philosophers to further racial subjugation, and he also formulated a theory of governance that combines emphasis on ethnic nationality with the Platonic ideal of the "natural ruler." More specifically, Sekyi critiqued what he saw as the amoral view of nature taken by Mill, Huxley, and Hobhouse—its "ruthless self-assertion," in Huxley's famous words—in favor of a theory whereby it is granted a moral and cosmological capacity. The relevant upshot of Sekyi's philosophical work is that his views culminate in what we might call an anti-colonial incrementalism. He espouses an anti-colonial politics rooted not in revolution but in "[mounting] nature's ladder step by step, lest we fail to reach a rung too far ahead, lose our balance thereby, and break limbs, possibly necks." His philosophical publications likewise hinge on this seeming paradox, focusing on habits of reflection as they serve a long-term project of self-governance. The bookends of his philosophical career are tellingly titled "The Relation between the Individual and the State" (1918) and "Thoughts for the Reflective" (1930).

10. This is part of a larger recuperative project on Armah's part, which notably includes his interest in Egyptian hieroglyphs as a common African language. This is thematized and formalized (as chapter headings) in his novel *Osiris Rising* (1995),

as well as in the "ancestral idea" of Armah's Per Ankh publishing cooperative. See http://stores.bbkwan.com.

11. It is worth noting that this is also true of how another "peer" postcolonial Ghanaian novel about an intellectual's psychological breakdown, Kofi Awoonor's Ewe-infused *This Earth, My Brother* (1971), is structured. In that case, the work both begins and concludes with imagery of mermaids meant to allegorize a "dream" Africa.

12. *Nananom* is the plural for *Nyiakropon*, the word for the traditional Fante gods that sit below the almighty God. (The word also means "chiefs," in a secular context.) *Nananom* is also a more specific term for a regional eighteenth-century oracle and god of war; Rebecca Shumway's *The Fante and the Transatlantic Slave Trade* (2011) provides a detailed description (134–40).

Chapter 2. Between the House of Stone and a Hard Place: Stanlake Samkange's Philosophical Turn

1. The Southern Rhodesian chapter of the African National Congress is distinct from, and in merging with an organization called the City Youth League gave rise to, the better-documented Southern Rhodesia African National Congress in 1957. Led by Joshua Nkomo, later founder of the Bulawayo-originating Zimbabwe African People's Union (ZAPU) party and second vice president under Robert Mugabe from 1987 to 1999, the SRANC was outlawed by the white minority government in 1959.

2. The authoritative source on the Samkanges' Methodist background is Terence Ranger's copiously detailed *Are We Not Also Men?* (1995), a deep dive into the Samkange family archive. Given Ranger's unparalleled access to and documentation of otherwise unavailable source materials, I will make frequent reference to the book's contents.

3. For more on Zhii, see Francis Nehwati's *African Affairs* essay "The Social and Communal Background to 'Zhii': The African Riots in Bulawayo, Southern Rhodesia in 1960" (1970).

4. I use the male pronoun here because Said and Samkange are both men. It should not be taken to indicate that public intellectualism is or should be a masculine concept.

5. Following Tarisayi A. Chimuka's essay "Ethics among the Shona," the Shona word *kuenzanisa/kuenzaisa* would best correspond to this sense of "justice conceived as fairness" (34). I think it is worth adding here that *kuenzanisa* can also be translated as "to compare." Interestingly, Chimuka then follows Herbert Chimhundu in seeing the Shona tendency to offer proverbs in contradictory pairs as evidence of a cultural bias toward moderation (ibid.).

6. For an informed and extremely clear discussion of civility's fraught position in African and decolonial studies, see the philosopher Olúfẹ́mi O. Táíwò's recent essay for the American Philosophical Association website, "What Incivility Gets Us (and What It Doesn't)."

7. Readers who are familiar with Samkange's oeuvre will know that this chapter omits sustained discussion of his return to the historical novel form with *Year of the Uprising* (1978). This is because I do not see it as marking any significant formal or conceptual turn in his career (which is not to say it is not worth reading in its own

right). As a semifictional treatment of Rhodes in the aftermath of the Rudd Concession (when Lobengula signed away all mineral rights to his territory), it traverses much of the same ground as *On Trial for My Country*, but without incorporating documentary forms, as the latter does. Instead, it describes the Shona and Ndebele uprisings—the First Chimurenga—against administration by Rhodes's British South Africa Company mostly through often-tedious dialogue. Samkange's intentions for the novel are transparently to inscribe himself into a celebratory nationalist history, as evidenced by the book's dedication to "All / men and women / young and old / living and dead / who / struggled and suffered / for / THE BIRTH OF ZIMBABWE" (i). On this front, then, I largely agree with Musaemura Zimunya that *Year of the Uprising* "offers no sense of a new literary experience" (16). I have chosen to focus on touchstone points of Samkange's career instead.

8. See, for example, Neil Ten Kortenaar's chapter in *Contemporary African Fiction*, "Doubles and Others in Two Zimbabwean Novels" (1997).

9. The kingdom or empire of Mutapa, often written elsewhere as Mwenemutapa, lasted from 1430 to 1760, and the Rozwi empire, which emerged from Mwenemutapa, ruled from 1684 to 1834. The Samkanges' main purpose in introducing them is to show the diverse origins of what is collectively referred to as "Shona" culture.

10. See, for example, Thad Metz's much-debated essay "Toward an African Moral Theory" (2007), in which he postulates an ubuntuist moral theory as one in which "an action is right just insofar as it promotes shared identity among people grounded on good-will; an act is wrong to the extent that it fails to do so and tends to encourage the opposites of division and ill-will" (338). For a more socially contextualized discussion of ubuntu and its limitations, see Bernard Matolino and Wenceslaus Kwindingwi's essay "The End of Ubuntu" (2013).

11. The most notable such effort is Masaemura Zimunya's *Those Years of Drought and Hunger: The Birth of African Fiction in Zimbabwe* (1982), which remains a powerful artifact of its time even as it has not aged well in terms of critical self-reflexivity.

Chapter 3. A Forked Path, Forever: Kintu *between Reason and Rationality*

1. See Taiye Selasi's "Bye-Bye Babar" (2005), as well as Binyavanga Wainaina's counterposition as detailed by Stephanie Bosch Santana in 2013. For a more scholarly version of Afropolitanism, Achille Mbembe's "Afropolitanism" (2007) is usually considered definitive.

2. This term also refers to the landmark book *The Empire Writes Back: Theory and Practice in Post-Colonial Literature* by Bill Ashcroft, Helen Tiffin, and Gareth Griffith (1989). See also Achebe's lecture "An Image of Africa: Racism in Conrad's *Heart of Darkness*" (1975). Finally, for a nuanced take on the practical ramifications of an indigenized literary practice, see Simon Gikandi, "Traveling Theory: Ngugi's Return to English" (2000).

3. The South African writer Fred Khumalo, author of *Dancing the Death Drill*, a novel that treats the sinking of the warship *SS Mendi* in 1917, writes in the *Johannesburg Review of Books*: "I want to suggest that the historical novel, once the preserve

of cosseted heroines and doughty heroes, warlike hordes pouring across bleak landscapes on foot or settlers making grim progress in small groups of ox wagons, is back in favour—but it is dressed in new clothes."

4. See, for example, the significant body of work by Robert Bernasconi, including *Race* (2001) and "Kant's Third Thoughts on Race."

5. Alasdair MacIntyre's *Whose Justice? Which Rationality?* (1988) is an important earlier touchstone in the canon of broad philosophical thinking about the fate of reason amid hyperplurality.

6. Appiah returns to this distinction in his *New York Review of Books* piece (2019), this time formulating it as one "between cognitive and practical procedures that are likely to be successful, given the way the world is (which I've called 'rational'); and procedures that a normal human being in a society has no reason to doubt will be effective, whether or not, in fact, they are (which I've called 'reasonable')." As an example of irrational but reasonable behavior, he uses his Asante father's refusal to eat bush meat as a way of following invisible spirits' rules.

7. Ogundele's argument in his essay is "not that religious beliefs, the supernatural, magic, and myth have no place in the historical novel," but that "belief in them may be a locomotive force in history or an explanation for deeds done by men. To the extent that they open a window to the inner life of a people and their worldview, supernatural beliefs and myths are grist to the mill of the historical imagination. But they belong in the realm of the eternal, whereas history belongs in the ever-changing world of human society" (2002, 130).

Chapter 4. Bodies Impolitic: African Deaths of Philosophical Suicide

1. Much of the most compelling recent work on "global modernisms" makes precisely this connection between European high modernism and African postcolonial realism: the two eras, while ostensibly divergent in their formal paradigms, are in fact two deeply interconnected parts of the same moment. See, for example, Jed Esty's *Unseasonable Youth: Modernism, Colonialism, and the Fiction of Development* (2013), as well as J. E. Casely Hayford's repositioning as a modernist in chapter 2 of this book.

2. For an example outside of African literary studies, see Alex Woloch's *The One vs. the Many: Minor Characters and the Space of the Protagonist in the Novel* (2003), and for one within African literary studies, see Eleni Coundouriotis's *The People's Right to the Novel: War Fiction in the Postcolony* (2014).

3. Wazha Lopang at the University of Botswana, for example, writes about suicide in Elechi Amadi's *The Great Ponds* as a point from which other characters interpret individual choice. See "Suicide as Redemption: An Analysis of Elechi Amadi's *The Great Ponds*" (2014).

4. See Paperno (1997), esp. 143–51.

5. See Jackson, "Plurality in Question: Zimbabwe and the Agonistic African Novel" (2018).

6. See also Gaurav Desai's *Commerce with the Universe* (2013), winner of the 2014 René Wellek Prize from the American Comparative Literature Association; and

Françoise Lionnet's lecture "Shipwrecks, Slavery, and the Challenge of Global Comparison: From Fiction to Archive in the Colonial Indian Ocean" (2012). South Africa, especially, has also been a key site for the development of the timely Indian Ocean studies subfield. The Centre for Indian Studies in Africa, established at Wits University in Johannesburg in 2007, has played a prominent role in bringing the field to interdisciplinary prominence, with literary studies among its chief areas of focus. Indian Ocean scholars' unifying aims are unassailable: they seek to escape the limitations of Anglo-American cultural history *and* counterhistory that a focus on either the Atlantic or Pacific worlds tends to imply. Aware of both the "dangers of Occidentalism and the inversion of binaries" (Moorthy and Jamal, 6), they favor instead an emphasis on cosmopolitanism and circulation in "an area whose boundaries are both moveable and porous" (4).

7. In Wicomb's novel *Playing in the Light* (2006), for example, a Cape Town woman who is unaware of her mixed-race heritage must navigate relations with her first black employee. In *October* (2014), the main character struggles to negotiate between fraught family and social-racial relations in South Africa and those of her diasporic home of Scotland.

8. The most-cited example of this widespread line of critique is probably the Nigerian writer Helon Habila's 2013 *Guardian* review of Zimbabwean writer NoViolet Bulawayo's debut novel *We Need New Names*.

9. A number of major initiatives have emerged to support Africa-based writers. The Etisalat Prize for Literature, for example, rewards a first-time African novelist with £15,000, a "high end device," and a book tour of African cities as well as distribution of 1,000 copies of all short-listed books across the continent. The funds attached to the Nigeria Prize for Literature are still more ample: it comes with a cash prize of $100,000. Meanwhile, a number of presses, including Kwani Trust (Kenya) and Cassava Republic (Nigeria), along with literary festivals such as Writivism (Uganda), Aké (Nigeria), and Jalada (which last covered twelve towns across Kenya, Tanzania, Uganda, Rwanda, and the DRC), have formed highly visible transnational partnerships that prioritize intracontinental cooperation.

10. Note that titles are only sometimes italicized in Huchu's text.

11. It is worth noting here that this gesture also places Huchu more firmly in line with the market zeitgeist of global African fiction. Genre fiction has received a huge amount of attention in recent years, focusing on writers such as Mukoma wa Ngugi, who is most prominently the author of the Kenyan murder thriller *Nairobi Heat* (2009); the Nigerian Nnedi Okorafor, whose speculative fiction novel *Who Fears Death* (2010) was commissioned in 2017 as the basis of a script for a new HBO series; and South Africa's Lauren Beukes, author of the international hit novel *The Shining Girls* (2013), among other works. In an indication that his "literary" novels fulfill a related, but ultimately distinct, creative role, Huchu himself, in fact, also writes short "spec fic" pieces under the name T. L. Huchu.

12. For more on Shona in this light, see Flora Veit-Wild's "'Zimbolicious'—The Creative Potential of Linguistic Innovation: The Case of Shona-English in Zimbabwe" (2009).

13. In order of publication, these are *The Wedding* (2001), *Green-Eyed Thieves* (2006), *High Low In-Between* (2009), and *The Institute for Taxi Poetry* (2012).

14. For a more in-depth treatment of South Africa's literary "de-exceptionalization" after the apartheid and even post-apartheid years, see Leon De Kock's *Losing the Plot: Crime, Reality, and Fiction in Postapartheid Writing* (2016).

15. As of the time of this book's writing, the list of African-identified writers who have received million-dollar book advances includes Yaa Gyasi, for *Homegoing* (2016); Imbolo Mbue, for *Behold the Dreamers* (2017); and Tomi Adeyemi, for a young-adult trilogy. See, for example: "Tomi Adeyemi's Million Dollar Book and Movie Deal" (2017).

16. The conversation between Coovadia and Ntshanga is archived on Twitter at: twitter.com/LieslJobson/status/530762126445780992.

17. There is a significant body of political, economic, and epidemiological literature on Mbeki's beliefs and policies surrounding antiretroviral treatment, but for a brief overview, see Dugger (2008). For examples of American reviews of *The Reactive*, see Ryan (2016) and Schuman (2016).

Epilogue: Speculations on the Future of African Literary Studies

1. For example, see Saint (2017).

2. See *Triangulum*'s book page on the Two Dollar Radio website, which also cheekily describes the novel as a combination of James Baldwin, Margaret Atwood, and the 1974 Terrence Malick film *Badlands*: twodollarradio.com/products/triangulum.

WORKS CITED

Achebe, Chinua. "An Image of Africa: Racism in Conrad's *Heart of Darkness*." Chancellor's Lecture delivered at the University of Massachusetts at Amherst, 18 February 1975.
———. *Things Fall Apart*. London: Heinemann, 1958.
Adéèkọ́, Adélékè. "My Signifier Is More Native than Yours: Issues in Making a Literature African" (1998). In *African Literature: An Anthology of Criticism and Theory*, edited by Ato Quayson and Tejumola Olaniyan. Malden, MA: Wiley-Blackwell, 2007, pp. 234–41.
———. "Okonkwo, Textual Closure, Colonial Conquest." *Research in African Literatures*, vol. 42, no. 2, 2011, pp. 72–85.
———. *Proverbs, Textuality, and Nativism in African Literature*. Gainesville: University Press of Florida, 1998.
Adichie, Chimamanda Ngozi. *Americanah*. New York: Anchor, 2013.
Aidoo, Ama Ata. *Our Sister Killjoy*. London: Longman, 1977.
Ajeluorou, Anote. "Socrates and Orunmila . . . Putting Premium on Africa's Indigenous Philosophy." *Guardian* (Nigeria), 25 August 2015. guardian.ng/art/socrates-and-orunmila-putting-premium-on-africas-indigenous-philosophy/.
Alpert, Avram. *Global Origins of the Modern Self, from Montaigne to Suzuki*. Albany: State University of New York Press, 2019.
Anderson, Amanda. *Bleak Liberalism*. Chicago: University of Chicago Press, 2016.
Andindilile, Michael. "'You Have No Past, No History': Philosophy, Literature, and the Re-Invention of Africa." *International Journal of English Literature*, vol. 7, no. 8, 2016, 127–34.
Appiah, Kwame Anthony. "Akan and Euro-American Concepts of the Person." In *African Philosophy: New and Traditional Perspectives*, edited by Lee M. Brown. Oxford: Oxford University Press, 2003, pp. 21–34.
———. "Dialectics of Enlightenment." *New York Review of Books*, 9 May 2019. www.nybooks.com/articles/2019/05/09/irrationality-dialectics-enlightenment/.
———. *In My Father's House: Africa in the Philosophy of Culture*. Oxford: Oxford University Press, 1992.
Armah, Ayi Kwei. *Fragments*. London: Heinemann, 1974.
———. *Osiris Rising*. Popenguine, Senegal: Per Ankh, 1995.
Ashcroft, Bill, Gareth Griffiths, and Helen Tiffins, eds. *The Empire Writes Back: Theory and Practice in Post-Colonial Literatures*. London: Routledge, 1989.
Attridge, Derek. "The South African Novel Today" (review of *Tales of the Metric System* by Imraan Coovadia). *Public Books*, 7 February 2017. https://www.publicbooks.org/south-african-novel-today/.
Awoonor, Kofi. *This Earth, My Brother*. London: Heinemann, 1971.
———. "Tradition and Continuity in African Literature." *Dalhousie Review* vol. 53, no. 4, 1974, pp. 665–71.

Bady, Aaron. "Let's Tell This Story." *The New Inquiry*, 8 October 2014. thenewinquiry.com/lets-tell-this-story/.

———. "Post-Coloniality Sells" (interview with Jennifer Nansubuga Makumbi). *The New Inquiry*, 8 October 2014. thenewinquiry.com/post-coloniality-sells/.

Bal, Mieke. "Working with Concepts." *European Journal of English Studies*, vol. 13, no. 1, 2009, pp. 13–23.

Baraka, Carey. "The Kenyan Literary Hustle," Brittle Paper, 1 August 2019. brittlepaper.com/2019/08/the-kenyan-literary-hustle-carey-baraka/.

Barnard, Rita. "Fictions of the Global." *Novel: A Forum on Fiction*, vol. 42, no. 2, 2009, pp. 207–15.

Bell, Duncan. *Reordering the World: Essays on Liberalism and Empire*. Princeton, NJ Princeton University Press, 2016.

Benhabib, Seyla. "Models of Public Space: Hannah Arendt, the Liberal Tradition, and Jürgen Habermas." In *Habermas and the Public Sphere*, edited by Craig Calhoun. Cambridge, MA: MIT Press, 1992, pp. 73–98.

Bernasconi, Robert. "Kant's Third Thoughts on Race." In *Reading Kant's Geography*, edited by Stuart Elden and Eduardo Mendieta. Albany: State University of New York Press, 2011, pp. 291–318.

———. *Race*. Malden, MA: Blackwell Publishers, 2011.

Bewes, Timothy. "Late Style in Naipaul: Adorno's Aesthetic and the Postcolonial Novel." In *Adorno and Literature*, edited by David Cunningham and Nigel Mapp. London: Bloomsbury, 2009, pp. 171–87.

Beukes, Lauren. *The Shining Girls*. New York: Little, Brown, 2013.

Brooks, Peter. "Must We Apologize?" In *Comparative Literature in an Age of Multiculturalism*, edited by Charles Bernheimer. Baltimore: Johns Hopkins University Press, 1995, pp. 97–106.

Bulawayo, NoViolet. *We Need New Names*. New York: Little, Brown, 2013.

Casely Hayford, J. E. *Ethiopia Unbound* (1911). London: Frank Cass & Co., 1969.

———. *Gold Coast Native Institutions: With Thoughts upon a Healthy Imperial Policy for the Gold Coast and Ashanti*. London: Sweet and Maxwell, 1903.

Chakrabarty, Dipesh. *Provincializing Europe: Postcolonial Thought and Historical Difference*. Princeton, NJ: Princeton University Press, 2007.

Cheah, Pheng. *What Is a World? On Postcolonial Literature as World Literature*. Durham, NC: Duke University Press, 2016.

Chibber, Vivek. *Postcolonial Theory and the Specter of Capital*. New York: Verso, 2013.

Chimuka, Tarisayi A. "Ethics among the Shona." *Zambezia*, vol. 28, no. 1, 2001, pp. 23–37.

Chirere, Memory. "Marechera Mania and Zimbabwean Literature." Archived, undated, on *Mazwi: A Zimbabwean Journal*, essays section. www.mazwi.net/essays/marechera-mania-and-zimbabwean-literature (no longer accessible).

Chow, Rey. *Ethics after Idealism: Theory, Culture, Ethnicity, Reading*. Bloomington: Indiana University Press, 1998.

Coetzee, J. M. *Foe: A Novel*. London: Martin Secker & Warburg Ltd., 1986.

Colmer, Rosemary. "The Human and the Divine: *Fragments* and *Why Are We So Blest?*" *Kunapipi*, vol. 2, no. 2, 1980, pp. 77–90.

Comaroff, Jean, and John Comaroff. *Modernity and Its Malcontents: Ritual and Power in Postcolonial Africa*. Chicago: University of Chicago Press, 1993.

Coovadia, Imraan. *Green-Eyed Thieves*. Johannesburg: Umuzi, 2006.

———. *High Low In-Between: A Novel.* Cape Town: Umuzi, 2009.
———. *The Institute for Taxi Poetry.* Johannesburg: Umuzi, 2012.
———. *A Spy in Time.* Los Angeles: Rare Bird Books, 2018.
———. *Tales of the Metric System.* Cape Town: Umuzi, 2014.
———. *The Wedding.* London: Picador, 2001.
Corrigan, Yuri. "Donna Tartt's Dostoevsky: Trauma and the Displaced Self." *Comparative Literature* 70, no. 4, 2018, pp. 392–407.
Coundouriotis, Eleni. *The People's Right to the Novel: War Fiction in the Postcolony.* New York: Fordham University Press, 2014.
Culler, Jonathan. "Omniscience." *Narrative*, vol. 12, no. 1, 2004, pp. 22–34.
———. "Whither Comparative Literature?" *Comparative Critical Studies*, vol. 3, no. 1, 2006, pp. 85–97.
De Bolla, Peter. *The Architecture of Concepts: The Historical Formation of Human Rights*, Kindle ed. New York: Fordham University Press, 2013.
De Kock, Leon. *Losing the Plot: Crime, Reality, and Fiction in Post-Apartheid South African Writing.* Johannesburg: Wits University Press, 2016.
Desai, Gaurav. *Commerce with the Universe: Africa, India, and the Afrasian Imagination.* New York: Columbia University Press, 2013.
De Silva, Mark. "Distant Visions: Putdownable Prose and the State of the Art-Novel." *3:AM Magazine*, 4 December 2015. www.3ammagazine.com/3am/a-distant-vision-putdownable-prose-and-the-state-of-the-art-novel/.
DiGiacomo, Mark. "The Assertion of Coevalness: African Literature and Modernist Studies." *Modernism/modernity*, vol. 24, no. 2, 2017, pp. 245–62.
Dostoevsky, Fyodor. *The Brothers Karamazov*, translated by Richard Pevear and Larissa Volokhonsky. New York: Farrar, Straus and Giroux, 2002.
———. *Demons*, translated by Richard Pevear and Larissa Volokhonsky. New York: Vintage, 1994.
Dugger, Celia W. "Study Cites Toll of AIDs Policy in South Africa." *New York Times*, 25 November 2008. www.nytimes.com/2008/11/26/world/africa/26aids.html.
During, Simon. *Against Democracy.* New York: Fordham University Press, 2012.
Esty, Jed. *Unseasonable Youth: Modernism, Colonialism, and the Fiction of Development.* Oxford: Oxford University Press, 2011.
Eze, Emmanuel Chukwudi. *On Reason: Rationality in a World of Cultural Conflict and Racism.* Durham, NC: Duke University Press, 2008.
Eze, Michael Onyebuchi, and Thaddeus Metz. "Emergent Issues in African Philosophy: A Dialogue with Kwasi Wiredu." *Philosophia Africana*, vol. 17, no. 2, 2015/2016, pp. 75–87.
Fanon, Frantz. *Black Skin, White Masks*, translated by Richard Philcox. New York: Grove Press, 2008.
———. "Racism and Culture." Speech to the Congress of Black African Writers, 1959. Anthologized in *Toward the African Revolution: Political Essays*, translated by Haakon Chevalier. New York: Grove Press, 1967, pp. 29–44.
———. *The Wretched of the Earth*, translated by Richard Philcox, Grove Press, 2004.
Fawcett, Edmund. *Liberalism: The Life of an Idea.* Princeton, NJ: Princeton University Press, 2014.
Forna, Aminatta. "Don't Judge a Book by Its Author." *Guardian*, 15 February 2015. www.theguardian.com/books/2015/feb/13/aminatta-forna-dont-judge-book-by-cover.

Frenkel, Ronit. Interview with Imraan Coovadia. *Current Writing*, vol. 28, no. 1, 2016, pp. 96–105.

———. "Preface" to special issue on Imraan Coovadia. *Current Writing*, vol. 28, no. 1, 2016, p. 1.

Freud, Sigmund. "The Uncanny." *The Standard Edition of the Complete Psychological Works of Sigmund Freud*, vol. 17 (1917–1919), *An Infantile Neurosis and Other Works*, edited and translated by James Strachey. Hogarth Press, 1955, pp. 217–56.

Friesen, Alan R. "Okonkwo's Suicide as an Affirmative Act: Do Things Really Fall Apart?" *Postcolonial Text*, vol. 2, no. 4, 2006.

Gagiano, Annie. Review of *The House of Hunger* by Dambudzo Marechera. Archived, undated, on *Litnet*, African library section. http://www.oulitnet.co.za/africanlib/hunger.asp (no longer accessible).

Ganguly, Debjani. *This Thing Called the World: The Contemporary Novel as Global Form*. Durham, NC: Duke University Press, 2016.

Getachew, Adom. *Worldmaking after Empire: The Rise and Fall of Self-Determination*. Princeton, NJ: Princeton University Press, 2019.

Geuss, Raymond. *Changing the Subject: Philosophy from Socrates to Adorno*. Cambridge, MA: Harvard University Press, 2017.

Gikandi, Simon. "Contested Grammars: Comparative Literature, Translation, and the Challenge of Locality." In *A Companion to Comparative Literature*, edited by Ali Behdad and Dominic Thomas. Malden, MA: Wiley-Blackwell, 2011, pp. 254–72.

———. *Reading Chinua Achebe*. Melton, UK: James Currey, 1991.

———. *Reading the African Novel*. Melton, UK: James Currey, 1987.

———. *Slavery and the Culture of Taste*. Princeton, NJ: Princeton University Press, 2011.

———. "Traveling Theory: Ngugi's Return to English." *Research in African Literatures*, vol. 31, no. 2, 2000, pp. 194–209.

Ghosh, Amitav. *The Sea of Poppies*. New York: Viking Press, 2008.

Girard, René. *The Scapegoat*, translated by Yvonne Freccero. Baltimore: Johns Hopkins University Press, 1989.

Gordimer, Nadine. "The Interpreters: Some Themes and Directions in African Literature."

Kenyon Review, vol. 32, no. 1, 1970, pp. 9–26.

Gorman-DaRif, Meghan. "In Search of the Transformative Imaginary: Literary Representations of Non-State Violence in the Globalized Postcolony." *Interventions*, vol. 20, no. 5, 2018, pp. 605–22.

Goyal, Yogita. *Romance, Diaspora, and Black Atlantic Literature*. Cambridge: Cambridge University Press, 2010.

Graham, James. *Land and Nationalism in Fictions from Southern Africa*. New York: Routledge, 2009.

Gray, John. *Enlightenment's Wake: Politics and Culture at the Close of the Modern Age*. London: Routledge, 1995.

Gros, Frédéric. *A Philosophy of Walking*, translated by John Howe, online ed. New York: Verso, 2014.

Gyasi, Yaa. *Homegoing*. New York: Alfred A. Knopf, 2016.

Gyekye, Kwame. "Person and Community in Akan Thought." In *Person and Community: Ghanaian Philosophical Studies I*. Washington, DC: Council for Research in Values and Philosophy, 2010, pp. 101–22.

Habermas, Jürgen. *The Structural Transformation of the Public Sphere: An Inquiry into a Category of Bourgeois Society*. Cambridge, MA: MIT Press, 1991.

Habila, Helon. "On Dambudzo Marechera." *Virginia Quarterly Review*, vol. 82, no. 1, 2006, 251–60.

———. Review of *We Need New Names* by NoViolet Bulawayo. *Guardian*, 20 June 2013. www.theguardian.com/books/2013/jun/20/need-new-names-bulawayo-review.

Hallward, Peter. *Absolutely Postcolonial: Writing between the Singular and the Specific*. Manchester: Manchester University Press, 2001.

Hapanyengwi-Chemhuru, Oswell, and Ngoni Makuvaza. "Hunhu: In Search of an Indigenous Philosophy for the Zimbabwean Education System." *Journal of Indigenous Social Development*, vol. 3, no. 1, 2014, pp. 1–15.

Harootunian, Harry. "Some Thoughts on Comparability and the Space-Time Problem." *boundary 2*, vol. 232, no. 2, 2005, pp. 23–52.

Harris, Ashleigh. *Afropolitanism and the Novel: De-Realizing Africa*, Kindle ed. New York: Routledge, 2020.

Head, Bessie. *Maru*. London: Heinemann, 1971.

Hensley, Nathan. *Forms of Empire: The Poetics of Victorian Sovereignty*. Oxford: Oxford University Press, 2017.

Hofmeyr, Isabel. "The Complicating Sea: The Indian Ocean as Method." *Comparative Studies of South Asia, Africa, and the Middle East*, vol. 32, no. 3, 2012, pp. 584–90.

Hogg, Emily J. "Human Rights, the Family, and the Bildungsroman in Goretti Kyomuhendo's *Waiting: A Novel of Uganda at War*." *Textual Practice*, vol. 34, no. 2, 2018, pp. 1–19.

Hountondji, Paulin J. *African Philosophy: Myth and Reality*, translated Henri Evans and Jonathan Ree. Bloomington: Indiana University Press, 1983.

Huchu, Tendai. *The Hairdresser of Harare*, Kindle ed. Athens: Ohio University Press, 2010.

———. *The Maestro, the Magistrate, and the Mathematician*. Athens: Ohio University Press, 2014.

Hutcheon, Linda. "Historiographic Metafiction: Parody and the Intertextuality of History." In *Intertextuality and Contemporary American Fiction*, edited by Patrick O'Donnell and Robert Con Davis. Baltimore: Johns Hopkins University Press, 1989, pp. 3–32.

Ibrahim, Abubakar Adam. *Season of Crimson Blossoms*. Abuja, Nigeria: Cassava Republic, 2016.

Iheka, Cajetan. *Naturalizing Africa: Ecological Violence, Agency, and Postcolonial Resistance in African Literature*. Cambridge: Cambridge University Press, 2017.

Irele, Abiola. "The African Imagination." *Research in African Literatures*, vol. 21, no. 1, 1990, pp. 49–67.

———. "The Crisis of Cultural Memory in Chinua Achebe's *Things Fall Apart*." *African Studies Quarterly*, vol. 4, no. 3, 2000.

Irr, Caren. *Toward the Geopolitical Novel: US Fiction in the Twenty-First Century*. New York: Columbia University Press, 2013.

Iser, Wolfgang. *The Fictive and the Imaginary: Charting Literary Anthropology*. Baltimore: Johns Hopkins University Press, 1993.

Jackson, Jeanne-Marie. "Plurality in Question: Zimbabwe and the Agonistic African Novel." *Novel: A Forum on Fiction*, vol. 51, no. 2, 2018, pp. 339–61.

Jackson, Jeanne-Marie, and Nathan Suhr-Sytsma. "Introduction: Religion, Secularity, and African Writing." *Research in African Literatures*, vol. 48, no. 2, 2017, pp. vii–xvi.

———, and the students of the Johns Hopkins University "Writing Africa Now" seminar (spring 2017). Interview with Masande Ntshanga. Brittle Paper, 27 March 2017. brittlepaper.com/2017/03/writing-africa-class-interview-masande-ntshanga/.

Jaji, Tsitsi Ella. *Africa in Stereo: Modernism, Music, and Pan-African Solidarity*. Oxford: Oxford University Press, 2013.

Jaji, Tsitsi, and Lily Saint. "Introduction: Genre in Africa." *Cambridge Journal of Postcolonial Literary Inquiry*, vol. 4, no. 2, 2017, pp. 151–58.

Janz, Bruce. "The Geography of African Philosophy." *The Palgrave Handbook of African Philosophy*, edited by Adeshina Afolayan and Toyin Falola. New York: Palgrave Macmillan, 2017, pp. 155–66.

———. "Reason and Rationality in Eze's *On Reason*." *South African Journal of Philosophy*, vol. 27, no. 4, 2008, pp. 296–309.

Jeyifo, Biodun. "The Nature of Things: Arrested Decolonization and Critical Theory" (1990). In *African Literature: An Anthology of Criticism and Theory*, edited by Ato Quayson and Tejumola Olaniyan. Malden, MA: Wiley-Blackwell, 2007, pp. 432–43.

Julien, Eileen. *African Novels and the Question of Orality*. Bloomington: Indiana University Press, 1992.

July, Robert. *The Origins of Modern African Thought*. London: Faber and Faber, 1968.

Just, Daniel. "The Modern Novel from a Sociological Perspective: Towards a Strategic Use of the Notion of Genres." *JNT: Journal of Narrative Theory*, vol. 38, no. 3, 2008, pp. 378–97.

Kahari, George. *The Rise of the Shona Novel*. Gweru, Zimbabwe: Mambo Press, 1990.

Kant, Immanuel. "What Is Enlightenment?" (1784), translated by Mary C. Smith. http://www.columbia.edu/acis/ets/CCREAD/etscc/kant.html#note1.

Khumalo, Fred. *Dancing the Death Drill*. Cape Town: Umuzi, 2017.

———. "Historical Fiction Is Back—With a Fire in Its Belly: Fred Khumalo Reflects on How Writing Can Be a Powerful Tool for an Activist." *Johannesburg Review of Books*, 7 May 2018. johannesburgreviewofbooks.com/2018/05/07/historical-fiction-is-back-with-a-fire-in-its-belly-fred-khumalo-reflects-on-how-writing-can-be-a-powerful-tool-for-an-activist/.

Kimani, Peter. *Dance of the Jakaranda*. New York: Akashic Books, 2017.

Kirsch, Adam. *The Global Novel: Writing the World in the 21st Century*, Kindle edition. New York: Columbia Global Reports, 2017.

Korang, Kwaku Larbi. *Writing Ghana, Imagining Africa: Nation and African Modernity*. Rochester, NY: University of Rochester Press, 2003.

Krishnaswamy, Revathi. "Toward World Literary Knowledges: Theory in the Age of Globalization." *Comparative Literature*, vol. 62, no. 4, 2010, pp. 399–419.

Kyomuhendo, Goretti. "Goretti Kyomuhendo in Conversation with Jennifer Nansubuga Makumbi." *Wasafiri*, vol. 33, no. 3, 2018, pp. 39–42.

———. *Waiting: A Novel of Uganda at War*. New York: City University of New York Press, 2007.

Langa, James. *Shaka*. London: Longmans, 1982.

Lazarus, Neil. *The Postcolonial Unconscious*. Cambridge: Cambridge University Press, 2011.

———. "Representations of the Intellectual in *Representations of the Intellectual*." *Research in African Literatures*, vol. 36, no. 3, 2005, pp. 112–23.

Lessing, Doris. *The Grass Is Singing*. New York: Thomas Y. Crowell, 1950.

Levin, Harry. *Grounds for Comparison*. Harvard Studies in Comparative Literature 32. Cambridge, MA: Harvard University Press, 1972; reissued 2013.

Lionnet, Françoise. "Shipwrecks, Slavery, and the Challenge of Global Comparison: From Fiction to Archive in the Colonial Indian Ocean." *Comparative Literature*, vol. 64, no. 4, 2012, pp. 446–61.

Lobb, Edward. "Armah's *Fragments* and the Vision of the Whole." *ARIEL*, vol. 10, no. 1, 1979, pp. 25–38.

Lopang, Wazha. "Suicide as Redemption: An Analysis of Elechi Amadi's *The Great Ponds*." *International Journal of Humanities and Social Science*, vol. 4, no. 5, 2014, pp. 162–68.

Lopez, Alfred J. "Introduction: Comparative Literature and the Return of the Global Repressed." *The Global South*, vol. 1, no. 1, 2007, pp. 1–15.

Lowe, Lisa. *The Intimacies of Four Continents*. Durham, NC: Duke University Press, 2015.

Lukacs, Georg. *The Theory of the Novel*. Translated by Anna Bostock. Cambridge, MA: MIT Press, 1971.

MacIntyre, Alasdair. *Whose Justice? Which Rationality?* South Bend, IN: University of Notre Dame Press, 1988.

Magosvongwe, Ruby. "Shona Philosophy of Unhu/Hunhu and Its Onomastics in Selected Fictional Narratives." *Journal of the African Literature Association*, vol. 10, no. 2, 2016, pp. 158–75.

Magubeni, Unathi. *Nwelezelanga: The Star Child*. Johannesburg: BlackBird Books, 2016.

Makumbi, Jennifer Nansubuga. *Kintu*. Oakland, CA: Transit Books, 2017.

Malaba, Mbongeni. "'A Series of Seemings': Inclusion and Exclusion in the Religious Environment Explored in Stanlake Samkange's *The Mourned One* and Charles Mungoshi's 'Sacrifice.'" *Current Writing*, vol. 24, no. 2, 2012, pp. 177–85.

Malec, Jennifer. Interview with Ayesha Harruna Attah. *Johannesburg Review of Books*, 6 August 2018. johannesburgreviewofbooks.com/2018/08/06/historical-fiction-is-a-way-of-fighting-rootlessness-ayesha-harruna-attah-discusses-her-new-novel-the-hundred-wells-of-salaga/#comments.

Mang, Riley. Interview with Bibi Bakare-Yusuf. *Los Angeles Review*, 2014. losangelesreview.org/interview-with-bibi-bakare-yusuf/.

Manshel, Alexander. "The Rise of the Recent Historical Novel." Post45, 29 September 2017. post45.research.yale.edu/2017/09/the-rise-of-the-recent-historical-novel/.

Marechera, Dambudzo. "The African Writer's Experience of European Literature" (1987). In *African Literature: An Anthology of Criticism and Theory*, edited by Ato Quayson and Tejumola Olaniyan. Malden, MA: Wiley-Blackwell, 2007, pp. 186–92.

———. *Black Sunlight*. London: Heinemann, 1980.

———. *The House of Hunger*. London: Heinemann, 1978.

Matolino, Bernard, and Wenceslaus Kwindingwi. "The End of Ubuntu." *South African Journal of Philosophy*, vol. 32, no. 2, 2013, pp. 197–205.

Mbembe, Achille. *Critique of Black Reason*, translated by Laurent Dubois. Durham, NC: Duke University Press, 2017.

———. "Afropolitanism." In *Africa Remix: Contemporary Art of a Continent*, edited by Simon Njami. Johannesburg: Jacana Media, 2007, pp. 26–30.

Mbue, Imbolo. *Behold the Dreamers*. New York: Penguin Random House, 2016.

Melas, Natalie. *All the Difference in the World: Postcoloniality and the Ends of Comparison*. Stanford, CA: Stanford University Press, 2006.

———. "Merely Comparative." *PMLA*, vol. 128, no. 3, 2013, pp. 652–59.

Metz, Thaddeus. "Toward an African Moral Theory." *Journal of Political Philosophy*, vol. 15, no. 3, 2007, pp. 321–41.

Mitchell, David. *Ghostwritten*. London: Hodder & Stoughton, 1999.

Moorthy, Shanti, and Ashraf Jamal, eds. *Indian Ocean Studies: Cultural, Social, and Political Perspectives*. London: Routledge, 2009.

Mudimbe, V. Y. *The Invention of Africa: Gnosis, Philosophy, and the Order of Knowledge*. Oxford: James Currey Ltd., 1988.

Mudimbe, V. Y., and Kwame Anthony Appiah. "The Impact of African Studies on Philosophy." In *Africa and the Disciplines: The Contributions of Research in Africa to the Social Sciences and Humanities*, edited by Robert H. Bates, V. Y. Mudimbe, and Jean F. O'Barr. Chicago: University of Chicago Press, 1993, pp. 113–38.

Muponde, Robert. *Some Kinds of Childhood: Images of History and Resistance in Zimbabwean Literature*. Trenton, NJ: Africa World Press, 2015.

———, and Ranka Primorac. "Introduction: Writing against Blindness." In *Versions of Zimbabwe: New Approaches to Literature and Culture*, edited by Robert Muponde and Ranka Primorac. Harare, Zimbabwe: Weaver Press, 2005.

Murphy, Laura T. *Metaphor and the Slave Trade in West African Literature*. Athens: Ohio University Press, 2012.

Mwesigire, Bwesigye Bwa. "Beyond the Afropolitan Postnation: The Contemporaneity of Jennifer Makumbi's *Kintu*." *Research in African Literatures*, vol. 49, no. 1, 2018, pp. 103–16.

Ndebele, Njabulo S. *Rediscovery of the Ordinary: Essays on South African Literature and Culture*. Manchester, UK: Manchester University Press, 1994. https://www.google.com/books/edition/South_African_Literature_and_Culture/UCG9AAAAIAAJ?hl=en&gbpv=1&bsq="What%20matters%20is%20what%20is%20seen.%20Thinking%20is%20secondary%20to%20seeing.%20Subtlety%20is%20secondary%20to%20obviousness"%20.

Nehwati, Francis. "The Social and Communal Background to 'Zhii': The African Riots in Bulawayo, Southern Rhodesia in 1960." *African Affairs*, vol. 69, no. 276, 1970, pp. 250–66.

Newell, Stephanie. *Literary Culture in Colonial Ghana: How to Play the Game of Life*. Manchester, UK: Manchester University Press, 2002.

Ngũgĩ wa Mũkoma. *Nairobi Heat*. Melville House, 2011.

Ngũgĩ wa Thiong'o. *Decolonising the Mind: The Politics of Language in African Literature*. Nairobi, Kenya: East African Educational Publishers, 1986.

Ntshanga, Masande. *The Reactive*. Cape Town: Umuzi, 2014.

———. *Triangulum*. Columbus, OH: Two Dollar Radio, 2019.

Nyabola, Nanjala. "Bessie Head: A Life of Letters." *Popula*, 17 July 2018. popula.com/2018/07/17/bessie-head-a-life-of-letters/.

Nyamfukudza, Stanley. *The Non-Believer's Journey*. London: Heinemann, 1980.

———. "To Skin a Skunk: Some Observations on Zimbabwe's Intellectual Development." In *Skinning the Skunk: Facing Zimbabwean Futures*, edited by Mai Palmberg and Ranka Primorac. Uppsala: Nordic Africa Institute, 2005, pp. 16–25.

Nyong'o, Tavia, and Kyla Wazana Tompkins. "Eleven Theses on Civility," *Social Text Online*, 11 July 2018. https://socialtextjournal.org/eleven-theses-on-civility/.

Obiechina, Emmanuel. "Narrative Proverbs in the African Novel." *Research in African Literatures*, vol. 24, no. 4, 1993, pp. 123–40.

Ochieng, Omedi. *The Intellectual Imagination: Knowledge and Aesthetics in North Atlantic and African Philosophy*. South Bend, IN: University of Notre Dame Press, 2018.

———. "W. E. B. Du Bois and the Imagination of the Public Intellectual." *African Journal of Rhetoric*, vol. 8, no. 1, 2016, pp. 107–24.

Ogundele, Wole. "Devices of Evasion: The Mythic versus the Historical Imagination in the Postcolonial African Novel." *Research in African Literature*, vol. 33, no. 3, 2002, pp. 125–39.

Okorafor, Nnedi. *Who Fears Death*. New York: DAW, 2010.

Olaniyan, Tejumola. "African Literature in the Post-Global Age: Provocations on Field Commonsense." *Cambridge Journal of Postcolonial Literary Inquiry*, vol. 3, no. 3, 2016, pp. 387–96.

Omotoso, Yewande. *Bom Boy*. Cape Town: Modjadji, 2011.

———. *The Woman Next Door*. London: Chatto & Windus, 2016.

Ouologuem, Yambo. *Le Devoir de violence*. Paris: Éditions du Seuil, 1968.

Paperno, Irina. *Suicide as a Cultural Institution in Dostoevsky's Russia*. Ithaca, NY: Cornell University Press, 1997.

Pavel, Thomas G. *The Lives of the Novel: A History*. Princeton, NJ: Princeton University Press, 2015.

Primorac, Ranka. *The Place of Tears: The Novel and Politics in Modern Zimbabwe*. London: Tauris, 2006.

Puchner, Martin. "J. M. Coetzee's Novels of Thinking." *Raritan: A Quarterly Review*, vol. 30, no. 4, 2011, pp. 1–12.

Quayson, Ato. *Calibrations: Reading for the Social*. Minneapolis: University of Minnesota Press, 2003.

———. *Oxford Street, Accra: City Life and the Itineraries of Transnationalism*. Durham, NC: Duke University Press, 2014.

———. *Strategic Transformations in Nigerian Writing: Orality and History in the Work of Rev. Samuel Johnson, Amos Tutola, Wole Soyinka, and Ben Okri*. Bloomington: Indiana University Press, 1997.

———. "Symbolization Compulsion: Testing a Psychoanalytical Category on Postcolonial African Literature." *University of Toronto Quarterly*, vol. 73, no. 2, 2004, pp. 754–72.

Ramose, Mogobe B. "Introduction: The Struggle for Reason in Africa." In *The African Philosophy Reader*, edited by P. H. Coetzee and A. P. J. Roux. London: Routledge, 2003, pp. 1–9.

Rand, Erin J. "Bad Feelings in Public: Rhetoric, Affect, and Emotion." *Rhetoric and Public Affairs*, vol. 18, no. 1, 2015, pp. 161–75.

Ranger, Terence. *Are We Not Also Men? The Samkange Family and African Politics in Zimbabwe 1920–64*. Harare, Zimbabwe: Baobob Press, 1995.

Robbins, Bruce. "Everything Is Not Neoliberalism." *American Literary History*, vol. 31, no. 4, 2019, pp. 840–49.

Rosenblatt, Helena. *The Lost History of Liberalism: From Ancient Rome to the Twenty-First Century*. Princeton, NJ: Princeton University Press, 2018.

Rugero, Roland. *Baho! A Novel*, translated by Christopher Schaefer. Los Angeles: Phoneme Media, 2016.

Rhys, Jean. *Wide Sargasso Sea*. London: André Deutsch, 1966.

Ryan, Marian. "Ten Years Ago, I Helped a Handful of Men Take My Little Brother's Life" (review of Masande Ntshanga, *The Reactive*). *Slate*, 6 July 2016.

Said, Edward W. *Humanism and Democratic Criticism*. New York: Columbia University Press, 2004.

———. *Representations of the Intellectual*. New York: Pantheon Books, 1994.

Saint, Lily. "The Danger of a Single Author." *Africa Is a Country*, 14 April 2017. africasacountry.com/2017/04/the-danger-of-a-single-author.

Saint-Amour, Paul. "The Medial Humanities: Toward a Manifesto for Meso-Analysis." *Modernism/modernity* Print Plus, vol. 3 cycle 4, 1 February 2019. modernismmodernity.org/forums/posts/medial-humanities-toward-manifesto-meso-analysis.

Samin, Richard, and Es'kia Mphahlele. "Richard Samin with Es'kia Mphahlele." *Research in African Literatures*, vol. 28, no. 4, 1997, pp. 182–200.

Samkange, Stanlake. *The Mourned One*. London: Heinemann, 1975.

———. *On Trial for My Country*. London: Heinemann, 1966.

———. *Year of the Uprising*. London: Heinemann, 1978.

Samkange, Stanlake, with Tommie Marie Samkange. *Hunhuism or Ubuntuism: A Zimbabwe Indigenous Political Philosophy*. Salisbury (Harare, Zimbabwe): Graham Publishers, 1980.

Santa, Stephanie Bosch. "Exorcising Afropolitanism: Binyavanga Wainaina Explains Why 'I Am a Pan-Africanist, Not an Afropolitan,' at ASAUK 2012." *Africa in Words*, 8 February 2013. https://africainwords.com/2013/02/08/exorcizing-afropolitanism-binyavanga-wainaina-explains-why-i-am-a-pan-africanist-not-an-afropolitan-at-asauk-2012.

Saussy, Haun. "Comparative Literature: The Next Ten Years." In *Futures of Comparative Literature: ACLA State of the Discipline Report*, edited by Ursula K. Heise. New York: Routledge, 2017, pp. 24–39.

———. "Exquisite Cadavers Stitched from Fresh Nightmares: Of Memes, Hives, and Selfish Genes." In *Comparative Literature in an Age of Globalization*, edited by Haun Saussy. Baltimore: Johns Hopkins University Press, 2006, pp. 3–42.

Schuman, David. Review of *The Reactive* by Masande Ntshanga. *The Rumpus*, 6 June 2016. therumpus.net/2016/06/the-reactive-by-masande-ntshanga/.

Scott, Joan W. "The Evidence of Experience." *Critical Inquiry*, vol. 17, no. 4, 1991, pp. 773–97.

Sekyi, Kobina. *The Blinkards* (1915). London: Heinemann, 1974.

———. "The Relation between the State and the Individual Considered in Light of Its Bearing on Concept of Duty." MA thesis, University College, London, 1918.

———. "Thoughts for the Reflective." Unpublished, 1930. Kobina Sekyi Papers, Cape Coast branch of the National Archives of Ghana.

Sekyi-Otu, Ato. *Left Universalism, Africacentric Essays*. London: Routledge, 2019.

Selasi, Taiye. "Bye-Bye Babar." *The Lip*, 3 March 2005. http://thelip.robertsharp.co.uk/?p=76.

———. *Ghana Must Go*. New York: Penguin Books, 2013.

Serpell, Namwali. "The Great Africanstein Novel." *New York Review of Books*, 12 September 2017. www.nybooks.com/daily/2017/09/12/the-great-africanstein-novel-kintu/.

Shih, Shu-mei. "World Studies and Relational Comparison." *PMLA*, vol. 130, no. 2, 2015, pp. 430–38.

Shumway, Rebecca. *The Fante and the Transatlantic Slave Trade*. Rochester, NY: University of Rochester Press, 2011.

Sibanda, Patrick. "The Dimensions of 'Hunhu/Ubuntu' (Humanism in the African Sense): The Zimbabwean Conception." *IOSR Journal of Engineering*, vol. 4, no. 1, 2014, pp. 26–29.

Siedentop, Larry. *Inventing the Individual: The Origins of Western Liberalism*. Cambridge, MA: Harvard University Press, 2017.

Singh, Julietta. *Unthinking Mastery: Dehumanism and Decolonial Entanglements*. Durham, NC: Duke University Press, 2018.

Slaughter, Joseph. *Human Rights, Inc.: The World Novel, Narrative Form, and International Law*. New York: Fordham University Press, 2007.

———. "The Novel and Human Rights." In *The Novel in Africa and the Caribbean since 1950*, edited by Simon Gikandi. Oxford: Oxford University Press, 2016, pp. 198–216.

Smith, Justin E. H. *Irrationality: A History of the Dark Side of Reason*. Princeton, NJ: Princeton University Press, 2019.

———. *The Philosopher: A History in Six Types*. Princeton, NJ: Princeton University Press, 2016.

Soyinka, Wole. *Death and the King's Horseman: A Play*. New York W. W. Norton, 2002.

———. *Myth, Literature, and the African World*. Cambridge: Cambridge University Press, 1976.

Spivak, Gayatri. *A Critique of Postcolonial Reason: Toward a History of the Vanishing Present*. Cambridge, MA: Harvard University Press, 1999.

Sterling, Cheryl. "Can You Really See through a Squint? Theoretical Underpinnings in Ama Ato Aidoo's *Our Sister Killjoy*." *Journal of Commonwealth Literature*, vol. 45, no. 1, 2010, pp. 131–50.

Summit, Jennifer, and Blakey Vermeule. *Action versus Contemplation: Why an Ancient Debate Still Matters*. Chicago: University of Chicago Press, 2018.

Táíwò, Olúfẹ́mi. "Exorcising Hegel's Ghost: Africa's Challenge to Philosophy." *African Studies Quarterly*, vol. 1, no. 4, 1998, pp. 3–16.

Táíwò, Olúfẹ́mi O. "What Incivility Gets Us (and What It Doesn't)." Blog of the American Philosophical Association, 3 September 2019, https://blog.apaonline.org/2019/09/03/what-incivility-gets-us-and-what-it-doesnt/.

Taylor, Charles. *A Secular Age*. Cambridge, MA Harvard University Press, 2007.

———. *Sources of the Self: The Making of the Modern Identity*. Cambridge, MA: Harvard University Press, 1989.

Taylor, Christopher. *Empire of Neglect: The West Indies in the Wake of British Liberalism*. Durham, NC: Duke University Press, 2018.

Taylor, Christopher. "Postcolonial Studies and the Specter of Misplaced Polemics against Postcolonial Theory: A Review of the Chibber Debate." *Cambridge Journal of Postcolonial Literary Inquiry*, vol. 5, no. 2, 2018, pp. 234–249.
Tembo, Nick Mdika. "Reading the Trauma of Internally Displaced Identities in Goretti Kyomuhendo's *Waiting*." *Eastern African Literary and Cultural Studies*, vol. 3, nos. 2-4, 2017, pp. 91–106.
Tempels, Placide. *Bantu Philosophy*, translated by Colin King. Paris: Presence Africaine, 1959.
Ten Kortenaar, Neil. "Doubles and Others in Two Zimbabwean Novels." In *Contemporary African Fiction*, edited by Derek Wright. Bayreuth: Bayreuth African Studies, 1997, pp. 19–41.
Thamm, Marianne. "Dangerous Mind: What Rick Turner Still Has to Offer Free South Africa." *Daily Maverick*, 26 June 2014. https://www.dailymaverick.co.za/article/2014-06-26-dangerous-mind-what-rick-turner-still-has-to-offer-free-south-africa/.
"Tomi Adeyemi's Million Dollar Book and Movie Deal." Brittle Paper, 25 July 2017. http://brittlepaper.com/2017/07/nigerian-harvard-university-grad-milliondollar-book-deal/.
Trilling, Lionel. *The Liberal Imagination*. New York: New York Review Books, 1950.
Turgenev, Ivan. *Fathers and Sons*. New York: W. W. Norton, 1966.
Turner, Rick. *The Eye of the Needle—Towards Participatory Democracy in South Africa* (1978), rev. ed. Kolkata, India: Seagull Books, 2015.
Tutuola, Amos. *The Palm-Wine Drinkard*. New York: Grove Press, 1953.
Van der Vlies, Andrew. *Present Imperfect: Contemporary South African Writing*. Oxford: Oxford University Press, 2017.
Veit-Wild, Flora. *Teachers, Preachers, Non-Believers: A Social History of Zimbabwean Literature*. London: Hans Zell Publishers, 1992.
———. "'Zimbolicious'—The Creative Potential of Linguistic Innovation: The Case of Shona-English in Zimbabwe." *Journal of Southern African Studies*, vol. 35, no. 3, 2009, pp. 683–97.
Verissimo, Jumoke. *A Small Silence*. Abuja, Nigeria: Cassava Republic Press, 2019.
Virilio, Paul. *Negative Horizon: An Essay in Dromoscopy*, translated by Michael Degener. London: Bloomsbury, 2008.
Wainaina, Binyavanga. *One Day I Will Write about This Place: A Memoir*. Minneapolis: Graywold Press, 2011.
Walkowitz, Rebecca. *Born Translated: The Contemporary Novel in an Age of World Literature*. New York: Columbia University Press, 2015.
Wanner, Zukiswa. *Men of the South*. Capetown: Kwela, 2012.
Warner, Michael. "The Mass Public and the Mass Subject." In *Habermas and the Public Sphere*, edited by Craig Calhoun. Cambridge, MA: MIT Press, 1992, pp. 377–401.
Warwick Research Collective. *Combined and Uneven Development: Towards a New Theory of World-Literature*. Liverpool, UK: Liverpool University Press, 2015.
Wenzel, Jennifer. *The Disposition of Nature: Environmental Crisis and World Literature*. New York: Fordham University Press, 2019.
Wicomb, Zoë. *October*. New York: New Press, 2014.
———. *Playing in the Light*. New York: New Press, 2006.

———. "To Hear the Variety of Discourses." 1990. *Current Writing: Text and Reception in Southern Africa*, vol. 2, 2011, pp. 35–44.

Williams, Jeffrey L. "The New Modesty in Literary Criticism." *Chronicle Review*, 5 January 2015. https://www.chronicle.com/article/The-New-Modesty-in-Literary/150993.

Wingo, Ajume. "Akan Philosophy of the Person." *Stanford Encyclopedia of Philosophy*, 27 December 2006. plato.stanford.edu/entries/akan-person/.

Wiredu, Kwasi. "An Oral Philosophy of Personhood: Comments on Philosophy and Orality." *Research in African Literatures*, vol. 40, no. 1, 2019, pp. 8–18.

———. "Toward Decolonizing African Philosophy and Religion." *African Studies Quarterly*, vol. 1, no. 4, 1998, pp. 17–46.

Wiredu, Kwasi, and Kwame Gyekye, eds. *Person and Community: Ghanaian Philosophical Studies I*. Washington, DC: Council for Research in Values and Philosophy, 2010.

Woloch, Alex. *The One vs. the Many: Minor Characters and the Space of the Protagonist in the Novel*. Princeton, NJ: Princeton University Press, 2003.

Young, Robert J. C. "The Postcolonial Comparative." *PMLA*, vol. 128, no. 3, 2013, pp. 683–89.

Zeleza, Paul Tiyambe. "The Troubled Encounter between Postcolonialism and African History." *Journal of the Canadian Historical Association*, vol. 17, no. 2, 2006, pp. 89–129.

Zimunya, Masaemura. *Those Years of Drought and Hunger: The Birth of African Fiction in Zimbabwe*. Gweru, Zimbabwe: Mambo Press, 1982.

INDEX

Achebe, Chinua, 8, 20, 35, 110, 133, 145, 148–150, 151
Action versus Contemplation (Summit and Vermeule), 50–51
Adéẹ̀kọ́, Adélékè, 8, 35–36, 148
Adichie, Chimamanda Ngozi, 154, 156, 167, 182, 188–189
Africa in Stereo (Jaji), 186
Africa in Words (website), 14
"The African Imagination" (Irele), 9
African literature: and absence or loss, 145; and Eurocentric criticism, 9–10, 145–146, 154–155; and genre, 164, 168–169, 187–188; and globality (*see* globality); and linguistic nativism, 35; literary prizes and Eurocentrism, 154–155; and localization, 9–10, 26, 28, 35, 39, 154, 185; and marginalization in the marketplace, 22; as multi-lingual, 153, 157, 166, 183, 188; and postcolonial contexts, 1–2, 21, 26, 37–38, 138–139, 145; and postcolonial critical theory, 3–4, 6, 9–10, 36–37, 110–111 (*see also* Eurocentric criticism *under this heading*); publishing and circulation of, 23, 109, 147, 176, 181–182; subversion and resistance in, 110, 183; and universality, 183–184
African National Congress (ANC), 70–72, 168
African Novels and the Question of Orality (Julien), 126
African Philosophy: Myth and Reality (Hountondji), 15
African Writers Conference (1962), 183
African Writers Series, 110
Afrocentrism, 31, 40–42, 50, 52, 67
Afropolitanism, 35–36, 107, 123, 136–137, 188–189; *Kintu* and, 107, 123, 136
Afropolitanism and the Novel (Harris), 188
Against Democracy (During), 160
Aidoo, Ama Ata, 21, 24, 60–61, 65–66
AIDS/HIV, 27, 131, 168, 177–178

Akan ethnicity and culture, 40–41; in Casely Hayford's *Ethiopia Unbound*, 57–58; and comparative projects, 33, 40–41, 43–46, 67; and conceptuality, 42–43, 60; personhood in, 4–5, 18, 45; "talking drums," 15–16; theology and cosmology, 16, 18, 43–45, 54, 57–58
alienation: in Casely Hayford's *Ethiopia Unbound*, 61–62; cultural, 61; Ngũgĩ wa Thiong'o on, 110–111; self-alienation and public intellectuals, 75; social, 24, 26, 61–62, 110–111, 133, 178; and subjectivity, 101–102
All the Difference in the World (Melas), 37–38
Americanah (Adichie), 154, 156, 167, 188–189
Anderson, Amanda, 7, 52
Andindilile, Michael, 154
Appiah, Kwame Anthony, 15–16, 18, 21, 33, 41–42, 44–47, 53, 60, 113–114, 116
The Architecture of Concepts: The Historical Formation of Human Rights (de Bolla), 42
Are We Not Also Men? (Ranger), 78–79
argument. *See* dialogues, philosophical
Armah, Ayi Kwei, 24, 60–64
Attah, Ayesha Harrunah, 111
Attridge, Derek, 168
autonomy, 18–19, 127, 149, 189. *See also* free will
Awoonor, Kofi, 13, 60–61
Awotwi, David Eyiku (Nana Ekow Eyiku I), 5–6

Bady, Aaron, 110, 111
Baho! (Rugero), 23
Bakare-Yusuf, Bibi, 182
Bakhtin, Mikhail, 17, 85
Bantu Mirror (newspaper), 72
Bantu Philosophy (Tempel), 15
Barnard, Rita, 161
Bell, Duncan, 7
Benhabib, Seyla, 82, 88
Bewes, Timothy, 145

[213]

Biko, Steve, 169, 173
Black Consciousness, 169, 173–174
Black Skin, White Masks (Fanon), 48
Black Sunlight (Marechera), 25, 26, 70, 97, 102–103
Bleak Liberalism (Anderson), 7, 52
Blyden, Edward, 54–55
Boethius, 158–160, 162, 167
Born Translated (Walkowitz), 158
Bound to Violence (Ouologuem), 139
"bracketing," 14
Brinkema, Eugenie, 178
Brittle Paper (website), 176–177
Brooks, Peter, 36
The Brothers Karamazov (Dostoevsky), 161
"Bye-Bye Babar" (Selasi), 35–36

Caine Prize, 154–155
Calibrations (Quayson), 48
capitalism, 4, 6, 7, 11, 38–39
Casely Hayford, J. E., 5, 21, 40–41, 51, 65, 70, 146, 193n9; and comparison as methodology, 59–60; and conceptual comparability, 32–35, 49, 59–61; and decolonization, 24, 41, 47, 49, 59–61, 67; and Fante Confederacy, 23; and globality, 19; and lateralization, 24, 41; and mediation, 23–24, 49–50, 55; and objective exchange, 32; and philosophical dialogue, 24, 55, 58; and reciprocity, 55–56; and reflection, 5; and syncretism, 49–50, 53; and utopian futurism, 59–60. See also *Ethiopia Unbound* (Casely Hayford)
Cassava Republic Press, 182
causality, 108, 112, 131, 139, 143
Central Africa Party (CAP), 72
centralizing *vs.* lateralizing ideologies, 24
Chakrabarty, Dipesh, 114–115
character development, 31–32, 53, 63, 85, 101, 141, 158. See also philosophizing individuals as characters
Cheah, Pheng, 152–153
Chibber, Vivek, 4, 37
Chirere, Memory, 101
Chow, Rey, 9
civility, 12, 22; critiques of, 76–79, 94, 95; and political injustice, 77–78; Samkange's formulation of, 69, 73–79; and self-moderation, 94–96; social harmony and rational choice, 93

Coetzee, J. M., 14, 20, 25, 110
collectivism, 120; African communalism *vs.* Western individualism binary, 8, 95–96; African literature and opposition of individualism and, 8–9; African novel and collective consciousness, 125, 127; Gyekye on balance of individual and collective, 18–19; hunhuism and relationship of individual to collective, 93–95, 97; and individual agency, 18–19; individuation or disaggregation from collective, 15–16, 98; and intellection (ordered thought), 14; liberal communitarianism, 18–19; philosophical practice and individuation, 15–16; philosophy as collective work, 47; and property ownership, 95–96; radical collectivity, 97, 146; and social alienation, 26; and social obligation or duty, 6, 148
Colmer, Rosemary, 61
Comaroff, Jean, 115–116
Comaroff, John, 115–116
Combined and Uneven Development (WReC), 38
comparability: Aidoo and rejection of, 65–66; and categorization as philosophical problem, 49–50; conceptual, 32–35, 39; decolonization and, 46; and dehierarchization, 47, 55–56; and equality, 57–58; and globalization *vs.* localization, 39; and lateralization, 24, 32–33, 46–47, 60; "mere" *vs.* relational, 41; and power inequalities, 34
Comparative Literature in an Age of Globalization (Saussy), 36
comparative literature studies: and African literary studies, 32–34; and "comparability," 33–36, 41; and marginalization of African literature, 28, 46, 181–185, 188–189; as Western- or Eurocentric, 33–37, 46
comparison: and identity formation, 48; *vs.* mediation, 55; as racial ontology, 48
conceptuality, 51, 60, 63; in Casely Hayford's *Ethiopia Unbound*, 58–59, 60; and language, 16, 42–43, 45, 119–120; and lateralization, 47
consciousness, 13–14, 67; African novel and collective, 125, 127; Black Consciousness, 169, 173–174; cultural identity

and individual critical consciousness, 149
The Consolation of Philosophy (Boethius), 158
"Contested Grammars: Comparative Literature, Translation, and the Challenge of Locality" (Gikandi), 46
contrapuntalism, 24, 168–169
Coovadia, Imraan, 19, 22–23, 27, 147, 149, 157, 166–175, 187; and genre experimentation, 168; and intellection as response, 180; as Ntshanga's mentor, 176; as speculative fiction writer, 187. See also *Tales of the Metric System* (Coovadia)
Corrigan, Yuri, 14
cosmologies, 43–44
Critique of Black Reason (Mbembe), 6–7
A Critique of Postcolonial Reason (Spivak), 114
Culler, Jonathan, 33–36, 41–42, 45, 88
cultural reclamation, 35, 51–52, 87–89
cultural studies and critical theory, 9
curses: in African historical novels, 137–144; belief as interpretive practice, 112, 117, 123–125, 127–133, 139–140; as constraint on freedom or individual agency, 109, 131; in Kimani's *Dance of the Jakaranda*, 109, 141–143; in Kyomuhendo's *Waiting*, 109, 137–141; in Makumbi's *Kintu*, 26, 108; mental health as alternative explanation of events, 108, 112, 125–126, 129, 135, 136; postnational novels and, 26; rationality and belief in traditional, 26, 108, 112–114; in Samkange's *The Mourned One*, 84–85; as socially transmitted, 139–140; twins and, 85, 109, 123–124, 128, 139

Dance of the Jakaranda (Kimani), 26, 109, 141–144
Death and the King's Horseman (Soyinka), 148–149
de Bolla, Peter, 42–43, 47, 80
Declaration of the Rights of Man and Citizen, 12
decolonization: Casely Hayford and, 24, 41, 47, 49, 59–61, 67; and Casely Hayford's *Ethiopia Unbound*, 67; comparative literature studies and, 33, 37, 40–49; and critique of Western methodologies, 48 (*see also* ethnocentrism); and lateralization, 24, 41; solitary reflection and, 57; and subjectivity, 67
Decolonizing the Mind (Ngũgĩ wa Thiong'o), 110–111
Demons (Dostoevsky), 27, 147, 149–151, 158, 166, 177
de Silva, Mark, 14
dialogues, philosophical, 14, 22; Casely Hayford's use of analogy and, 24, 49, 55, 58; in fictional correspondence, 24; fictional letters and presentation of, 66; Habermas and faith in, 75–76; and hunhuism, 94–95; internal monologue, 24, 102, 170–171; morality and, 66; and the philosophizing individual, 22–23; Socratic, 24, 66, 158, 174; written correspondence, 66
diaspora, 35–36, 154, 157, 162–163, 165, 182; and audience for *Our Sister Killjoy*, 66; Huchu as diasporic writer, 151
dichronicity, 63
DiGiacomo, Mark, 52–53
disillusionment, 20, 26, 52–53, 61, 65, 78–79, 84, 159, 160; in Samkange's *The Mourned One*, 83–84
dispassion: and reflective distance, 79; and victimization, 83
distance, analytic: narrative techniques and creation of, 13–14; and philosophy, 13–14
Dostoevsky, Fyodor, 27, 149–151, 159, 161, 167, 169, 171, 180
"dromosphere," 164
During, Simon, 160

education reform, 94–95
"Eleven Theses on Civility" (N'yongo and Tompkins), 77
Elmina, 5
Empire of Neglect (Taylor), 7
Enlightenment's Wake (Gray), 114
"Enlightenment values," 5–6, 47, 50, 52, 107, 113, 118, 121, 187
equality: and African individualism, 12–13; Casely Hayford and civilizational equality, 24, 49, 67; and comparability, 57–58; comparability and power inequalities, 34; comparative literature and inequalities, 36–37; and

equality (*continued*)
  critical individualism, 75–76; and dis-passion, 67; freedom and global inequality, 11; Kimani's *Dance of the Jakaranda* and social inequality, 79, 142–143; and lateralization, 43, 47; liberalism and, 12; Samkange and racial, 72–73, 79. *See also* comparability
Ethics after Idealism (Chow), 9
Ethiopia Unbound (Casely Hayford), 5, 31; argument and reflection in, 22–23; as decolonial literary comparatism, 49; incremental structure of, 24; and individuality, 56–57; and interaction among traditions, 24; narrative structure in, 56, 58, 59; and the philosophizing individual as character, 22, 58; racial segregation debate in, 55–56; reflection in, 24, 56–57; as syncretic, hybrid text, 49–54
ethnocentrism: and literary criticism, 9–10, 145–146, 154–155; philosophy and embedded, 113–115; reason and elitism, 113–114; and "world fiction," 137–138
ethnophilosophy, 91–92
Eurocentrism, 8–9
"Exorcising Hegel's Ghost" (Táíwò), 184
experience: *vs.* acquired knowledge, 65; Aidoo's *Our Sister Killjoy* and subjective, 65; *vs.* "conceptuality," 48–49; novels and subjective, 21–24; and philosophy in the novel of ideas, 23, 32; and reflection, 32
The Eye of the Needle (Turner), 172
Eze, Emmanuel Chukwudi, 26, 109, 113, 190; on difference between freedom and liberty, 127; and "everyday reason," 118–122
Eze, Michael Onyebuchi, 15

fairness: narrative fairness, 83–85; and neutrality, 82, 88; as principle of hunhuism, 92–93, 94; Samkange's commitment to, 70, 76, 79, 82, 84–85, 88–89, 92, 96–97; and unbiased intellect, 79–80
Fanon, Frantz, 31, 48, 57, 67, 152
Fante Confederacy, 23–24, 51–52, 59

Fante intellectualism, 25, 32, 51–52, 57
Fathers and Sons (Turgenev), 151
Fawcett, Edmund, 10
"Federation" period as context, 71–72
Foe (Coetzee), 110
Forna, Aminatta, 185
Fragments (Armah), 24–25, 61–64, 66
freedom, 161–162; difference between freedom and liberty, 127, 131; and disenfranchisement, 149; and language, 119
free will: African self-determination, 12–13; and disenfranchisement, 149; Dostoevsky's Kirillov and suicide as choice, 180; Nyamfukudza and self-expiration, 103
Frenkel, Ronit, 167
Friesen, Alan, 149
Futures of Comparative Literature (Saussy), 37

Gagiano, Annie, 101
gender, 1, 11, 22, 67, 87–88, 182, 185
"The Geography of African Philosophy" (Janz), 115
Getachew, Adom, 10
Geuss, Raymond, 3–4
Ghana Must Go (Selasi), 154
Ghosh, Amitav, 153
Ghostwritten (Mitchell), 161, 162, 167
Gikandi, Simon, 8–9, 46–47, 54
Gikuyu movement, 51
Girard, René, 170–171
Glissant, Édouard, 41
globality: and connectivity, 152–153; and the "dromosphere," 164; and hyperconnectivity, 145–146, 161–162; intellection as incompatible with, 158; as literary genre, 157–158; philosophical reflection as relief from, 180; and publishing as transnational, 19; and spatial mobility, 146, 154, 167; and spatial rather than temporal narrative structure, 167; and systematicity, 162; and "totality," 152
The Global Novel (Kirsch), 157
Gordimer, Nadine, 20, 68, 72
Gorman-DaRif, Meghan, 141
Goyal, Yogita, 50, 55
Graham, James, 86–87, 86–88
Gray, John, 114
Gros, Frédéric, 5

guerrilla insurrections, 72–73, 99
Gyasi, Yaa, 154, 189
Gyekye, Kwame, 4, 18–19, 114

Habermas, Jürgen, 74–79, 82, 94
Habila, Helon, 102–103
The Hairdresser of Harare (Huchu), 1–2, 156
Hallward, Peter, 9, 37
Hapanyengwi-Chemhuru, Oswell, 94–95
Harootunian, Harry, 38–39
Harris, Ashleigh, 188
Head, Bessie, 13
Hearn, Lafcadio (Koizumi Yakumo), 60
Hegel, Georg Wilhelm Friedrich, 11, 150, 184
historiographic novels, 112
HIV/AIDS, 27, 131, 168, 177–178
Homegoing (Gyasi), 154, 189
Hountondji, Paulin J., 15
House of Hunger (Marechera), 101–102
Huchu, Tendai, 1–3, 19, 22–23, 27; as diasporic writer, 151; and Dostoevsky's Kirillov, 147–151, 155, 159–161, 166, 169, 171–172, 180; and intellection as response, 180; speculative fiction written as T. L. Huchu, 187; and sphere of private thought, 156. See also *The Maestro, the Magistrate, and the Mathematician*
Humanism and Democratic Criticism (Said), 168–169
Human Rights, Inc. (Slaughter), 7, 146, 152
hunhuism (Shona moral system): and cultural embeddedness, 91–92, 96; and distinction between reciprocity and generosity, 91–92, 94; human relationships as priority in, 73–74, 91–92, 94, 97; as individualized but not subjectivized, 95–96; and moderation of behavior, 94; novel form and representation of, 95; and relationship of individual to collective, 93–95, 97; as replicable way of being, 90, 96–97, 102
Hunhuism or Ubuntuism: A Zimbabwe Indigenous Religious Philosophy (Samkange and Samkange), 25, 69–70, 73–74, 76, 79, 90–96; narrative framing device in, 90–91

Ibrahim, Abubakar Adam, 155
identity: "Africanstein" identity in Makumbi's *Kintu*, 134–135; comparison and formation of, 48; gender and sexuality, 1–3, 13, 66, 185; individualism and sense of self, 13; individuation *vs.* group affiliation in formation of, 146; individuation *vs.* subjectivization in *Kintu*, 123–137; Kimani's *Dance of the Jakaranda* and exploration of, 141–142; Kyomuhendo's *Waiting* and national, 137; national identity as construct, 75; and racial alienation, 133; self-identification as philosopher, 22; twins and individuation, 112; and universality, 185; writers and, 185; writers and resistance to locality as classification, 185
Iheka, Cajetan, 186
Indian Ocean Studies, 153
individualism: African authors and investment in, 10; African literature and opposition of collectivism and, 8–9; and autonomy, 18–19, 127, 149, 189 (*see also* free will); and *bildungsroman* tradition, 140, 146, 180; in Casely Hayford's *Ethiopia Unbound*, 56–57; and communality, 18; and equality, 12–13, 75–76; and Eurocentrism, 6; and experience, 21–22; and globalization, 23; individuation as distinct from subjectivization, 21–22, 65; individuation or disaggregation from collective, 98; and intellectual rebellion, 15–16; in liberalism, 7–8; and "the liberal subject," 6; and liberty, 127, 131; in Marechera's *Black Sunlight*, 102–103; moral status of the individual, 98; Mphahlele's African individuality, 13; as narratological practice, 13–14; novel as fantasized space for, 4; Samkange's individualized (not subjectivized) representational mode, 96–97; and self-actualization, 109, 147–148, 177, 179; solitary reflection as decolonizing force, 57; subjectivization *vs.* individuation, 21–22, 96–97; suicide and autonomy, 149–150; and traditional cultural belonging, 127–128; and universality, 21–22; Western individualism *vs.* African communalism, 8, 95–96; Western notions of progress and focus on, 6, 146

In My Father's House (Appiah), 21, 44–46, 116
integrity, individual, 3, 8, 22, 79–80, 135
intellection, 13–14, 27, 51, 61, 146, 158, 171–172, 176, 180; and alienation from community, 171; globality as incompatible with, 158; replicable systems of, 55, 79 (*see also* hunhuism (Shona moral system)); self-abstraction and, 79; and setting, 13; setting or location and, 13; solitary reflection as decolonizing force, 57
intellectual rebellion, 15–16
interiority, 11, 14, 53, 58, 65–66, 98, 101–102
The Interpreters (Soyinka), 20
Inventing the Individual (Siedentop), 10
Irele, Abiola, 9, 149–150
Irrationality (Smith), 113
Iser, Wolfgang, 132–133

Jaji, Tsitsi, 164, 186
Jameson, Fredric, 38
Janz, Bruce, 115, 120–121, 185–186
Jest, Daniel, 18
Julien, Eileen, 17, 111, 126

Kahari, George, 97–98
Kant, Immanuel, 5–6, 50, 113, 150
Kimani, Peter, 26, 109, 126, 141–144
Kintu (Makumbi), 22, 25–27, 107–109, 116–117, 126–127, 136; and "Africanstein" identity, 134–135; agency and reason in, 108; and collision of tradition and "global" views, 26, 123, 127, 134–137; decolonization as issue in, 133; distinction between rationality and reason in, 112–113; framing devices in, 131–132; as historical fiction, 111–112; individuation vs. subjectivization in, 122–137; and liberty in Eze's sense, 131; and locality, 27, 109–110; and meaning making, 112, 129, 133; as "meta-interpretive," 111–112, 117–118, 123, 126, 129–130, 132; narrative structure of, 112; as novel of ideas, 23–24; pluralized reason in, 107–108, 112, 115, 118–122, 135; publication of, 109; racial dynamics in, 133–134; twins or doubling in, 109, 117, 123–124, 128

Kirsch, Adam, 157
Korang, Kwaku, 51
Krishnaswamy, Revathi, 39–40
Kunipipi (Colmer), 61
Kyomuhendo, Goretti, 26, 109, 137–141, 143–144

La Guma, Alex, 98
Land and Nationalism in Fictions from Southern Africa (Graham), 86–88
Lange, James, 97
language: and concepts, 16, 42–43, 45, 119–120; linguistic nativism, 35; thought as the need for, 119
lateralization: and comparability, 32–33, 46–47, 60; and decolonization, 24, 41; and equality, 43, 47; *vs.* recentralizing, 24, 35, 38
Lazarus, Neil, 9, 37, 74–75, 84, 110
Left Universalism (Sekyi Otu), 1, 7
liberal communitarianism, 18–19
The Liberal Imagination (Trilling), 50
liberalism, 6–10, 24; in Casely Hayford's *Ethiopia Unbound*, 24, 50, 52; colonialism and, 7; "global liberalisms," 8; and the individual, 12; individualism and, 7–8; novels and, 17; and ordered thought, 50; pluralism and, 9; and Samkange's works, 79–80, 84, 88–89; settler colonies and, 7. See also individualism
The Lives of the Novel (Pavel), 17–18
locality or localization, 9–10, 35; and African literature, 154; and comparability, 39; generalization *vs.* localization, 28; and Makumbi's *Kintu*, 27, 109–110; and postnational novels, 26; writers and resistance to classification by, 185
locatedness and African literature, 185
Lopez, Alfred J., 37–38
Lukács, Georg, 145

The Maestro, the Magistrate, and the Mathematician [MMM] (Huchu), 157–166; and Coovadia's *Tales of the Metric System*, 166–167, 172; and disillusionment, 159; and Dostoevsky's *Demons*, 147; and free will, 156, 159; and globality, 156; and mediation of experience, 159–164; narrative

structure of, 161–162; as novel of ideas, 23–24, 180; and philosophers as pariahs, 22–23; and philosophical suicide, 27, 156; and private introspection, 156; publication and circulation of, 147, 176; reading and intertextuality in, 160–164; and suicide as an idea, 160
Magosvongwe, Ruby, 93
Magubeni, Unathi, 23
Makumbi, Jennifer Nansubuga, 19, 23–24; and cultural plurality as theme, 107–108; as historical novelist, 107; *Kintu* as an historical novel, 111–112, 137, 144. See also *Kintu* (Makumbi)
Makuvaza, Ngoni, 94
Malaba, Mbongini, 84–86
Manshel, Alexander, 112
Marechera, Dambudzo, 22, 25, 32, 70, 97–98, 101–103
Maru (Head), 13
Mbembe, Achille, 6–7
meaninglessness, as choice, 100–101
meaning making, 112–113, 122
Melas, Natalie, 37–38, 41, 46
meso-analysis, 20–21
Metaphor and the Slave Trade in the West African Literature (Murphy), 63
Methodist Church, 70–71, 86
Metz, Thaddeus, 15
Mieke, Bal, 45
mind-body dualism, 170
Mitchell, David, 161
Modernism/modernity (Saint-Amour), 21
modernity, 4, 38; Casely Hayford and Fante, 49, 59, 61; Digiacomo and African, 52–54; *vs.* tradition, 17, 26; and Western-centric definition of the world, 39
Modernity and Its Malcontents (Comaroff and Comaroff), 115–116
moral authority, 2; in Akan culture, 57–58; hunhuism and, 91
The Mourned One (Samkange): and civility, 69–70; compared and contrasted with *The Non-Believer's Journey*, 97–101; and cultural reclamation, 87–88; and disillusionment, 83–84; as "failed novel," 83; and fairness, 70; gender identity in, 87–88; as philosophical turning point, 22, 25, 69–70;

and self-abstraction, 103; and theme of institutional betrayal, 83–84; and universality, 22
Mphahlele, Es'kia, 13–14
Mudimbe, V. Y., 15, 92
Muponde, Robert, 87
Murphy, Laura, 63
Mwesigire, Bwesigye Bwa, 123
Myth, Literature, and the African World (Soyinka), 13–14

narrative structure: and analytic distance, 13–14; in Armah's *Fragments*, 62; in Casely Hayford's *Ethiopia Unbound*, 56, 58, 59; of Coovadia's *Metric System*, 166–168, 175; framing devices and, 82; globality and spatial, 167; and historiographic novels, 112; multiple plot lines and diffused, 157–158, 166–167, 177; Samkange and fragmentation of, 102; of Samkange's *On Trial for My Country*, 82–83; transnationalism and, 157–158; twins or doubling and ambivalence, 124; "zooming in" in hunhuism, 90–91
National Democratic Party (NDP), 72–73, 78
nationalism, 75, 97
national *vs.* global literature, 19
nativism, 8–9, 24, 31, 35–36, 183
Naturalizing Africa (Iheka), 186
Ndebele, Njabulo, 98
"The Necklace" (Coovadia), 169–171
Nemapare, Esau, 71
neutrality, 24, 52, 70, 82, 88, 94; *vs.* fairness, 82; in Makumbi's *Kintu*, 108; Samkange and "unbiased intellect," 80
Newell, Stephanie, 49–50, 53
ngangas, 96
Ngũgĩ wa Thiong'o, 20, 35, 51, 110–111, 185
Nkomo, Joshua, 72–73, 78
Nkrumah, Kwame, 18
No Longer at Ease (Achebe), 20
The Non-Believer's Journey (Nyamfukudza), 25, 70, 97–101
novel of ideas, 183–189; as instrument of disaggregation, 60; locality and ethnocentric perceptions of, 113–115; philosophy and, 1–3; and relationship between reason and rationality, 122; and subjectivity, 60–61

Ntshanga, Masande, 27–28, 147, 149, 175–180, 187; and intellection as response, 180
Nwelezelanga (Magubeni), 23
Nyabola, Nanjala, 13
Nyamfukudza, Stanley, 25, 70, 78, 97–99, 100–101, 103
Nyatsime College, Chitungwiza, 95
Nyong'o, Tavia, 77

Ochieng, Omedi, 79
Ogundele, Wole, 136, 138–139
Okorafor, Nnedi, 182, 187
Olaniyan, Tejumola, 145, 182–183
Oluwole, Sophie, 3
omniscient narrators, 84, 86–89, 96
Omotoso, Yewande, 155
One Day I Will Write about This Place (Wainaina), 154
On Reason (Eze), 118–123, 131
On Trial for My Country (Samkange), 79–80, 81–84, 91, 97
orality or oral tradition: and African literature, 9, 15–17; and collective consensus, 15–16; textuality vs., 15–17
"An Oral Philosophy of Personhood" (Wiredu), 15–16
Osiris Rising (Armah), 64
Ouologuem, Yambo, 139
Our Sister Killjoy (Aidoo), 24, 61, 65–66; as feminist novel, 67; narrative structure of, 65; and rejection of learned knowledge, 65
Oxford Street, Accra (Quayson), 186

The Palm-Wine Drinkard (Tutuola), 139
Paperno, Irina, 150
particularism, cultural, 4
Pavel, Thomas, 17–18
p'Bitek, Okot, 46
Person and Community (Wiredu and Gyeke, eds.), 18
personhood, 4–5, 18, 45–46, 135
Phillips, Caryl, 158
The Philosopher (Smith), 3
philosophizing individuals as characters, 22–23, 54–55; and alienation, 149; in Casely Hayford's *Ethiopia Unbound*, 22–23; in Coovadia's *Tales of the Metric System* and fictionalized Rick Turner, 27, 172–175; Hunter as fictionalized Turner in Coovadia's *Tales of the Metric System*, 172–175; and introspection in Ntshanga's *The Reactive*, 176; marginalization and, 27; and mediation in the novel, 3–4; and subjectivity, 63; as target of derision, 64; as unreliable narrator, 63
philosophy (narrow scope intentional): and analytic distance, 14–15; as "character," 17; as collective work of individuals, 47; as connection between individual and national community, 22; and distance, analytic, 13–14; as individual, 3–4; as method of inquiry, 10, 33; and methodology, 4–5; and the novel as, 16–17; and ordered thought, 14–15, 50; shift from philosophical orientation in African literature, 21; as written text, 15–16
A Philosophy of Walking (Gros), 5–6
The Place of Tears (Primorac), 73
pluralism, 6, 50; and choice, 161–162; and cultural syncretism, 107–109; Eze on, 113–114, 119–120; global hyperpluralism, 6, 113–114, 162; and localization, 9, 118–119; and multiple modernities, 115; pluralized reason in Makumbi's *Kintu*, 107–108, 112, 115, 118–122, 135; and rationality, 113–114, 118, 120–122, 188; and universality, 113–114
postcolonial theory, 3–6, 9–11, 37, 110–111
The Postcolonial Unconscious (Lazarus), 9, 110–111
post-independence novels, Samkange and, 97–98
Post45 (website), 112
Present Imperfect (Van der Vlies), 178–179
Primorac, Ranka, 73, 85, 97
Proverbs, Textuality, and Nativism in African Literature, 8–9
Provincializing Europe (Chakrabarty), 114
public intellectualism, 60, 69–70, 74–79
Puchner, Martin, 14

Quayson, Ato, 8, 48, 101, 186

racism: civility and perpetuation of, 76–79; comparison and racial ontology, 48; "Enlightenment values" and, 113–114; Kimani's *Dance of the*

Jakaranda and, 142–143; racial segregation debate in Casely Hayford's *Ethiopia Unbound*, 55–56; and universality, 183–184. *See also* ethnocentrism

"Racism and Culture" (Fanon), 31, 67, 152

radicalism, 87, 97, 99, 135; in Casely Hayford's *Ethiopia Unbound*, 52; and civility, 77; opposition between liberalism and, 8, 17, 71, 73; radical collectivity in African literature, 97, 146; Samkange and, 8, 69–71, 87, 99

Ramose, Mogobe, 114, 185

Rand, Erin J., 76

Ranger, Terence, 71–73, 78–80

rationality: as abstract, 121; Africans allowed reason, but not rationality, 121; as distinct from reason, 120, 122; and experience, 119–120; and ideal of truth, 116; plurality and, 113–114, 118, 121; as a process, 115–116, 119–120; as a property of the individual person, 120; victimization and dispassion, 83

Rawls, John, 19

The Reactive (Ntshanga), 27, 147, 175–179, 187; and introspection, 176; publication and circulation of, 176

Reading Chinua Achebe (Gikandi), 8

Reading the African Novel (Gikandi), 8

reason: Africans allowed reason, but not rationality, 121; conflated with rationality, 115–116; elitist ethnocentrism and, 113–114; "everyday reason" in Eze, 118–121, 128; and experience, 122; and freedom, 131; and individual will, 123, 127; pluralized, 113–114, 118, 121–122; as pursuit of meaning, 113; rationality as distinct from, 120, 122, 123; and truth, 117–118; as universal, 118

recentralizing *vs.* lateralizing culture, 24, 35, 38

reciprocity, 56, 79–80; *vs.* generosity, 91–92, 94–96; and hunhuism, 91–92, 94

Rediscovery of the Ordinary (Ndebele), 98

reflection: action *vs.* contemplation, 50–51; in Casely Hayford's *Ethiopia Unbound*, 22, 24, 50, 54–55; and ordered thought, 14–15; solitary reflection as decolonizing force, 57

religion: in Casely Hayford's *Ethiopia Unbound*, 54; and decolonization, 42

replicability: hunhuism (Shona moral system) and, 90, 94, 96–97, 102; philosophical systems and, 55

representation, Eurocentric notions of universality and, 151–152, 188

Representations of the Intellectual (Said), 74–75

Rhys, Jean, 110

Romance, Diaspora, and Black Atlantic Literature (Goyal), 50, 55

Rosenblatt, Helena, 10

Rugero, Roland, 23

Said, Edward, 74–75, 168–169

Saint, Lily, 164

Saint-Amour, Paul, 20–21

Samkange, Stanlake, 19; and ANC, 70–72; and character as narrative frame, 83; and civility, 69–70, 76–79, 94, 95; and determination of right and wrong, 81; and dispassion, 80; and education reform, 94–95; and fairness, 70, 88; and fragmentation, 102; and globality, 19; and historical/autobiographical approach, 90–91; as historical novelist, 79–82, 91; and hunhuism as replicable way of being, 102–103; and individual/community binary, 95; and institutional racism, 86–90, 93–94; and liberalism, 79–80; and narrative fairness, 84–85; narrative structure of *On Trial*, 82–83; and neutrality, 88; and novel as means of expression, 95; and omniscient narrator, 84, 86–89, 96; and philosophical turn, 25, 69, 91, 95; political dimension of works, 95; and political protest novels, 97–98; and priority of individual character, 96–97; as public intellectual, 69–70, 74–79; and relationship of politics to writing, 68–73; and replicability way of being, 79, 90, 92, 96–97; and self-abstraction, 76–79, 82, 88–89, 94, 96, 103; and systematization, 79; and "unbiased intellect," 79–80; and use of historical evidence, 91, 96

Samkange, Thompson, 70–71, 88–89

Samkange, Tommie, 69–70, 90

Sarbah, John Mensah, 51

Saussy, Haun, 36–37, 39–40

The Scapegoat (Girard), 170–171
Scott, Joan W., 21–22
Sea of Poppies (Ghosh), 153
A Secular Age (Taylor), 162
Sekyi, Kobina, 51, 193n9
Sekyi-Otu, Ato, 1, 7, 28
Selasi, Taiye, 35–36, 154, 188
self-abnegation, 147–148
self-abstraction, 76–79, 82, 87, 88–89, 94, 103
self-actualization, 109, 147–148, 177, 179
self-alienation, public intellectualism and, 73, 75
self-relativization, 130, 185
Serpell, Namwali, 14, 134–135
sexuality: in Aidoo's *Our Sister Killjoy*, 66; in Huchu's *Hairdresser*, 1–3
Shaka (Lange), 97
Shih, Shu-Mei, 38
Sibanda, Patrick, 93
Siedentop, Larry, 10
Singh, Julietta, 10–11
Slaughter, Joseph, 7, 95, 146, 152
slavery, 6, 12, 63–64
Slavery and the Culture of Taste (Gikandi), 54
A Small Silence (Verrismo), 23
Smith, Justin E. H., 3, 113
social subjectivity, 179
Social Text (Nyong'o and Tompkins), 77
solitude, 6, 7, 32, 56–57; as loneliness, 61
Some Kinds of Childhood (Muponde), 87
"Some Thoughts on Comparability and the Space-Time Problem" (Harootunian), 39
Song of Lawino (Okot p'Bitek), 46
Sources of the Self (Taylor), 179
Soyinka, Wole, 13–14, 20, 145, 148, 151
spiritual bankruptcy, 97
Spivak, Gayatri, 114
A Spy in Time (Coovadia), 187
Sterling, Cheryl, 67
Strategic Transformation in Nigerian Writing (Quayson), 186
subjectivity: in Casely Hayford's *Ethiopia Unbound*, 55, 58; *vs.* conceptuality in *Fragments*, 63; as distinct from individuality, 65; Marechera and subjective experience, 63; and Marechera's *House of Hunger*, 101; and the novel of ideas, 61; and philosophical individual, 63; Samkange and, 97
subjectivization, 25, 109, 122–137

suicide, philosophical, 27; African literature and tradition of suicide, 147–148; in Dostoevsky's *Demons*, 27, 149–152; in Huchu's *MMM*, 27, 156, 160, 169; and individual autonomy, 149–150; and Ntshanga's *The Reactive*, 175–176; and social duty, 148–149
Summit, Jennifer, 50–51
sunsum (hereditary will or personality, Akan), 45

Tales of the Metric System (Coovadia), 22–23, 27; and Dostoevsky's *Demons*, 164–165, 171–172; and generic hybridity, 164–165; and globality, 157–158, 166–167; and literary suicide, 172–175; narrative structure of, 166–168, 175; and perspectival switch, 175; and philosophy as by-product of violence, 166–167; publication of and circulation of, 147, 176; and Said's contrapuntalism, 168–169; and spatial connectedness, 166–167; visual design of text, 168
talking drums, 15–16
Taylor, Charles, 162, 179
Taylor, Chris, 7, 10–12
Teachers, Preachers, Non-Believers (Viet-Wild), 69
Thamm, Marianne, 172
The Theory of the Novel (Lukács), 145
Things Fall Apart (Achebe), 110, 133, 139, 148–149
"To Hear the Variety of Discourse" (Wicomb), 153–154
Tompkins, Kyla Wazana, 77
"Toward Decolonizing African Philosophy and Religion" (Wiredu), 42
"Tradition and Continuity in African Literature" (Awoonor), 13
Triangulum (Ntshanga), 187
Trilling, Lionel, 50
truth: and consciousness, 67; and dispassion, 80; a priori, 2; rationality and ideal of, 116; and reason or rationality, 117–118
Turner, Richard "Rick": as fictionalized in Coovadia's *Tales of the Metric System*, 27, 172–175
Tutuola, Amos, 139
twins or doubles, 84–85, 89, 109, 112, 129, 139–140
Two Thousand Seasons (Armah), 64

ubuntuism: and communal/individual binary, 95–96; as culturally embedded, 91–92; as embodied experience, 91–92; and human relationships, 73–74, 90–91, 95; and origin in absence, 92–93; property ownership systems in, 95–96; as rational choice, 93; and reciprocity, 94; Samkange on value of, 90; as universally replicable, 90–91

Universal Declaration of Human Rights, 7

universality: and common experience, 6; and generalization, 119–120; and individualism, 21–22; localization *vs.* generalization, 28; morality and, 89–90; of moral principles, 12–13; and pluralism, 113–114; postcolonial contexts and claims of, 150–151; and racism, 183–184; and representation, 151–152; self-relativization and, 184–185; as Western-centric, 13–14; writers and resistance to classification by locality, 185

Unthinking Mastery (Singh), 10–11

Veit-Wild, Flora, 69, 70–71, 73, 80
Vermeule, Blakey, 50–51
Verrismo, Jumoke, 23
Virilio, Paul, 164
viscerality, 22

Waddilove Institute, 70, 86–89, 95
Wainaina, Binyavanga, 35–36, 154

Waiting: A Novel of Uganda at War (Kyomuhendo), 26, 109, 137–141, 143–144; and the European *bildungsroman* tradition, 140–141; and mingling of mythic and historical events, 138–139; and national identity, 137; temporality in, 138

Walkowitz, Rebecca, 158
war of liberation novels, 97
Warwick Research Collective (WReC), 38
What Is a World? (Cheah), 155–156
"Whither Comparative Literature" (Culler), 33–35
Wicomb, Zoe, 153–154
Wide Sargasso Sea (Rhys), 110
will: African self-determination and free will, 12–13; disenfranchisement and free, 149; Nyamfukudza and self-expiration, 103; *sunsum* (Akan), 45
Williams, Jeffrey L., 47
Williams, Raymond, 145
Wiredu, Kwasi, 4–5, 15–16, 18, 33, 41–47, 53, 58, 60, 114–115
"wolf and lamb" tale, 58–59
"Working with Concepts" (Bal), 45
"World Studies and Relational Comparison" (Shih), 38
The Wretched of the Earth (Fanon), 57

Young, Robert J. C., 39–40, 48

Zukiswa, Wanner, 155

A NOTE ON THE TYPE

THIS BOOK has been composed in Miller, a Scotch Roman typeface designed by Matthew Carter and first released by Font Bureau in 1997. It resembles Monticello, the typeface developed for The Papers of Thomas Jefferson in the 1940s by C. H. Griffith and P. J. Conkwright and reinterpreted in digital form by Carter in 2003.

Pleasant Jefferson ("P. J.") Conkwright (1905–1986) was Typographer at Princeton University Press from 1939 to 1970. He was an acclaimed book designer and AIGA Medalist.

The ornament used throughout this book was designed by Pierre Simon Fournier (1712–1768) and was a favorite of Conkwright's, used in his design of the *Princeton University Library Chronicle*.

Lightning Source UK Ltd.
Milton Keynes UK
UKHW012249080121
376694UK00007B/348